J. P. Wilson

Scriptural Proofs

That God Offers us in Our Lord Jesus Christ Perfect Deliverance from all Sin...

J. P. Wilson

Scriptural Proofs
That God Offers us in Our Lord Jesus Christ Perfect Deliverance from all Sin...

ISBN/EAN: 9783337259440

Printed in Europe, USA, Canada, Australia, Japan

Cover: Foto ©Lupo / pixelio.de

More available books at **www.hansebooks.com**

SCRIPTURAL PROOFS

THAT GOD OFFERS US IN OUR LORD JESUS CHRIST PERFECT DELIVERANCE FROM ALL SIN, INWARD AS WELL AS OUTWARD, IF WE WILL BUT RECEIVE HIM AND BELIEVE ON HIS NAME FOR ALL THAT GOD HAS MADE HIM TO BE TO US. (*John* i. 12; 1 *Cor.* i. 30.)

BY

J. P. WILSON.

"Holiness by faith in Jesus,
   Not by effort of thine own,
Sin's dominion crushed and broken
   By the power of grace alone.
God's own holiness within thee,
   His own beauty on thy brow;
This shall be thy pilgrim brightness
   This thy blessed portion now."
                        Miss HAVERGAL.

FOURTH TO SIXTH THOUSAND

LONDON:
S. W. PARTRIDGE & CO., 9 PATERNOSTER ROW, E.C.
1888.

Promise.

"Let Israel hope in the Lord: for with the Lord there is mercy, and with him is plenteous redemption. And *he shall redeem Israel from all his iniquities.*" (Ps. cxxx. 7, 8.)

Fulfilment.

"Blessed be the Lord God of Israel; for *he hath visited and redeemed his people,* and hath raised up an horn of salvation for us in the house of his servant David; as he spake by the mouth of his holy prophets, which have been since the world began; that we should be saved from our enemies, and from the hand of all that hate us; to perform the mercy promised to our fathers, and to remember his holy covenant; the oath which he sware to our father Abraham, that he would grant unto us, *that we being delivered out of the hand of our enemies might serve him without fear, in holiness and righteousness before him, all the days of our life.*" (Luke i. 68-75.)

Type of the Spiritual Cleansing.

"And it came to pass, when he was in a certain city, behold *a man full of leprosy*: who seeing Jesus fell on his face, and besought him, saying, Lord, if thou wilt, thou canst make me clean. *And he put forth his hand, and touched him, saying, I will: be thou clean. And immediately the leprosy departed from him.*" (Luke v. 12, 13.)

INDEX TO THE HEADINGS

OF THE

SECTIONS AND PARAGRAPHS.

	PAGE
Note in place of Preface	xxiii
Cleansing from all Filthiness and from all Idols: A New Heart: Loving God with all the Heart and with all the Soul	1
Objection and Answer	2
All the Promises ours	3
Judge the Tree by its Fruit	4
Those Two Promises Enough	5
God's Law in our Minds and Hearts	6
"They shall all know Me"	7
Each of us in himself an Israel	7
Fulfilment of Old Testament Figures	8
"Yield yourselves unto God" (Rom. vi. 13)	10
"Healeth all thy Diseases"	11
Suppose only partial bodily healing	11
"Healing in his Wings"	12
Our Lord's Works of Bodily Healing	12
Has He two Sorts of Healing?	13

A 2

	PAGE
"As Moses lifted up the Serpent"	14
All who looked, perfectly cured	14
Time of Healing	15
Greek Tenses of the New Testament	17
"Second blessing": "Higher life"	19
What is the Gospel?	20
"What God hath joined——"	21
According to your Faith	21
Sanctification at Death	22
The Cry of every Awakened Heart	23
Why no Promise of Deliverance at Death?	24
Why that Time in Particular?	25
What a Pity to Wait!	26
Prayers and Armour in Ephesians	27
The Prayers	28
The Armour	29
None against any inside Enemy	29
"In the heavenlies"	30
The "whole armour" sufficient	31
"The Helmet of Salvation"	31
A Case in Point	32
Abundance of cases of perfect victory	33
God's Pictures of Holiness	34
To be realised in us	35
"The Way of Holiness"	35

This also for us	36
Practical Illustration	37
Further Blessing	38

"Put on thy strength, O Zion" . . . 39
"*All the ends of the earth*"	40

"God is my Salvation" 42

Redemption 43
The Right of Redemption	43
The Extent of Redemption	44

"Ransomed" 45

"I am thine, save me" . . . 46
How much can He save?	47

Grace "much more" Abounding . . . 49

"Whosoever abideth in Him" . . 50
Sin active or inactive still Sin	50
"*In Him is no Sin*"	51
"*Shall save his People from their Sins*"	52
"*Taketh away the Sin of the World*"	52
Him who knew no Sin made to be Sin	53

"Hath Established My Goings" . . 53
Established in Christ	54
Made the Goodness of God in Him	55

Peter on and in the Water 55
Even little Faith very blessed	56

	PAGE
Looking only at Jesus	57
This only an Illustration	57

Walking with God 57

| *" The Kingdom of Heaven "* | 58 |
| *Christ in us as well as for us* | 59 |

"Remission" or "Forgiveness of Sins" . . 60

Deliverance and Setting at Liberty	60
" Loosed us from our Sins "	61
" He hath done all Things Well "	61
" Won't let Him "	61

The Law of the Spirit of Life . . 62

Power of Evil over us	63
The blessed Deliverance	64
Grace here again abounding	64

Christ declaring the Father's Name . . 65

All blessings through the Father's Name	66
Does God say we must have Sin in us?	66
Dare any of us say this?	67

Trusting in the Name of the Lord . . 68

"O Lord, my Strength" . . 69

"Deliver us from Evil" . . 71

"That which he requested" . . 72

"Hath cast out thine enemy" . . 73

	PAGE
"I the Lord do keep it"	74
"Judgment" for the "Oppressed"	75
How much	76
"Shall he find faith?"	77
God and his People of old	78
Their short time of obedience and blessing	78
We have "a better hope"	79
In our ever-living Joshua	79
"Holiness and Righteousness before Him"	80
A heading to St. Luke's Gospel	80
For present fulfilment in us	81
"To the Uttermost"	81
What is "the uttermost"?	82
The Land of Blessing	82
God's care over it	83
And their great blessedness in it	83
The spiritual fulfilment to us	84
"Righteousness and Strength"	84
"From all Iniquity"	85
To be fulfilled in our hearts now	85
"A New Creature"	86
"Taketh away all his armour"	86

INDEX TO HEADINGS OF

	PAGE
"Fear not"	87
Call to us to trust for entire deliverance	88
Blessedness following upon it	89
"Delivered." "Translated"	89
Agrees with Prayers in Ephesians	90
Christ's finished work	90
"Delivered" and "Translated" how much?	91
"Having no part Dark"	91
"Full of light"	92
"Ask of Me"	92
To be fulfilled in us	93
The Potter and the Clay	94
The vessel entirely remade	94
Our "marred" state and our hope in it	95
"The Son of God manifested"	95
One healthy one against the world	96
"These Abominations"	96
Where is the line?	97
Are we "delivered to do" any sin?	98
Preventing others accepting deliverance	99
"Let God arise"	90
"He shall preserve thy soul"	100
Promise of deliverance from all sin	100
"In the Strength of the Lord God"	101
Which is the stronger, Christ or sin?	101

SECTIONS AND PARAGRAPHS.

	PAGE
"Free indeed"	102
From indwelling sin	103
"Thy Light and thy Truth"	103
Who shall ascend into the hill of the Lord?	104
"Behold I make a Covenant"	105
Unbelief shuts out from the blessing	105
"The Lord thy God is with thee"	106
"Mindful of his Covenant"	107
Christ is the Covenant	107
Our unmindfulness of the Covenant	108
Or "Testament"	108
Our elder brother's will	109
Spiritual dwarfs	110
"Shall not turn away from me"	111
God's fear in our hearts	112
"Prone to wander"	113
"Satisfied"	114
No satisfaction where sin is	115
Heartfelt experience of this dissatisfaction	115
Let us believe for perfect healing	117
"The Travail of his Soul"	117
The earthly type of it	118
The reward our Lord looks for	118
And at the present time	119
"All that is within me"	120
A great difficulty	120
God must deal with it	120

	PAGE
"He will bind us up"	121
Only as we realise our resurrection with Christ . .	121
Blessedness of perfect healing	122
"As the days of heaven upon the earth" . . .	123
"Thy Word have I hid in mine heart"	124
Christ dwelling in our hearts by faith . . .	124
"Loose him and let him go"	125
Lazarus a type of ourselves	125
Are we not to be set free as he was? . . .	126
"All our works in us"	127
No peace where sin is	128
"Hallowed be thy name" . . .	129
In all the earth hereafter	129
And surely in us now	129
"According to that a man hath" . . .	130
The way provided for it	130
"In the presence of mine enemies" . .	131
"Christian" and "Giant Pope"	132
"The cup of salvation"	132
The price and the purchase equal . . .	133
Fulness of blessing ours now	134
"I will take"	135
Coming but not drinking	135
"Do give me a cup of tea"	136
Do not some of us here see ourselves? . .	138
Let us not only "come," but also "drink" . .	138
How we drink	139

	PAGE
Undoubting faith	140
Another lively instance of it	140
We need it for holiness	140
"*Subdued kingdoms*"	141

"𝔍𝔣 𝔊𝔬𝔡 𝔟𝔢 𝔣𝔬𝔯 𝔲𝔰 𝔴𝔥𝔬 𝔠𝔞𝔫 𝔟𝔢 𝔞𝔤𝔞𝔦𝔫𝔰𝔱 𝔲𝔰?" . 142

God for us	142
God with us	142
God in us	142
"*Let us cleanse ourselves*"	143
"*Perfecting holiness*"	143
God in us ready to do his part . . .	144
Can God and sin dwell together? . . .	144

𝔈𝔩𝔢𝔞𝔫𝔰𝔦𝔫𝔤 𝔣𝔯𝔬𝔪 𝔞𝔩𝔩 𝔲𝔫𝔯𝔦𝔤𝔥𝔱𝔢𝔬𝔲𝔰𝔫𝔢𝔰𝔰 . . 145

Corruptions in the early Church . .	145
Which were still to increase . . .	146
Much increased when St. John wrote . .	146
The creed of the heretical sects . .	147
Their views about our Lord	147
St. John's antidote to their poison . .	148
As to our Lord's human body . . .	148
As to fellowship with God while in sin .	148
Their professed inherent sinlessness . .	149
All his writing clear and consistent . .	149
But read carelessly, may be misunderstood .	150
Those two passages above sufficient . .	150
It's further testimony to freedom from sin .	151
Attempted answer to these passages . .	152
But the attempt vain	153
The old nature dead in full believers .	153

"𝔗𝔥𝔢 𝔡𝔢𝔰𝔦𝔯𝔢𝔰 𝔬𝔣 𝔱𝔥𝔦𝔫𝔢 𝔥𝔢𝔞𝔯𝔱" . . . 154

"𝔖𝔴𝔢𝔢𝔱 𝔚𝔞𝔱𝔢𝔯 𝔞𝔫𝔡 𝔅𝔦𝔱𝔱𝔢𝔯" . . . 155

Of ourselves judging what is right . .	156
Works of the Flesh	157
Fruit of the Spirit	157

	PAGE
"An horrible pit"	157
Pollution of the living water	158
"Instead of—"	159
"Sanctify you Wholly"	159
Expectation of not sinning any more	160
"Christ liveth in me"	160
In what capacity did he speak?	161
Only as a saved sinner	162
"None of Self and all of Thee"	162
Several Texts excluding Sin	164
"To me to live is Christ"	164
"Holiness and godly sincerity"	164
"Holily, righteously, and unblamably"	165
"Children of God without blemish"	165
"Without blemish, before Him in love"	165
"Preserved blameless"	166
Take all the above together	166
"Without spot, unrebukable"	167
But how if this is impossible?	167
Extract from Dr. Mahan	168
"Dead unto Sin"	169
The two Natures	169
Till one of them is dead	170
"Reckoning" Ourselves Dead to Sin	170
God says we have died	171
And I believe it	172

"To the law and to the testimony" . . . 173
Not to "make a Man an Offender for a Word" . . 173
But must not alter the Word of God 174
Explaining away "Healing" 174
And Redemption "from all iniquity" 175
Asserted Benefit of Remaining Sin 175
Explaining away "Salvation" 176
And "Plenteous Redemption" 176
And "Ransomed" 177
Objection and Answer 177
And "The Strong Man Armed" 178
And "A New Creature" 178
"Holiness and Righteousness before Him" . . . 178
"The Serpent in the Wilderness" 179

The Twelve Spies 180
Their good and evil Report 180
Ten of them dishearten the People 181
Joshua and Caleb urge them to go up . . . 181
God's Anger because they will not 182
Much of this repeated now 183
The few Joshuas and Calebs 183
The great majority of the other spies . . . 184
"The congregation" 184
The Children entering in 185
"Bade stone them with Stones" 185
Extract from "Milestone Papers" 186

David and Goliath 187
Goliath's Challenge 187
David's inquiry about it 188
How David felt about it 188
David's Weapons 189
His Answer to Goliath 189
His Victory over him 190
We may here see ourselves 191
God be praised for a few full believers . . . 191
Eliabs still to be met with 192

	PAGE
The above put into verse	192
"In Christ"	194
Noah in the Ark	195
Our Hymns	196
"Make me, keep me pure within" . . .	197
"A Heart to praise my God"	198
God forgive our Unbelief	200
Unbelief meetings	200
What shall we do with the Hymns? . .	201
The only right Course	202
Let none of us continue in unbelief . .	202
"Who is this that cometh—?"	203
Song of rejoicing in the Lord	204
Powerlessness of evil to resist Christ . .	204
He wants to destroy it in us	204
"A peaceable habitation"	205
The desolation and its remedy . . .	206
How the remedy is applied in us . . .	207
Is there any place for sin here? . . .	207
"One of these least Commandments" . .	208
"Except your righteousness exceed— —" .	208
Doing the Father's will and our Lord's sayings	209
Obedience of St. Paul to that Word of our Lord	210
And of St. James	211
And of St. Peter	211
And of St. John	212
And of all the inspired writers . . .	212
Disobedience to it	213
Keeping of God's Law	214
By abiding in Christ and He in us . .	214

	PAGE
"The end of the law"	215
Believers only in part	215
Not unto us, O Lord	216
"Turned aside unto vain jangling"	217
"A pure heart, and a good conscience"	218
What was the "vain jangling"?	218
Guarding against being misunderstood	219
Dean Alford upon the "vain jangling"	220
"Possible and Impossible"	221
Toplady on Perfection	221
Dr. Mahan's answer	221
Toplady's stand-point	222
An earthly case in illustration	222
Letters respecting this book	224
The first letter	224
A sequel to the above letter	225
"Rescued from the Snares"	226
Sinning and repenting	226
"From all your idols will I cleanse you"	226
"And cause you to walk in my statutes"	227
An Experiment	228
Obedience at last	228
God's Answer to it	229
"The Obedience of Faith"	229
"Do all to the Glory of God"	230
"If any man will do his will"	230
Digression on "dead flies"	231
Separation of faith and practice	232
The reward of obedience	233

	PAGE
The seventh of Romans	233
Objection to what I said upon it	234
This chapter so much debated	235
Alford on Seventh Romans	236
Correction of the sentence objected to	236
More kind criticism invited	237
Rejoicing in full deliverance	237
Definite Testimony needed	238
Especially personal testimony	239
Trying to find a saved preacher	240
Finding one at last	240
"Thou canst make me clean"	241
The teaching of our Lord's miracles	242
Leprosy the type of indwelling sin	242
We come with one trouble at a time	243
Because we are so slow to learn	243
Note on the above letter	244
Time of Cleansing	245
Cleansing needed for full service	245
And for the keeping of the law	246
"Make the tree good"	246
Isaiah's felt uncleanness; and his cleansing	247
God's way and man's way	248
The Gospel according to Isaiah	249
Sickness and the Gospel	249
Relief from sickness—when?	250
Certainly at death or at our Lord's coming	250
But surely also now if we believe for it	250
Scripture Proofs	251

	PAGE
" *These signs shall follow* "	253
" *Them that believe* "	253
Not necessarily every one who believes	254
" *My words shall not pass away* "	255
Passages at first sight on the other side	255

A little more on Faith-healing 257

For the uprooting of unbelief	257
Sickness a work of the devil	258
Faith-healing and entire sanctification	259
Promises of old dependent on holiness	260
First, healing of soul; then, of body	261
The requirement in the workers	261
Prominence given to faith in the original	262
Do not let us limit God (Ps. lxxviii. 41)	263
Looking only at the promise	264

Another word on 1 John i. 8 265

All the difficulty in ourselves	265

Difficulty of a strong intellect 266

The difficulty expressed	267
The blessing which was future now present	268
" *Freely given to us of God* "	268
But we must take it	269
" *An appointed time* " *for* " *the vision* "	270
The promises to and in Christ	270
" *Angels of God ascending and descending* "	270
" *Upon the Son of Man* "	271
The blessing for every one of us	271
" *Christ liveth in me* "	272
" *I in them, and thou in me* "	272
Bearing on the intellectual difficulty	273

Illustration of " I will take " 274

The sister conducting the meeting	274

	PAGE
Blessed with the knowledge of full salvation	275
" Go work to-day in my vineyard"	276
" Endure hardness".	276
Diligent obedience	277
A stranger in the meeting	277
His statement	278
The cause of his failure shown to him	279
Set at liberty	280
By accepting God's free gift	281
Our seal to God's truth	281
God's seal to our faith	282
He manifests Himself to us	283
As not to the world	283
The two seals in the present case	284
Bearing of his case on this book	285

"Searched the Scriptures daily" 285

| *Some carefully testing this book by the Bible* | 286 |
| *Word of strong approval* | 286 |

Germ of obedience in saving faith 287

Loss of the joy of pardon 288

| *No safety but in pressing on* | 289 |

"Longing for more light" 290

Hindrances	290
Remedy for this evil	291
" An honest and good heart"	291

Doctors administering poison 292

Teaching young converts to expect to sin	293
Sinning and repenting	293
A difficult question	294
Meetings for deepening the Christian life	294

	PAGE
Blessedness of even a half Gospel	295
" *Make the tree good* "	296
" *If they drink any deadly thing* "	297

Definite testimony again 298

A little bit more 298

And another little bit 299

Very definite 300

" A little child " (Matt. xviii. 2) 301

Limiting God's power to save 301

Seeing full salvation 303

Even Methodists objecting 303
And off-shoots from them	304
" *All the days of Joshua* "	304
And of John Wesley	305
Sanctification and Aggressive Power	306
" *Primitives* " *and others raised up*	306
And now " *The Salvation Army* "	307
" *Scavengers* "	307
But if they don't keep to their work	308

All guilty alike 308
An average congregation	309
Dare not throw stones at each other	310
A word respecting all of us	310
" *Guilty concerning our brother* "	310
The channel choked	311
Through unbelief for full sanctification	311

	PAGE
Sanctification and Missionary Success	312
Missionary Societies some time back	313
The choice of missionaries	313
Their comparative failure	314
Cost of some of the converts	314
Exceptions	315
Happy contrast now	315
"To Him the porter openeth"	316
A good little book	316
Practical unbelief in the Holy Ghost	317
Questions put to a missionary candidate	318
"Are we filled with the Holy Ghost?"	318
Preaching powerless without this	319
Christ in us the power	320
We must all be holy	320
Faith and Holiness: then Power	321
Unsuccessful prayer	322
Possible clue to our failure	323
"Private Thoughts" by Thomas Adam	323
Asking amiss	324
A bit of ministerial experience	325
No longer the old nature	326
Case of Holiness before Power	326
Working hard in the Gospel	326
But thirsting for power	326
But needing holiness first	327
Case in point	327
Deep soul trouble	328
The want supplied	328
To the praise of God's grace	329
Still increasing blessedness	330
Increased power of testimony	330
Fresh opportunities for service	331

	PAGE
Subsequent testimony and service	332
Especially among "Brethren"	333

All included in love ... 334

After purity, only more love	334
Seek nothing else	335
Another witness	336

"If we let God make us holy——" ... 337

| All blessings in Christ | 337 |
| With Him in us right working begins | 338 |

Not yet "established" ... 340

| Statement of a common experience | 340 |
| And of the cause of it | 341 |

Not an "experience," but Christ ... 342

Many longing for rest from sin	343
Clear conversion, but wanting something more	344
Wrongly directed by one brother	344
But then rightly by another	345
Early fervour gradually subsiding	345
Earnest struggles for deliverance	346
Clearer sight of Christ as the Way	347
Help coming in a strange disguise	347
Able to attend a Holiness Convention	348
But still seeking wrongly	348
Putting away the "evil heart of unbelief"	349
Not to seek gifts, but the Giver	350
Trusting only in Christ	351
"Waiting for the fire"	351
"Joy unspeakable, and full of glory"	352
In fulfilment of the promises	352
To the perfect satisfying of his soul	353
Subsequent experience	354
Temptations and trials in abundance	354
Caution to the reader	355

	PAGE
Out of Galatians into Ephesians	355
First out of Egypt: then into Canaan	356
Risk of missing our way	357
Need of being definite	358
Canaan a type of Ephesians	358
Ephesians as real as Galatians	359
Difference of the two conflicts	359
All victory when Jesus has come in	360
Enemies all the way along	361
"All the way 'long it is Jesus"	361
"The gift of God"	363
Christ Himself the gift	364
Mere doctrinal oneness with Christ	364
Living union with Christ	365
God shining into his heart	366
And his mouth showing forth God's praise . . .	367
"Living Water"	368
"Jesus only"	368
"Jesus comes, He fills my soul"	369
"Simply trusting"	370
"I struggled and wrestled"	370
"Jesus saves me now"	371
Jehoshaphat's Victory	373
His sin against God	373
Caught in a snare	374
Inquiring of a prophet of the Lord	374
Going on in spite of warning	375
Death of Ahab	376
God's reproof of Jehoshaphat	376
"A great multitude" come up against him . . .	376
God's promise of deliverance	377

SECTIONS AND PARAGRAPHS.

	PAGE
They believe and praise the Lord	378
And God fulfils his promise	379
And " exceeding abundantly " more	379
Faith in God's bare Word	380
His answer to it	380
Bearing upon our own case	381
No matter what his weakness	382
Or the power of his enemies	382
If only he believed	382
And so with us.	383

Conclusion of this Volume 384

Note in place of Preface

To any who may have the three parts of this book as issued successively as " First Sheets," " Further Sheets," and " Third Series of Scriptural Proofs," I shall be glad to send copies of the above Index and Title-page to bind up with them.

I am trying to prepare full " Tables of Contents," including especially references to all the passages of Scripture dealt with in the book, and am putting into shape much that I wish to say in the way of preface to it: but there are reasons for which I do not like to delay the publication of the " Proofs " themselves the very considerable time still needed to complete satisfactorily these additions to them. If they should be completed hereafter they can go out as a small supplementary volume; of which I shall be happy to supply copies to all who may have procured copies of this one.

NOTE IN PLACE OF PREFACE.

To prevent the appearance of setting myself up as an instructor of the Church in general—an expounder to all my brothers and sisters in Christ of "the way of God more perfectly" (Acts xviii. 26)—I must mention that the preparing and printing of the "Proofs" was not by desire or choice of my own; but was almost forced upon me by circumstances which I cannot here enter into; and that they were first sent out, part by part, only to applicants by letter for them; and that their publication now as a volume is in consequence of letters from readers of the separate parts expressing the great benefit they have derived from them.

My hope is that, of the many more who may see them as thus issued than would be likely to see them if continuing to be sent out only in parts in that comparatively private way, some may receive similar benefit from them in this their collected form to that received from the separate parts by those who have written so warmly respecting them.

I now once more, as on the paper covers of all the separate parts, beg for "brotherly and sisterly criticisms" from readers who may feel led to make any. I do this the more earnestly because of the great benefit I have derived from letters received in answer to those previous requests.

J. P. WILSON,

88 NORTH SIDE, WANDSWORTH COMMON,
LONDON S.W.

Scriptural proofs that God gives us in our Lord Jesus Christ perfect deliverance from all sin, inward as well as outward, if we will but receive Him and believe on his name for all that God has made Him to be to us (John i. 12; 1 Cor. i. 30).

Cleansing from all Filthiness and from all Idols: A New Heart. Loving God with all the Heart and with all the Soul.

"The Lord thy God will circumcise thine heart, and the heart of thy seed, *to love the Lord thy God with all thine heart, and with all thy soul*, that thou mayest live" (Deut. xxx. 6).

"Then will I sprinkle clean water upon you, and *ye shall be clean: from all your filthiness, and from all your idols, will I cleanse you. A new heart also will I give you, and a new spirit will I put within you:* and I will take away the stony heart out of your flesh, and I will give you an heart of flesh. And *I will put my Spirit within you*, and cause you to walk in my statutes, and ye shall keep my judgments, and do them" (Ezek. xxxvi. 25-27).

More entire cleansing of the heart, or more perfectly bringing it into a right state towards God, especially in perfecting it in love to Him, than is put before us in these two most blessed promises cannot be expressed.

Objection and Answer.

But here a dear brother dashes in with the bold assertion that we have nothing to do with either of them, either as Christians or as living in this dispensation, as they both belong exclusively to the Jews in the next.

To which I answer, " Let me fall now into the hand of the Lord; for very great are his mercies: but *let me not fall into the hand of man*" (1 Chron. xxi. 13), even though of ever such dear brethren. "For as the heavens are higher than the earth, so," He says, "are *my ways higher than your ways, and my thoughts than your thoughts*" (Isa. lv. 9).

He has given us the whole Bible. The devil formerly set his slaves to burn it up out of the earth as a whole; and failing in that, he now sets some of God's children to cut it up and rob themselves and their brothers and sisters of many of its most blessed parts. But we cannot afford to lose the least bit of it; and so let us not yield to him in this matter the thousandth of an inch.

Our heavenly Father has told us that "Whatsoever things were written aforetime were written *for our learning*, that we through patience and comfort of the scriptures might have hope" (Rom. xv. 4); and that "No prophecy of the scripture is of any *private*" (in the margin of the revised version "*special*") "interpretation" (2 Pet. i. 20). And we find accordingly in the New Testament many instances of the application to our dispensation of declarations and promises in the Old Testament appearing to refer in their first meaning only to the Jews.

"Behold the days come, saith the Lord, that I will make a new covenant *with the house of Israel, and with the house of Judah*: not according to the covenant that I made with their fathers in the day that I took them by the hand to bring them out of the land of Egypt; which my covenant they brake, although I was an husband unto them, saith the Lord" (Jer. xxxi. 31, 32).

What could seem to belong more exclusively to the Jews than this promise? And yet it is brought forward in the Epistle to the Hebrews and elaborately reasoned upon there (Heb. viii. 8-13; ix. 15-18; x. 16-18; xii. 24), as spoken of us of this dispensation, without a hint of possibility of doubt as to the rightness of so applying it.

On no conceivable ground can the two promises quoted above, of the circumcision of the heart to love the Lord our God with all the heart and with all the soul, and the giving of a new heart and a new spirit, be restricted to the Jews, and to the next dispensation, that would not at least equally restrict to them and to it this one of a new covenant, shown in that inspired epistle so certainly to belong to us.

All the Promises ours.

And lastly—and perhaps best of all, in the way of preserving to us every word of promise that God has spoken—we have his word by St. Paul, "All the promises of God in him" (our Lord Jesus Christ) "are yea, and in him Amen, unto the glory of God by us"; or, as it stands in the revised version, "*How many soever be the promises of God*, in him is the yea: wherefore also through him is the Amen, unto the glory of God *through us*" (2 Cor. i. 20).

Judge the Tree by its Fruit.

In the life of Mrs. Fletcher, of Madeley, or, as she was at the time, the little girl, Mary Bosanquet, there is a specimen of the results naturally to be looked for of our taking God's promises less freely and fully than He gives them to us:—

"I was now, I believe, about ten years old, and can recollect many comfortable moments in reading the Word of God. The promises in Isaiah were in a particular manner applied to my soul: and I hardly ever opened the Bible but there was something for me: till one day I heard a person make the remark that 'many people take promises to themselves which do not belong to them.' Of some, she observed they belonged to the Church, others to the Jews, such and such to the Gentiles, &c., and then began to blame the presumption of those who applied them to their own souls!

"Such a thought had never entered my heart before. I knew the words were primarily spoken on particular occasions: but *the Lord had led me to believe that his Word was written to every soul so far as they were willing to receive it by faith.* But from the above conversation I was unhinged. I knew not what to choose or what to refuse; so that, being cast into reasonings, I lost all my love for reading the Scriptures; and sank into a very cold and lifeless state."

The poor child does not seem to have recovered from this shock to her faith for years. We may well distrust **a** tree bringing forth such fruit, and keep at the utmost distance from all *such views* of "Dispensational Truth."

It has been said of the dear brothers in the Lord chiefly holding these views that they "make the Jews their *waste-paper basket*"; throwing over to them in the next dispensation all promises beyond their experience, or which they cannot make fit into their theological system: so many of them and such blessed ones being thus treated by them that it might almost tempt us, if this view of the Bible were accepted as correct, to wish to be Jews in the next dispensation rather than Christians in this.

Those Two Promises Enough.

But if those two promises, the one for circumcising our heart to love the Lord our God with all our heart and with all our soul, and the other for cleansing us from all our filthiness, and from all our idols, and giving us a new heart and a new spirit, and putting God's Spirit within us, are thus indeed, as children say of any of their possessions which they particularly prize, "*our own very own*," that seems at once to settle the question as to whether God does or does not offer us in our Lord Jesus Christ—in whom, as declared in that Word above quoted, all his promises are yea, and in Him Amen, to the glory of God by us—perfect deliverance from all sin inward as well as outward.

For there manifestly cannot be sin in any heart in which those two promises are fulfilled. To say of any heart that there is sin still left in it is to say that these promises have not yet been fulfilled in it.

God's Law in our Minds and Hearts.

I referred above to God's promise by Jeremiah of a New Covenant with us. Here are some of the words declaring what this covenant is:—

"This shall be the covenant that I will make with the house of Israel; After those days, saith the Lord, *I will put my law in their inward parts*" (in the Epistle to the Hebrews "*into their mind*"), "*and write it in their hearts*; and will be their God, and they shall be my people" (Jer. xxxi. 33).

If the law were only that we are to *love God*, without saying *how much* we are to love Him, it is conceivable that it might be put into our minds and written in our hearts, and yet other loves be there which were not in subjection to this love to Him. For it is possible to love with some degree of love two persons or things opposed to each other. But it is that we are to love Him *with all our heart, and with all our soul, and with all our mind, and with all our strength* (Mark xii. 30); and there cannot in any heart in which this is fulfilled be any love not in subjection to this supreme love to Him: and where there is this supreme love to Him, and no other love not entirely subjected to it, there is of necessity the absence of sin.

And this is confirmed by the fact of the promise being not only of *putting* the law into our *mind*, but also of *writing* it in our *heart*; which must certainly mean the giving to it the command of all that is within us, whether intellectual or emotional; our affections, desires, motives, and will, as well as our thoughts and our judgment: involving, of course, the entire exclusion of sin.

"They shall all know Me."

But some may have difficulty in seeing how we can apply to ourselves the next following words: "And they shall teach no more every man his neighbour, and every man his brother, saying, Know the Lord: for they shall all know me, from the least of them unto the greatest of them, saith the Lord" (Jer. xxxi. 34); such a state of things being manifestly so contrary to the existing state of the Church.

But the difficulty disappears on our remembering that all God's promises are conditional on our belief for their fulfilment (Heb. iv. 2). The promise, for instance, to bring the Israelites into Canaan was to all who came up out of Egypt; yet through their unbelief it was fulfilled to scarcely any of them (Numb. xiv. 23, 28-30). But to the believers Joshua and Caleb it was fulfilled; and to any of the Levites who may have believed; for we are not told of them, as of those belonging to the other tribes, which among them did and which did not believe; as they were not "numbered" "among the children of Israel" (Numb. i. 49), and there was no "ruler" or "head" from their tribe with the twelve from the other tribes who went up to search the land (Numb. xiii. 1-16).

And to believers in his promises now the words we are considering are perfectly fulfilled: for they do "all know" Him "from the least of them unto the greatest of them."

Each of us in himself an Israel.

Moreover, the promise has a further sweet fulfilment in each of us individually if we believe for it.

We are each one of us in himself a complete little Israel, and, indeed, each in himself a complete little world; and so we may well *personify* the things in us which together make up our moral and spiritual being. David did this when he called upon "all" that was "within" him to "bless" God's "holy name" (Ps. ciii. 1). And St. Paul did it with respect to the thoughts of the heathen, when he said that they "show the work of the law written in their hearts, their conscience also bearing witness, and their *thoughts* the meanwhile *accusing or else excusing one another*" (Rom. ii. 15).

Now while we are believing in Christ only for pardon and deliverance from the overcoming power of sin, but not for the entire casting of it out of us, there is a continual effort by all that is of God in us to bring all else into a right state towards Him; a constant striving for the "casting down imaginations, and every high thing that exalteth itself *against the knowledge of God*, and bringing into captivity every thought to the obedience of Christ" (2 Cor. x. 5).

But when Christ has full possession of our hearts, and sitting "upon the throne" there, says, "*Behold I make all things new*" (Rev. xxi. 5), there is an end of all this inward striving (Gal. v. 17); for there is no longer anything in us to which it is necessary to say: "Know the Lord;" for "all that is within us" does know Him and serve Him and "bless his holy name."

Fulfilment of Old Testament Figures.

And then we have in us the fulfilment of the lovely Old Testament figures:—

"Violence shall no more be heard in thy land,

wasting nor destruction within thy borders; but thou shalt call thy walls Salvation, and thy gates Praise. The sun shall no more be thy light by day, neither for brightness shall the moon give light unto thee: but the Lord shall be unto thee an everlasting light, and thy God thy glory. Thy sun shall no more go down, neither shall thy moon withdraw itself: for the Lord shall be thine everlasting light, and the days of thy mourning shall be ended" (Isa. lx. 18–20).

For we " are " now indeed " come unto Mount Sion and unto the city of the living God" (Heb. xii. 22), "the mountain of his holiness, beautiful for situation, the joy of the whole earth," " the city of the great King" (Ps. xlviii. 1, 2), with nothing to "hurt" or "destroy" in all that "holy mountain;" "full of *the knowledge of the Lord* as the waters cover the sea" (Isa. xi. 9: lxv. 25): the fierceness of the wolf, and leopard, and bear, and lion, and the venom of the asp and cockatrice all gone, only their strength and wisdom (Matt. x. 16) left; and all under the rule of the child-like spirit in us of entire dependence upon our loving God and Father through our dear Lord and Saviour and by the power of our blessed Sanctifier and Comforter.

And so all the sweet word of prophecy is fulfilled in us spiritually that :—

" The wolf also shall dwell with the lamb, and the leopard shall lie down with the kid; and the calf and the young lion and the fatling together; and a little child shall lead them. And the cow and the bear shall feed; their young ones shall lie down together : and the lion shall eat straw like the ox. And the sucking child shall play on the hole of the asp, and the weaned child shall put his hand on the cockatrice' den. They shall not hurt nor destroy in all my holy mountain: for the earth shall be full of the knowledge of the Lord, as the waters cover the sea" (Isa. xi. 6-9).

And certainly this is a state of things in which there is no place for sin: and yet equally certainly it is all included in the "all spiritual blessings in heavenly places" with which God has "blessed us" "in Christ" (Eph. i. 3), and of which He is ready to put every one of us into possession by revealing Him in us (Gal. i. 16) by his Spirit (1 Cor. ii. 12) as their fulfilment (2 Cor. i. 20), if we will but, by putting away our unbelief, yield ourselves up to Him that He may do it.

"*Yield yourselves unto God*" (Rom. vi. 13).

I say "*yield ourselves up to Him that He may do it;*" because all that is written here about the fulfilment of the promises, supposes that we are *willing to be entirely yielded up to Him.* Any expectation without this of our being "strengthened with might by his Spirit in the inner man; that Christ may dwell in" our "hearts by faith" (Eph. iii. 16, 17), that we may ask (Ezek. xxxvi. 37) in his name and have them fulfilled in us (John xvi. 23, 24), would be expecting to obtain "the pearl of great price" without being willing to "sell all" to "buy it" (Matt. xiii. 46).

"*Healeth all thy Diseases.*"

In the list of "benefits" for which David, in the 103rd Psalm, calls upon his soul and all that

was within him to bless God's holy name, the first two are :—
" Who forgiveth all thine iniquities; who *healeth all thy diseases*."

Must we not understand that the Holy Spirit really meant " *healeth*," when He inspired David to write it?

Suppose only partial bodily healing.

If I were suffering from bodily disease, and the doctor so far cured me of it that he could say, " I trust it will not break out any more, nor interfere with your power to go about your work; you taking care, which I know you will, so to regulate your life as best to keep it under : but it must remain *lurking in your system* till your dying day; and I am afraid will often make you painfully conscious of its existence there : " I should, if I believed this was the best that could be done for me, say, " I thank you, doctor ; " and feel grateful to him for this extent of cure. But if on the strength of it he spoke of having "*healed my disease*," should I be able quite to go along with him in such a view of my case?

No one would think of using the word "heal," pure and simple, under such circumstances; but would of course add the necessary qualification and say "partial healing," or "healing to a great extent," or some other such words.

But this is all that so many dear children of God believe Him able to do, in the way of curing our poor sin-sick souls. If it were so, would He be less accurate in language than we should be in such a case? Would He call it " healing," without adding any qualification?

That any should thus limit the healing is the more strange because of the outcry they would raise if such a qualified meaning were proposed for the other "benefit," the "forgiveth all thine iniquities." For they know the result of merely partial forgiveness would be:—

> "Almost will not avail,
> Almost is but to fail;
> Sad, sad that bitter wail,
> Almost—but lost."

Is it not surprising that they should take in two such different ways the two halves of the one verse? And is not this as sad as it is strange: for is not our perfect healing as important to us, and as much to the glory of God by us, as our perfect forgiveness?

"Healing in His Wings."

Another passage in the Old Testament about "healing," is that in Malachi, "Unto you that fear my name shall the Sun of righteousness arise *with healing in his wings*" (Mal. iv. 2).

And in accordance with this prophecy, St. Peter in the first Christian sermon preached to us Gentiles, gave as a short account of the life on earth of our Lord Jesus Christ, that He "went about doing good, and *healing all that were oppressed of the devil*" (Acts x. 38).

Our Lord's Works of Bodily Healing.

Of his works of bodily healing the records are such as these:—

"They sent out into all that country round

about, and brought unto him all that were diseased; and besought him that they might only touch the hem of his garment: and as many as touched *were made perfectly whole* " (Matt. xiv. 35, 36).

"He saith unto the man, stretch forth thine hand. And he stretched it out: and his hand was restored *whole as the other* " (Mark iii. 5).

" Are ye angry at me, because I have made a man *every whit whole* on the Sabbath day ? " (John vii. 23.)

All the accounts of his bodily cures show that they were thus perfect—that in those whom He healed there was nothing left of the disease or infirmity from which they had been suffering.

Has He two Sorts of Healing?

Now can we believe, in the absence of any hint to this effect in the Word of God, that He has one sort of healing for the body, and another for the soul; a perfect healing for the less, and only an imperfect healing for the infinitely more important subject on which to exert his power as the " mighty to save "? (Isa. lxiii. 1.)

I am entirely unable to believe this ; and, so far as I can see, am never likely to be able to believe it; and I do not in the least wish to be able to believe it: and so if inability and unwillingness to believe that it is only partial healing which our dear Lord is ready to administer to our poor sin-sick souls—or, rather, that it is only a partial healing which He is *able to be to us by his indwelling in us by the Spirit* (Eph. iii. 17 ; Gal. ii. 20)—appears to any of my brothers and sisters in Him a dangerous heresy, I must be content to be given up by them as an incorrigibly dangerous heretic.

"As Moses lifted up the Serpent.'

Our Lord's words to Nicodemus about Moses lifting up the serpent in the wilderness have an important bearing upon the question of the extent of deliverance from sin purchased for us by his death on the cross:—

"And as Moses lifted up the serpent in the wilderness, even so must the Son of man be lifted up: that whosoever believeth in him should not perish, but have eternal life" (John iii. 14, 15).

In turning to the Book of Numbers, and there reading the account of the lifting up of the serpent and of the healing of the bitten Israelites on their looking upon it, we see no hint of any one of them being so foolish as to look for anything but a perfect cure. There plainly was not one who said with reference to his poor diseased body, "I think I may venture to believe I shall be saved from dying of the bite; but I cannot hope for more than that; I must, I know, go on suffering from some remains of the poison left in me all the rest of my days."

All who looked, perfectly cured.

No, the whole record shows that every one that looked at the serpent expected and experienced a *perfect cure*: the poison went entirely from his veins. Whether he was left weak or not from the bad effects of it during the time it was in him—as we, however perfectly cured from the poison of sin, are left thus weak through its injurious effects while in us—does not appear: but as regards real and entire riddance out of him of the actual poison itself, he was as though he had never been bitten; and this just because he believed it should be so to him on his obeying the word of good tidings "look and live."

But that was an earthly matter; and "the children of this world are in their generation wiser than the children of light:" and so the children of light do just exactly that foolish thing which those Israelites did *not* do, limit their faith, that is, as to the extent of cure. And as according to the faith exercised so always is the answer to it, they obtain only partial, instead of perfect healing. And any who do not follow them in this foolishness, but look for and obtain a perfect cure, are cried out against as poor deluded ones to believe in such an impossibility, and most of all for daring presumptuously to declare that in their own case it has been fulfilled.

We may be very sure that our Lord never used an illustration which should express more than the truth He took it to illustrate; or, to speak more correctly, that He never instituted a type which should be greater than its fulfilment. And so, if a perfect bodily cure was given by God to those that would in faith for it look on the serpent of brass lifted up on the pole, a perfect spiritual cure is given by Him to those who with faith for it will look at our Lord Jesus Christ lifted up on the cross: or, in other words, they are, on thus believing in Him for it, entirely delivered from all sin inward as well as outward.

Time of Healing.

But some may here say, Of course we are all agreed as to the perfection of healing for soul as well as body. You need not use so many words to prove *that.* But where we differ is as to the *time* of its completion. We hold that, commencing at regeneration, it is not complete till death or our Lord's coming again.

But this again is answered by reference to the cases of bodily healing :—

" There came a leper to him, beseeching him, and kneeling down to him, and saying unto him, If thou wilt, thou canst make me clean. And Jesus, moved with compassion, put forth his hand, and touched him, and saith unto him, I will; be thou clean. And *as soon as he had spoken, immediately the leprosy departed from him,* and he was cleansed" (Mark i. 40–42).

" Jesus said unto the Centurion, Go thy way, and as thou hast believed, so be it done unto thee. And his servant was healed *in the self-same hour*" (Matt. viii. 13).

" Simon's wife's mother lay sick of a fever, and anon they tell him of her. And he came and took her by the hand, and lifted her up; and *immediately the fever left her, and she ministered unto them*" (Mark i. 30, 31).

" A certain woman, which had an issue of blood twelve years, and had suffered many things of many physicians, and had spent all that she had, and was nothing bettered, but rather grew worse, when she had heard of Jesus, came in the press behind, and touched his garment. For she said, If I may touch but his clothes, I shall be whole. And *straightway the fountain of her blood was dried up; and she felt in her body that she was healed of that plague*" (Mark v. 25–29).

" He saith to the sick of the palsy, I say unto thee, Arise and take up thy bed, and go thy way into thine house. And *immediately he arose, took up the bed, and went forth before them all;* insomuch that they were all amazed, and glorified God, saying, We never saw it on this fashion" (Mark ii. 10–12).

"He took the damsel by the hand, and said unto her, Talitha cumi; which is, being interpreted, Damsel, I say unto thee, arise. And *straightway the damsel arose and walked;* for she was of the age of twelve years. And they were astonished with a great astonishment" (Mark v. 41, 42).

With only a very few exceptions—in each of which there seems to have been special reason for a little delay, but not in any one of them apparently so much as one hour—all our Lord's recorded works of bodily healing were thus as instantaneous as they were perfect.

Greek Tenses of the New Testament.

We are not, however, left merely thus to infer the instantaneous character of our Lord's works of spiritual healing from that of his works of bodily healing; but have direct proofs of it in many passages in the New Testament.

I must here mention, for those, like myself, with no Greek scholarship, that in our English translation two Greek tenses having very distinct meanings from each other, the "*Aorist*" expressing the *doing a thing completely at once,* and the "*Present*" expressing the doing a thing, and *continuing to do it,* have both in general to be translated by our one English present tense in which this distinction of meaning is lost.

Dr. Steele, in a treatise of deep interest on the "Tense Readings of the Greek Testament," in his

"Milestone Papers," shows by abundant examples that while the present tense, expressing continuous action, is constantly used respecting Christian graces or duties, such as "Rejoice in the Lord," "Obey your parents," "Love your wives," "Pray for us," "Let the peace of God rule in your hearts," "Let the word of Christ dwell in you richly," &c., the "aorist," signifying the doing a thing once for all, is as constantly used in passages respecting our sanctification; such as, "Mortify therefore your members which are upon the earth" (Col. iii. 5); "The very God of peace sanctify you wholly" (1 Thess. v. 23); "Let us cleanse ourselves from all filthiness of the flesh and spirit" (2 Cor. vii. 1); "That ye present your bodies a living sacrifice, holy, acceptable unto God" (Rom. xii. 1); "That ye put off concerning the former conversation the old man, which is corrupt according to the deceitful lusts" (Eph. iv. 22); "That ye put on the new man, which after God is created in righteousness and true holiness" (Eph. iv. 24); "Sanctify them through thy truth" (John xvii. 17); "Purifying their hearts by faith" (Acts xv. 9); "Purge out therefore the old leaven" (1 Cor. v. 7); &c.

Dean Alford, in his Greek Testament, entirely confirms the distinctness of meaning in which the New Testament writers, as well as the classical Greek authors, use the two tenses; and so does Bishop Ellicott; and so, apparently, do all the other good modern critical New Testament commentators and grammarians. The statement in "Green's Handbook to the Grammar of the New Testament," in speaking of the Imperative Mood, that while "the Present implies continuance or repetition, the Aorist implies that the action is *instantaneous or complete,*" and, in speaking of the

Subjunctive, that " The Present implies continuity, the Aorist *completion*," and in speaking of the Infinitive, that "the Present marks continuity, the Aorist *a single act*," appears rightly to give the views of all of them.

And as to the correctness of the statement that the Aorist, expressing a complete work done on the instant, is the tense constantly used in the New Testament in texts respecting cleansing and sanctification, any one merely able to read the Greek words, without critical knowledge of them, can test this for himself by referring to the original of all such passages, and, with the help, if need be, of a " parsing lexicon," noting the tenses of the verbs.

"Second blessing": "Higher life."

But it may be said, that those who contend the most earnestly for the entire deliverance from sin, generally protest against the idea of its taking place at conversion; and assert that it is a " second blessing " received, or a " higher life " entered upon, at an interval, longer or shorter as the case may be, after the acceptance of pardon.

I know they do: and they have this much to show in favour of their view, that most of those who profess to be thus delivered, and whose lives seem to accord with their profession, say they received the deliverance as a distinct gift from forgiveness, at some number of hours, or days, or weeks, or months, or years, as the case may be, after it.

But the fact seems to be, that the rule laid down by our Lord, " *According to your faith be it unto you* " (Matt. ix. 29), prevails as certainly in God's spiritual kingdom, as any law in his material creation; and that, accordingly, the deliverance is obtained only when, on a felt need of it, there is a believing coming to Him for it. He then by the Spirit (John vii. 37) reveals Himself to us as the supply of this need as He had before done for that of pardon (Phil. iv. 19).

And as, in the present state of the Church, the need of cleansing is not generally felt at the same time as the need of pardon—or if the need is felt there is not the same *preparedness to believe* in Him for the supply of it—there is generally an interval between the times of the reception of the two "good and perfect gifts;" which are yet both included in the one " Gospel of the grace of God" (Acts xx. 24).

What is the Gospel?

A dear minister was appointed to speak in a gathering specially for the promotion of holiness. But many persons coming into it who did not appear to be of the class of those who have made sure of the pardon of their sins, a Christian friend at his side said to him, "Oh! look at all these people, *you must not speak on holiness, you must preach the gospel.*"

When he stood up to speak he began with words which I cannot give literally here, as I have not the report at hand to refer to; but they were exactly to the following effect:—

" My dear brother here has told me that, so many strangers having come into this meeting, I must not speak on holiness, but must preach the Gospel. Now, I wish to ask what is the Gospel? I read, ' Unto you first God, having raised up his Son Jesus, sent him to bless you, in *turning away every one of you from his iniquities.*' What is that but the Gospel? and what is it but holiness?"

"*What God hath joined——*"

Surely he was right: and surely the right word for us is "What therefore God hath joined together, let not man put asunder" (Matt. xix. 6).

But unhappily this is what many are doing, by taking up with a half Gospel of the *entire forgiveness*, indeed, of sin, but only a *partial deliverance* from it; not perceiving what a poor substitute it is for the old original whole one, as stated in those words just now quoted, "turning away every one of you from his iniquities," and in the many other similar words by which it is described in God's Book.

And they are so persuaded that this only imperfect salvation is the real Gospel, that they look with extreme alarm upon any who, holding on to the old complete one, insist that God has indeed given us in Christ "plenteous redemption" (Ps. cxxx. 7), and by "*turning away*" means real turning away, full turning away, and by "*iniquities*" iniquities of heart as well as of life, and who declare that they by his grace have accepted Him for it, and that He fulfils it to them as a blessed fact (Ezek. xxxvii. 14; Luke i. 45; Rom. i. 16).

"*According to your Faith.*"

Under the operation of that law of the kingdom, it would appear that those who do not believe in our Lord Jesus Christ for either pardon of sin or cleansing from it, do not get either: that those who believe in Him for its pardon and for deliverance from its overcoming power now, but from its indwelling only at death, have in Him pardon and deliverance from its overcoming power now; and will, we may hope, have in Him deliverance from the indwelling at death; and that those who believe in Him first for its pardon and for deliverance from its overcoming power, and afterwards, by a separate act of faith, for deliverance from its indwelling without waiting for death, have also in Him just exactly these things that they believe in Him for, and at the times that they believe in Him for them.

And no doubt any, feeling their need sufficiently, and seeing clearly enough the "fulness" which there is in Him for us (John i. 16; Col. i. 19), to enable them to believe in Him for pardon and perfect deliverance both at once, would also have Him for both at once.

And the nearer we come to that and get others to come to it the better. For assuredly when God says, as He does to every one of us his children, "Oh! do not this abominable thing that I hate" (Jer. xliv. 4), and "Walk worthy of the vocation wherewith ye are called" (Eph. iv. 1), and "As he which hath called you is holy, so be ye holy in all manner of conversation; because it is written Be ye holy for I am holy" (1 Pet. i. 15, 16; Lev. xi. 44; xix. 2; xx. 7), it cannot be his will that any one of us should continue even one moment to have anything more to do with the "*abominable thing*" in any shape or of any sort outward or inward.

Sanctification at Death.

There is, I think, a strong confirmation of the view of an entire deliverance from sin being given to us on our believing on our Lord Jesus Christ, and in the power of the Holy Ghost given us through Him, and revealing Him in us for it, in the fact that there is not one word in the Bible—so far, at any rate, as I can see, and I have looked very carefully to try and see any, if any were there—of promise of our being freed from it hereafter, at either of the times at which alone so many dear Christians declare it is possible for us to be so; namely, at death, or at the coming again of our Lord.

From every other evil from which we are suffering we are then promised full and eternal deliverance: but not a hint is given, so far as I am able to find, of any at all from this the worst of all evils; and from which, therefore, we should expect at least as full promise of deliverance, if God intended that we should then be suffering from it, as from any others.

The Cry of every Awakened Heart.

A dear Christian lad dying in a country hamlet some time ago of consumption, the son of parents in very poor circumstances, so that he was suffering from the privations of poverty as well as from his disease, was being visited by another young Christian who was doing his best to comfort him in all that he was passing through, especially such pain from his terrible cough, that after one of his bad fits of coughing he could not for some considerable time bear even to be spoken to. His young comforter was putting before him all that sweet deliverance that was now close at hand for him, "No more death, neither sorrow, nor crying, *nor any more pain.*" The dear dying lad, to complete the list of deliverances with that which he felt to be the best of them all, added, " and *no more sin.*"

Another dear dying one, under different earthly circumstances, the wife of a manufacturer, who had long and lovingly toiled in Christ's service, especially in trying to bring to Him as many as she could of her husband's workpeople, also spoke of it as the best thing of all in that deliverance from all evil, which she was waiting for death to bring to her, that she should *have done for ever with sin.*

And I think the feeling of those two dying ones is that of every person really alive to God, thoroughly awakened to a sense of sin, and not yet fully delivered from it—namely, that full deliverance from it would be the greatest of all possible blessings; so that if they should think it could be had only by death, they would, like those two dear ones, consider it the greatest blessing in the way of deliverance which death could bring to them.

Why no Promise of Deliverance at Death.

And if this is so, as I feel sure all will agree with me that it is, then, on the theory that death or the coming of our Lord is the time that *God intends* —for that is the question; not whether or not many of his children through "lack of knowledge," or through unbelief, postpone their deliverance till then—to be the time of our deliverance from sin, how is it to be accounted for, that sorrow, and pain, and trouble, and crying, and persecution, and oppression, and affliction, and shame, and spoiling of our goods, and evil speakings against us, and privation, and hunger, and thirst, and weariness, and poverty, and sickness, and weakness, and ignorance, and imprisonment, and these bodies of humiliation, and death itself, and many other evils besides, should all be specifically mentioned, and some of them many times over, as things from which we are then to be delivered, but never once sin—how, I say, is this to be accounted for, except on the ground that *God assumes that we are entirely rid of that beforehand* by a full acceptance of his gift to us of his Son, who was called Jesus because He should " *save his people from their sins,*" and who " gave himself for us that he might *redeem us from all iniquity,* and purify us to himself a peculiar people, zealous of good works," and " his own self bare our sins in his own body on the tree, that we, being *dead to sin,* might live unto righteousness; by whose stripes we are healed"—"*are healed*"—now, already—not shall be at death, or at his coming again, unless we, ourselves, by failing to believe for it sooner, put it off till then?

On the supposition that God assumes that we have taken this perfect deliverance from sin already, as part of that *salvation of our souls* which we receive through believing in our Lord (1 Pet. i. 9), the absence of any word about sin in the promises of deliverance from all other evils at the coming of the Lord or at death is fully explained; but on the other supposition—that the deliverance from this, the greatest evil, like that from all those smaller ones, is only then to be—the absence of all mention of it in the Word of God as to take place then, seems entirely inexplicable.

Why that Time in Particular?

It seems a great mystery how *that particular time* should have been arrived at by so many Christians, as that at which so desirable an event is to take place. For surely they cannot in the teeth of our Lord's words, "*From within out of the heart of men proceed*" all evil things, including those which are carried out entirely through the agency of the body (Mark vii. 21), have adopted the theory of several heretical sects of old, *that the seat of sin is in the body.* And if not, what connection then can there be between getting rid of the body and getting rid of indwelling sin?

That many *temptations* are presented through the body of course all are agreed; but the question just now is not at all of *temptation*, but of *indwelling sin* responding to temptation; the traitor within the citadel in league with the open enemy without.

We should all alike, if on our entreating an unconverted one to turn immediately to God and be saved, he answered that *he meant to be converted at death*, cry out against the wicked folly of putting off the acceptance of salvation until that, the least favourable of all times for accepting it. But on what ground can we show that our *putting off until then the acceptance of this completion of salvation* is any less foolish; and if we really knew what we were doing, any less wicked?

What a Pity to Wait!

All this, however, is consistent with the hope already expressed that children of God believing that it is not his will to give them the deliverance until then, will receive it then. But does it not seem a sad pity that they should thus " ignorantly in unbelief" (1 Tim. i. 13) postpone until death the acceptance of that which if accepted in their health and strength would make so blessed a change in their lives, both as regards their happiness and their power to live to the glory of God?

A dear minister's wife was slowly dying. Her anxiety to be rid of heart-sin was intense: but her husband's and her own theological creed forbade her to think that this could be till the moment of death. She struggled desperately to get her feet out of such a net (Ps. xxv. 15); appealing to him whether, if God could do it at death, He could not do it some hours before? To which he was obliged to assent. Then if a few hours, could He not also do it a few days? Which also he could not deny. Then if a few days, could He not do it a few months? And here his theological cobwebs gave way altogether; and the dear soul was enabled to accept that full salvation which God in his infinite love had all the way through been pressing upon both of them as his glorious gift, purchased for them with the blood of his Son, and ready to be wrought in them by his Spirit revealing Him in them for it, but which "the traditions of men," in which they had been brought up, had been hitherto causing them to reject.

Prayers and Armour in Ephesians.

Along with the notice of the absence of any promise of deliverance from sin at death, or at the coming of the Lord, I would also call attention to the *absence of any allusion to inward sin* in the two prayers of St. Paul in the end of the first and end of the third chapters of the Epistle to the Ephesians; and also to the absence in his catalogue of "the whole armour of God" in the sixth chapter, of *any means of either defence or active war-*

fare against sin in us; which, if it were supposed to exist, would undoubtedly be by far our most dangerous enemy, and therefore the one against which we should expect God to provide us with means of fighting more than against any other.

The Prayers.

Here are the prayers:—

In the first chapter: "That the God of our Lord Jesus Christ, the Father of glory, may give unto you the spirit of wisdom and revelation in the knowledge of him: the eyes of your understanding being enlightened; that ye may know what is the hope of his calling, and what the riches of the glory of his inheritance in the saints, and what is the exceeding greatness of his power to usward who believe, according to the working of his mighty power, which he wrought in Christ, when he raised him from the dead, and set him at his own right hand in the heavenly places" (Eph. i. 17–20).

And then in the third chapter: "That he would grant you, according to the riches of his glory, to be strengthened with might by his Spirit in the inner man; that Christ may dwell in your hearts by faith; that ye, being rooted and grounded in love, may be able to comprehend with all saints what is the breadth, and length, and depth, and height; and to know the love of Christ, which passeth knowledge, that ye might be filled with all the fulness of God" (Eph. iii. 16–19).

Most blessed prayers they are for increase of knowledge and love and holiness, but *not a word about deliverance from sin*; because apparently it is assumed that we know this to have been already freely and fully given to us in Christ. And yet there are, further on in the Epistle, many injunctions both against sin in general and against particular sins; but only in the way of exhortation to realise in our hearts and lives what we thus know God has already wrought out for us in Him (Rom. vi. 6, 11, 17, 18; 1 Pet. ii. 24, &c.).

The Armour.

And here is his catalogue of "the whole armour."

"Finally, my brethren, be strong in the Lord, and in the power of his might. Put on the whole armour of God, that ye may be able to stand against the wiles of the devil. For we wrestle not against flesh and blood, but against principalities, against powers, against the rulers of the darkness of this world, against spiritual wickedness in high places. Wherefore take unto you the whole armour of God, that ye may be able to withstand in the evil day, and having done all, to stand. Stand therefore, having your loins girt about with truth, and having on the breastplate of righteousness; and your feet shod with the preparation of the Gospel of peace; above all, taking the shield of faith, wherewith ye shall be able to quench all the fiery darts of the wicked. And take the helmet of salvation, and the sword of the Spirit, which is the Word of God: praying always with all prayer and supplication in the Spirit, and watching thereunto with all perseverance and supplication for all saints" (Eph. vi. 10–18).

None against any inside Enemy.

It has been well observed that there is no word here of protection to the back. Christians being expected always to face all enemies in the strength of the Lord. But is not the absence of any means of contending with an inside foe equally worth noticing?

And not only is there no mention of weapons, offensive or defensive, against any inside enemy, but in the list of the enemies themselves, there is no mention of any inside one; the "principalities," "powers," "rulers of the darkness of this world" and "spiritual wickedness in high places" (revised version, "spiritual hosts of wickedness in the heavenly places"), which are all that are named, being all outside of us.

"*In the heavenlies.*"

For the scene of the warfare for which St. Paul is exhorting us to "put on the whole armour of God" is placed by him "*in the heavenlies*": for this, the Greek scholars say, is the meaning of the expression translated "high places." It is used only by St. Paul, and by him only in this Epistle, to describe, apparently, the heavenly state into which we are brought by believing in Christ for full salvation. And the very entrance into this state is through the casting out of us by Christ of all inside foes (Luke xi. 21, 22). And then, being "raised up together, and made to sit together *in the heavenlies* in Christ Jesus," (Eph. ii. 6) the chief of the fighting—as was the case with Israel after entering the promised land, *the type of the heavenlies*—begins; but, thank God, now only, as here shown by St. Paul, against outside enemies.

The one Greek word translated above "*whole armour*," and which we have in English, with but little change of spelling, in the word "panoply,"

occurs in the New Testament only here and in Luke xi. 22, where it is translated "*all armour*":—
"When a strong man armed keepeth his palace, his goods are in peace: but when a stronger than he shall come upon him, and overcome him, he taketh from him *all* his *armour* wherein he trusted, and divideth his spoils."

The "whole armour" sufficient.

The words "*keepeth his palace*" and "*his goods are in peace*" show that the "all armour" of the "strong man" was sufficient to keep him in undisturbed possession till "the stronger than he" came upon him. And we may be confident that the "whole armour" of the "stronger than he" will be sufficient to prevent him from entering again when he has been put out of possession. But for this we must ourselves "*put it on*," which we can only do by believing in it and in our Lord Jesus Christ for it: for it is by *putting Him on* (Rom. xiii. 14) by faith that we do indeed "put on the whole armour of God."

"The Helmet of Salvation."

I do not like to leave that "whole armour of God" without a word specially on the "*helmet of salvation*," or as it is in another place, "for an helmet *the hope of* salvation" (1 Thess. v. 8).

If, in our warfare with our spiritual enemies we have for our "helmet of salvation," or of "the hope of salvation" a steadfast trust in God, that the word will be fulfilled in us "O God the Lord, *the strength of my salvation*, thou hast *covered my head* in the day of battle" (Ps. cxl. 7), shall we not have in every conflict a victory answering to this our trust in Him?

But if, on the contrary, though trusting to be at last victorious, we expect to be wounded again and again before this happy final result, will it not be just so with us, because it will be just to that extent that our "helmet of salvation" or of "the hope of salvation" is imperfect?

A Case in Point.

I give here the case of one who tried both ways of entering into the battle, and who accordingly was in the one case frequently defeated, but in the other constantly victorious.

It is that of a young Christian, working earnestly for Christ, especially in the Sunday-school, but not unfrequently overcome in the course of the week by a naturally quick temper, to his deep shame and sorrow.

After one of these painful failures he said to a Christian friend, "I cannot bear this inconsistency; teaching those dear boys about Christ on the Sunday, and then being betrayed into this un-Christlike conduct in the week. I must give up my class till I am saved from this sad stumbling in my Christian course."

His friend showed him how wrong it would be so to act: that instead of giving up his service to Christ because of his failures, he must look to Him (Isa. xlv. 22; Phil. iv. 13) for deliverance from them. And he asked him whether he had ever prayed to Him about his temper. "Oh, yes," he said, "scores of times; and as earnestly as any man could ever pray about anything."

"And have you really trusted Him to save you from it?"

"Oh, yes, that I have."

"And do you expect ever to lose your temper again?"

"Yes," he answered, "I know I shall by my past bitter experience."

"Oh," his friend said, "I thought you had trusted Christ; and yet you say you know you shall lose your temper again! There must be some mistake somewhere, mustn't there? That is a curious sort of trust, isn't it, to say you have trusted Him against it, and yet you know it is going to overcome you again."

The young man saw the inconsistency of his two statements and admitted it to his friend, who then advised him to go away alone with our Lord, and see if by his grace he could not *really* trust Him. After a little time he returned with a bright face, saying that all was right now—that he did really trust Him, and knew He would keep him. And when they met again some weeks afterwards he was able rejoicingly to say that he had been perfectly kept by Him in circumstances which would before have been to him an occasion of stumbling.

Abundance of cases of perfect victory.

Not only do such examples abound of perfect victory by faith in Christ over individual spiritual enemies, but many are to be met with also of the same perfect victory by faith in Him over all of them together; in fulfilment of the words of triumph which God has given us to use with respect to them all, " I have pursued mine enemies and overtaken them, neither did I turn again *till they were consumed:*"

"Thou hast also given me the necks of mine enemies, that I *might destroy* them that hate me;" "Then did I beat them small as the dust before the wind, I did cast them out as the dirt in the streets" (Ps. xviii. 37, 40, 42): cases of those who—to pass from Old to New Testament language—having been crucified with Christ (Gal. ii. 20 revised version), are "dead indeed unto sin" in every shape, inward or outward, but, through his resurrection, "alive" again with a life now only "unto God" (Rom. vi. 11).

God's Pictures of Holiness.

I take as the next scriptural proofs that God offers to us in Christ deliverance from all sin two Old Testament descriptions of a perfectly holy life:—

"Blessed is the man that walketh not in the counsel of the ungodly, nor standeth in the way of sinners, nor sitteth in the seat of the scornful. But his delight is in the law of the Lord; and in his law doth he meditate day and night. And he shall be like a tree planted by the rivers of water, that bringeth forth his fruit in his season; his leaf also shall not wither; and whatsoever he doeth shall prosper" (Ps. i. 1-6).

"Blessed are the undefiled in the way, who walk in the law of the Lord. Blessed are they that keep his testimonies, and that seek him with the whole heart. They also do no iniquity: they walk in his ways" (Ps. cxix. 1-3).

Is God merely putting before us here a lovely ideal of impossible attainment? Is He not rather showing us that which He wishes and requires us to be, and which He has provided for us the means of our becoming, in our Lord Jesus Christ, and by the power of the Holy Ghost given us through Him, and revealing Him in us for it?

To be realised in us.

Is not each of the two passages a beautiful picture of the life on earth of our Lord Jesus Christ; held up before us that " beholding as in a glass the glory of the Lord," we may be " changed into the same image" (2 Cor. iii. 18)?

Do not both of them show the fruit of that " divine nature," of which we are made " partakers" by the " exceeding great and precious promises," if we are so united to Him by faith as to be in Him and He in us, for the fulfilment of them to us?

And then—delighting in the law of the Lord—meditating in it day and night—undefiled in the way—keeping his testimonies—seeking Him with the whole heart—doing no iniquity—walking in his ways—what sin can there be in us?

"The Way of Holiness."

Here is another of God's pictures of perfect holiness:—

"The wilderness and the solitary place shall be glad for them; and the desert shall rejoice, and blossom as the rose. It shall blossom abundantly, and rejoice even with joy and singing: the glory of Lebanon shall be given unto it, the excellency of Carmel and Sharon, they shall see the glory of the Lord, and the excellency of our God.

"Strengthen ye the weak hands, and confirm the feeble knees. Say to them that are of a fearful heart, Be strong, fear not: behold, your God will come with vengeance, even God with a recompence; he will come and save you.

"Then the eyes of the blind shall be opened, and the ears of the deaf shall be unstopped. Then shall the lame man leap as an hart, and the tongue of the dumb sing: for in the wilderness shall waters break out, and streams in the desert. And the parched ground shall become a pool, and the thirsty land springs of water: in the habitation of dragons, where each lay, shall be grass with reeds and rushes.

"And an highway shall be there, and a way, and it shall be called The way of holiness; the unclean shall not pass over it; but it shall be for those: the wayfaring men, though fools, shall not err therein. No lion shall be there, nor any ravenous beast shall go up thereon, it shall not be found there; but the redeemed shall walk there:

"And the ransomed of the Lord shall return, and come to Zion with songs and everlasting joy upon their heads: they shall obtain joy and gladness, and sorrow and sighing shall flee away" (Isaiah xxxv. 1–10).

This also for Us.

Whatever glorious fulfilment God may intend for these beautiful figures to his earthly Israel and to the world, in a dispensation yet to come, does He not intend also a glorious fulfilment of them now already spiritually in us as his spiritual Israel? ("*We are the circumcision* which worship God in the Spirit and rejoice in Christ Jesus and have no confidence in the flesh" Phil. iii. 3).

That the translators of the Bible believed this is shown by the heading they have put to the chapter:—

"*The joyful flourishing of Christ's kingdom. The weak are encouraged by the virtues and privileges of the gospel.*"

Practical Illustration.

I have heard of an infidel lecturer, in his confidence in the skill in argument with which God had endowed him, but which he was using in rebellion against Him, saying at the beginning of his lecture, that if, at the end of it, any one present should have a question to ask about anything he might have said, he should be happy to answer him.

At the end of the lecture a plain working man stood up and said, "I think, sir, you said you would be glad to answer any question any of us might wish to put to you."

'Yes," said the lecturer, "I am quite ready. What is that you wish to ask?"

"Just this, sir. Three weeks ago I was the wickedest man in the town; and my home a little hell through my wickedness: and now there is not a happier man in the town; and my home is being turned into a little heaven: and this has been brought about by the gospel of Christ, which you are telling us to throw aside as rubbish. My question is, *What have you to give us in its place which will produce the same effects?*"

The lecturer had not a word to answer. The simple statement of one of God's facts disposed in a moment of all the devil's lies which he had for the hour or two before been so boldly pouring forth.

Now is not every such case—and, God be praised! He gives us to hear of multitudes of them on every side—of a man becoming a "new creature" (2 Cor. v. 17) by the Gospel of Christ being the power of God to his salvation on his believing it (Rom. i. 16), a fulfilment of the above prophecy of Isaiah that "*the desert shall rejoice and blossom as the rose?*"

Further Blessing.

But the prophecy goes on: "It shall blossom *abundantly*, and rejoice *even with joy and singing.*" And then follows a picture of "beauty of holiness" (Ps. xxix. 2), in which there is no place for sin. "An highway shall be there, and a way, and it shall be called *the way of holiness; the unclean shall not pass over it.*" "*No lion shall be there, nor any ravenous beast shall go up thereon, it shall not be found there;* but the redeemed shall walk there: and the ransomed of the Lord shall return and come to Zion with songs and everlasting joy upon their heads: they shall obtain joy and gladness, and sorrow and sighing shall flee away."

And is not all this further blessedness to be looked for also as a matter of present experience by those who by God's grace have experienced that first blessed change (Heb. vi. 1) of our desert hearts and lives being made to rejoice and blossom at all?

And if it is fulfilled in us, and continues to be so by our continuing "in the faith grounded and settled," "not moved away from the hope of the Gospel" (Col. i. 23), are we not then living a **life free from sin**, outward or inward?

"Put on thy strength, O Zion."

There is another lovely, and most sweetly encouraging word of prophecy as regards deliverance from sin, in the fifty-second chapter of Isaiah. And here again, the translators have shown their belief of its application to ourselves by the heading:—

Christ persuadeth the church to believe his free redemption, to receive the ministers thereof, to joy in the power thereof, and to free themselves from bondage. Christ's kingdom shall be exalted.

"Awake, awake; put on thy strength, O Zion; put on thy beautiful garments, O Jerusalem, the holy city: for henceforth there shall no more come into thee the uncircumcised and the unclean. Shake thyself from the dust; arise, and sit down, O Jerusalem: loose thyself from the bands of thy neck, O captive daughter of Zion. For thus saith the Lord, Ye have sold yourselves for nought; and ye shall be redeemed without money" (Isa. lii. 1–3).

"Therefore my people shall know my name: therefore they shall know in that day that I am he that doth speak: behold, it is I. How beautiful upon the mountains are the feet of Him that bringeth good tidings, that publisheth peace; that bringeth good tidings of good, that publisheth salvation; that saith unto Zion, Thy God reigneth" (verses 6, 7).

"Break forth into joy, sing together, ye waste places of Jerusalem: for the Lord hath comforted his people, He hath redeemed Jerusalem. The Lord hath made bare His holy arm in the eyes of all the nations; and all the ends of the earth shall see the salvation of our God" (verses 9, 10).

I have said that the translators have shown their belief that all this is for us; but we have higher authority than theirs that it is so; for St. Paul, quotes the prophecy as certainly referring to our dispensation:—

"The word is nigh thee, even in thy mouth and in thy heart: that is, the word of faith, which we preach; that if thou shalt confess with thy mouth the Lord Jesus, and shalt believe in thine heart that God hath raised him from the dead, thou shalt be saved. For with the heart man believeth unto righteousness; and with the mouth confession is made unto salvation. For the scripture saith, Whosoever believeth on him shall not be ashamed. For there is no difference between the Jew and the Greek: for the same Lord over all is rich unto all that call upon him. For whosoever shall call upon the name of the Lord shall be saved. How then shall they call on him in whom they have not believed? and how shall they believe in him of whom they have not heard? and how shall they hear without a preacher? and how shall they preach, except they be sent? as it is written, *How beautiful are the feet of them that preach the gospel of peace, and bring glad tidings of good things!*" (Rom. x. 8–15).

We have here, then, inspired authority for saying that the above prophecy of Isaiah describes the salvation offered to us in the gospel.

All the ends of the earth.

The concluding words of it, "All the ends of the earth shall see the salvation of our God," accord well with those in the forty-fifth chapter:—

"*Look unto me, and be ye saved, all the ends of the earth: for I am God, and there is none else*" (Isa. xlv. 21, 22).

And with those in the sixty-fifth psalm:—

"By terrible things in righteousness wilt thou answer us, O God of our salvation; who art *the confidence of all the ends of the earth*, and of them that are afar off upon the sea" (Ps. lxv. 5).

And with those in the sixty-first psalm:—

"*From the end of the earth will I cry unto thee*, when my heart is overwhelmed: lead me to the rock that is higher than I" (Ps. lxi. 2).

And many of his children, with hearts overwhelmed with the evil of indwelling sin, causing them to feel as at "the ends of the earth" away from Him as regards power to obey his command "Be ye holy, for I am holy," have "cried unto" Him, and He has indeed "led" them "to the Rock that is higher than" they. ("The shadow of a great rock in a weary land," Isa. xxxii. 2.)

And this has been to them the "awaking" up to newness of life in Him (Eph. v. 14), and the "putting on" of their "strength," and of their "beautiful garments." And now He preserves them from the "coming into" them any more of "the uncircumcised and the unclean."

And they have "shaken" themselves "from the dust" and "loosed" themselves "from the bands of their neck." And they "break forth into joy" and "sing together," because "the Lord" has so blessedly "comforted" and so gloriously "redeemed" them, by thus "making bare" on their behalf "his holy arm." And all their desire is that "all the ends of the earth shall see the salvation of our God," a salvation worthy of Him as "The Holy One of Israel"; an entire salvation from sin, outward or inward.

"God is my Salvation."

The twelfth chapter of Isaiah is another of God's pictures of perfect holiness: and in this case also the translators have shown their belief of its application to all believers—whatever special application it may have to Israel and to the world hereafter—by the heading which they have put to the chapter:—

"*A joyful thanksgiving of the faithful for the mercies of God.*"

"And in that day thou shalt say, O Lord, I will praise thee: though thou wast angry with me, thine anger is turned away, and thou comfortedst me. Behold God is my salvation; I will trust, and not be afraid: for the Lord Jehovah is my strength and my song; he also is become my salvation. Therefore with joy shall ye draw water out of the wells of salvation.

"And in that day shall ye say, Praise the Lord, call upon his name, declare his doings among the people, make mention that his name is exalted. Sing unto the Lord; for he hath done excellent things; this is known in all the earth. Cry out and shout, thou inhabitant of Zion: for great is the Holy One of Israel in the midst of thee."

Can we doubt that God means all this to be realised spiritually in the present experience of every one of us his children, through our entering by faith into perfect oneness (John xvii. 21–23) with his Son, "holy, harmless, undefiled, separate from sinners, and made higher than the heavens" (Heb. vii. 26), but made "to be sin for us" "*that we might be made the righteousness of God in him*"? (2 Cor. v. 21).

And if it is fulfilled in us and *God* is our Salvation, and we are made in Christ the very *righteousness of God*, and by abiding in Him and He in us are kept in this salvation and righteousness, how can we fail of being always in a state of entire deliverance from sin?

Redemption.

There were different depths to which an Israelite might sink from which he would need to be redeemed.

He might be sunk so low as to be obliged to do that of which Naboth said, " The Lord forbid " that he should do it even to please the king—sell " the inheritance of" his " fathers " (1 Kings xxi. 3; Lev. xxv. 25). Or even much lower yet, he might have to sell himself and his children : or he and they might be taken for his debts (Lev. xxv. 39, 47, 54 ; 2 Kings iv. 1).

It is this lowest depth to which we are reduced in our need of redemption. For not only is our inheritance gone, the eternal life which was our birthright, but also we ourselves, and our children with us, have been " sold under sin " (Rom. vii. 14), sold into bondage to the world, the flesh and the devil (Eph. ii. 2, 3).

The right of redemption.

The Israelite might at any time redeem himself, and his children, and his inheritance, if he could (Lev. xxv. 26, 49): but in our case any such hope was far away out of our sight.

But if unable to do it himself, any "nigh of kin" to him might do it for him. ("One of his brethren may redeem him: either his uncle, or his uncle's son, or any that is nigh of kin unto him of his family may redeem him," Lev. xxv. 48, 49). And here it is that redemption comes within our reach, our Lord Jesus Christ having made Himself our Brother (Heb. ii. 11), for the very purpose of redeeming us and all belonging to us, and having paid the redemption price by his blood.

The Extent of Redemption.

Now, was it only a partial or a perfect redemption which the Israelite's nigh of kin effected for him and his? Did he take him and his children and his inheritance only partly away out of the power of the one to whom they had been sold; or did he take them entirely away from him, so that they were, with respect to his having any longer any power over them or part in them, just as if they had never been sold to him at all?

We know the answer: and shall any other be given to the same question asked about our elder Brother's redemption of us and ours? Must we say that the earthly redemption was so perfect that it was beyond his power to work out for us a spiritual redemption of equal perfection? Or shall we not rather say that here, as everywhere else in the spiritual fulfilment of the earthly types, if the type was "glorious," "much more doth the" fulfilment "*exceed in glory*" (2 Cor. iii. 7, 9).

And if so, are we not then indeed most blessedly "redeemed" "from all iniquity" (Titus ii. 14; Ps. cxxx. 8), whether of heart or life?

"Ransomed."

In connection with the word "Redeemed" God has made use of another word to confirm the completeness of the deliverance which He has given to us from the power of our spiritual enemies:—

"The Lord hath redeemed Jacob, and *ransomed* him from the hand of him that was stronger than he.

"Therefore they shall come and sing in the height of Zion, and shall flow together to the goodness of the Lord, for wheat, and for wine, and for oil, and for the young of the flock and of the herd: and their soul shall be as a watered garden; and they shall not sorrow any more at all" (Jer. xxxi. 11, 12).

This is in the same chapter as the promise of the "New Covenant with the house of Israel, and with the house of Judah," dwelt upon a little way back.

Now does not "Ransomed," as in the case of "Redeemed" considered above, mean that he who had been taken captive is bought back completely out of the power of him who had taken him captive; so that, so far as his having any further hold over him, he is as though he had never been in his power at all?

And so if the Lord has indeed "ransomed" us "from the hand of him that was stronger than" we —his and our evil enemy "the god" (2 Cor. iv. 4) of "this present evil world" (Gal. i. 4)—ought we not to be able to say in humble but yet very triumphant (Ps. xcviii. 1) glorying in our great Deliverer (1 Cor. i. 31), that which He could say in a yet much more blessed sense, as having ever been the perfectly sinless One, " The prince of this world cometh, and hath nothing in me" (John xiv. 30)?

And then with all sin thus destroyed out of us (1 John iii. 8), we may look for the fulfilment of the rest of the beautiful picture, in the abundance to us, in a spiritual sense, by "the goodness of the Lord," of "wheat," and "wine," and "oil," and of "the young of the flock and of the herd;" and in our "soul" being "as a watered garden," and our "not sorrowing any more at all"—which cannot be if there is sin in us: for, if our hearts are in anything of a right state towards God, so long as it is in us it must be a source of deep sorrow to us (Rom. vii. 24).

"I am thine, save me."

"*I am thine, save me*" (Ps. cxix. 94). Here again, as in the "healing" a little way back and the "redemption" and "ransoming" immediately above, the question arises, *What extent* of salvation may we look for from God?

Certainly for *as much as it is in his power to give to us.* This our Lord has taught us by referring us to our own conduct towards anything of ours needing exertion on our part to save it. "Which of you," He said, "shall have an ox or an ass fallen into a pit, and will not straightway pull him out?" (Luke xiv. 5.)

And He shows us that we should do this in spite of any obstacle in the way; for He supposes the case to occur on the Sabbath day, when the necessary exertion would, to a Jew, be absolutely forbidden, but He assumes that his ownership of the beast, and its crying need of his help, would, by common consent, be held to set all such difficulty aside.

And we may take it, not only from his teaching here, but from the whole tenor of the Word of God, that his ownership of us, and our crying need of his help—both of which are set forth in that prayer, "I am thine, save me"—will certainly cause Him to exert Himself for our salvation to the utmost of his power.

How much can He save?

The question then is, How much *can* He save us?

A poor negro said he liked his preacher because he "*made God big.*" And was he not right? Ought we not to have a view of salvation which exalts God (Ps. lxx. 4)?

Does not his Word lead us to form very high ideas indeed of his power to save? He asks:—

"Is anything too hard for the Lord?" (Gen. xviii. 14.) And again:—

"Behold, I am the Lord, the God of all flesh: is there anything too hard for me?" (Jer. xxxii. 27.)

And though "It is," our Lord says, "easier for a camel to go through the eye of a needle, than for a rich man to enter into the kingdom of God," yet even this, He says, is not too hard for God. "With men," He says, "it is impossible, but not with God: for with God all things are possible" (Mark x. 27).

He is "able to do exceeding abundantly above all that we ask or think" (Eph. iii. 20).

"Look unto me," He says, in words already

considered above, "and be ye saved, *all the ends of the earth*"—however extreme, that is, the distance from Him—"for I am God, and there is none else" (Isa. xlv. 22). "*Be ye saved*"—without limit as to the extent of the salvation.

And our Lord says: "I that speak in righteousness, *mighty to save*" (Isa. lxiii. 1).

He is able "to save them *to the uttermost* that come unto God by him, seeing he ever liveth to make intercession for them" (Heb. vii. 25).

But here again, some may say, "Of course we are all agreed that God is able to save to any extent whatever."

If so, then, we must all be agreed that He offers us, in our Lord Jesus Christ, in whom all his salvation is stored up for us, entire deliverance from all sin, inward as well as outward; to prove which by his Word is the object of this book.

But here the dear souls start back with, "Oh, no, we do not mean *that* when we speak of his being able to save to the uttermost."

And I would earnestly beg of them, if they *do not mean that*, then to try clearly to define to themselves *what it is that they do mean*; what they consider to be the utmost present salvation that God can give to us; and see whether they can bring themselves to draw the line anywhere short of that entire deliverance; which however, of course, still leaves unlimited room for growth for ever and ever in the blessedness and power of salvation; the entire deliverance from sin being that which puts us into a condition in which alone such growth is possible to us. This is "the grace" *in* which we are to "grow" (2 Peter iii. 18, revised version). But we cannot grow in it until we are in it.

Grace "much more" Abounding.

"Where sin abounded *grace did much more abound*" (Rom. v. 20).

How much has sin abounded? I suppose we shall all, of every variety of creed held by those "that love our Lord Jesus Christ in sincerity" (Eph. vi. 24), agree that it has abounded to the ruin of our whole nature. If then grace were to "abound" only as much, it would be to its perfect restoration: which surely would include the casting of all sin out of it; out of our nature itself, not merely out of our outward conduct.

But it does not thus merely abound as much, but "*much more*," even to the making us through the "exceeding great and precious promises" "*partakers of the divine nature*, having escaped the corruption that is in the world through lust" (2 Peter i. 4).

"Bless the Lord, O my soul: and all that is within me, bless his holy name. Bless the Lord, O my soul, and forget not all his benefits: who forgiveth all thine iniquities: who healeth all thy diseases; who redeemeth thy life from destruction; who crowneth thee with loving kindness and tender mercies; who satisfieth thy mouth with good things; so that thy *youth is renewed like the eagle's*" (Ps. ciii. 1–5).

Whosoever then has, when sin abounded in him, accepted God's much more abounding grace in our Lord Jesus Christ, and continues to live in the power of that grace by continuing to live a life of full faith in Him (Gal. ii. 20), is surely living a life free from sin outward or inward.

And surely in whatever degree the life of any

of us falls short of this, we are just to that extent, "receiving" "the grace of God in vain" (2 Cor. vi. 1).

"Whosoever abideth in Him."

"And now, little children; abide in him; that when he shall appear, we may have confidence, and not be ashamed before him at his coming" (1 John ii. 28).

"Ye know that he was manifested to take away our sins; and in him is no sin. Whosoever abideth in him sinneth not (1 John iii. 5, 6).

"*Abide in me, and I in you,*" is our Lord's commandment; and none of us will venture to say that in giving it to us, He was giving us one which we may not by his grace keep. But here we have his word by St. John that "Whosoever abideth in him *sinneth not.*" And if it is thus possible for us by his grace to "abide in him," and "whosoever abideth in him sinneth not," how can we avoid the conclusion that it is possible for us not to sin?

Sin active or inactive still Sin.

And if it be said that this "Whosoever abideth in him sinneth not," refers to *actual* sins, not to the existence of sin in the heart in a state of repression, I would ask where do we read in God's Word that He does not see sin to be as much sin in what we call a state of *repression* as in what we call a state of *activity?*

It may need to be *active* to be discerned *by us*, but to Him who "understands our thought afar off," and to whose "eyes" there is nothing that is "not naked and opened," and whose Word is "quick and powerful, and sharper than any two-edged sword, piercing even to the dividing asunder of soul and spirit, and of the joints and marrow, and is a *discerner of the thoughts and intents of the heart*," how can there be any need, if there be sin in us at all, that it should be in any way active to enable Him to see it, and to see it in its true character as indeed sin, actual sin, even in an ever so entirely repressed state, just as much as if it were in a state of ever so lively activity?

And if He thus sees all sin alike, whether active or repressed, as actual sin, and calls it always by its right name (Gen. i. 5), then when He says "whosoever abideth in him sinneth not," must He not mean that there is not in such a one sin of any sort either active or repressed?

"*In Him is no Sin.*"

And is not this confirmed by that word, "In him is no sin"? For if "*In him is no sin,*" and we are called to "*abide in him,*" is not this calling us to abide in a state of "*no sin*"?

And is it not also confirmed by that other word above: "Ye know that he was manifested to *take away our sins*"? For surely "taking away our sins" cannot mean taking away merely their guilt and outward *activities*, or even merely their guilt and *outward and inward* activities, and leaving the *sins themselves*—the pride, for instance, and deceit, and envy, and self-conceit, and covetousness, and worldliness, and uncleanness, and ungodliness, and idolatry, and unbelief—there as much as ever, though in an inactive instead of an active state; but must mean just what it says, the actual taking away of the sins themselves, leaving us *without their existence in us at all, in any state whatever, active or inactive.*

"*Shall save his People from their Sins.*"

And is not this entire taking away of sin out of us declared to us in our Lord's very name of Jesus, given to Him because He should "*save his people from their sins*" (Matt. i. 21)? Must not this mean save them not merely from the guilt of their sins, and from their outward workings, or even merely their guilt and both outward and inward workings, but just exactly what it says, "save them *from their sins,*" the very sins themselves?

"*Taketh away the Sin of the World.*"

And so also with his name of the "Lamb of God, which *taketh away the sin* of the world" (John i. 29). Must not this mean really the sin itself, not merely its condemnation and its workings? Does it not declare that truth, of which the counterpart is stated in St. Paul's words, "They that are Christ's have crucified *the flesh* with the affections and lusts" (Gal. v. 24), not merely "the affections and lusts," as the workings of the "flesh" as the evil principle, but the evil principle itself, along with its evil workings?

Him who knew no Sin made to be Sin.

And so also with respect to our Lord being made "sin for us," though He "knew no sin; that we might be made the righteousness of God in him" (2 Cor. v. 21): must not this mean that He and we are so entirely one that we are really *made in Him the very righteousness of God*, not merely *judicially accounted so* for his sake? I say "not merely" because of course this also is included. It is the "forgiveth all thine iniquities" to which that "healeth all thy diseases" (Ps. ciii. 3) is the twin-sister mercy of our loving God to us.

It being always remembered, however, that in all these cases, that which is declared is only so far realised in us as we believe for it; so that all those who do not at all believe for it, have all their experience to strengthen them in their unbelief, and those who only partially believe have all theirs to strengthen them in their only partial belief; and so both are united to condemn those who fully believe and dare to declare that it is to them according to their faith.

"Hath Established my Goings."

"I waited patiently for the Lord; and he inclined unto me, and heard my cry. He brought me up also out of an horrible pit, out of the miry clay, and set my feet upon a rock, and established my goings. And he hath put a new song in my mouth, even praise unto our God: many shall see it, and fear, and shall trust in the Lord" (Psalm xl. 1–3).

Many dear children of God seem to believe—at all fully, at any rate—in only about the first half of this beautiful cluster of the "all spiritual blessings" with which God has blessed us in Christ (Eph. i. 3).

They know God has brought them up out of the horrible pit of their mere earthly life, and has set their feet on the "strong" (Ps. xxxi. 2) and "tried" (Isa. xxviii. 16) rock, the glorious "Rock of ages" (Isa. xxvi. 4, margin). They sing with all their hearts—"On Christ the solid Rock I stand: All other ground is sinking sand."

But when it comes to the "hath established my goings," and they are asked, *Are* your goings really *established*? Is there no slipping and sliding on the Rock, though, thank God, you feel blessedly safe from being allowed by Him to slip right off, back again into the horrible pit? they have with sorrow to confess that they do very frequently thus slip and slide, even to the extent of thinking and feeling and saying and doing things which their consciences tell them at the time, or on reflection afterwards, really are sins against God, and sometimes against man also.

And it is well if they do not "limit the Holy One of Israel," by adding that they never expect in this life to be rid of these slippings and slidings, and do not believe that any of their brothers and sisters in his family, whatever they may say, are really any more without them than themselves.

Established in Christ.

But God be praised, He has a people, whatever these dear souls may think or say of them, who can go the length of the whole passage and, "to the praise of the glory of his grace, which he freely bestowed on us in the Beloved" (Eph. i. 6, revised version), can say that He has, so far as freedom from sin is concerned—the having "always a conscience void of offence toward God and toward men" (Acts xxiv. 16), whatever there may yet be in them of weakness and mistake and infirmity, and other such things—indeed "established" their "goings," and has as a consequence put the new song in their mouth, even praise unto our God, in such power that "many" do "see it and fear, and trust in the Lord."

And this comes to pass through "the eyes of" their "understanding being enlightened" (Eph. i. 18) to see Christ as their *entire deliverer from sin*, inward as well as outward, as well as *the bearer of it all for them*. Their "established" *walk* in Him is the result of their established inward *state* in Him. It is the fulfilment in them of that word, "As ye have therefore *received* Christ Jesus the Lord, so *walk* ye in Him" (Col. ii. 6).

Made the Goodness of God in Him.

"Either make the tree good," He said, "and his fruit good; or else make the tree corrupt and his fruit corrupt" (Matt. xii. 33).

And again He said, "A good man out of the good treasure of the heart bringeth forth good things: and an evil man out of the evil treasure bringeth forth evil things" (Matt. xii. 35).

But "none," He said, "is good, save one, that is, God" (Luke xviii. 19). But in our oneness with Him, and by our being "made the righteousness of God in Him," and by the "exceeding great and precious promises" which "in him are yea and in him Amen," "partakers of the divine nature," we have this one only goodness: and surely He means this to be the description of our whole *moral and spiritual* character.

And surely in such a character there is no sin outward or inward.

Peter on and in the Water.

"Jesus constrained his disciples to get into a ship, and to go before him unto the other side, while he sent the multitudes away. And when he had sent the multitudes away, he went up into a mountain apart to pray: and when the evening was come, he was there alone.

"But the ship was now in the midst of the sea, tossed with waves: for the wind was contrary. And in the fourth watch of the night Jesus went unto them, walking on the sea. And when the disciples saw him walking on the sea, they were troubled, saying, It is a spirit; and they cried out for fear. But straightway Jesus spake unto them, saying, Be of good cheer; it is I; be not afraid. And Peter answered him and said, Lord, if it be thou, bid me come unto thee on the water. And he said, Come. And when Peter was come down out of the ship, he walked on the water, to go to Jesus.

"But when he saw the wind boisterous, he was afraid; and beginning to sink, he cried, saying, Lord, save me. And immediately Jesus stretched forth his hand, and caught him, and said unto him, O thou of little faith, wherefore didst thou doubt? And when they were come into the ship, the wind ceased" (Matt. xiv. 22-32).

Even little Faith very blessed.

It is a blessed thing even to be in such a state as to make that reproof of our Lord to Peter applicable to us, "O thou of little faith, wherefore didst thou doubt;" a blessed thing, that is, to have any faith in Him at all, to lead us to call upon Him, in our slipping and sliding and sinning, for pardon and restoration, and to find it in Him.

But is this the best that God has for his children this side of his taking them home, to have done with failure of every sort for ever? Has He not the power of saving them from it as far as there is any sin in it, even already down here? Yes; on one condition, that they will believe that He has it, and that in Christ and by the Holy Ghost He will exercise it, and does exercise it, upon them.

Looking only at Jesus.

Then—not like Peter when with his eyes off Jesus, seeing the wind boisterous, he was afraid, and beginning to sink, but like him while, attending only to his sweet word "Come," he walked on the rough waves as if on firm ground—they, looking only to Him (Heb. xii. 2), and listening only to his voice (John x. 27), telling them of full salvation, walk on the top of the trials and troubles, and temptations, and sins, which make up together the "troubled sea" of this "present evil world" (Gal. i. 4), unhurt by any of them, to where He is calling them to come and be in safety for ever up above them all with Himself.

This only an Illustration.

Perhaps I should not be right in bringing this scene in the life of Peter forward as a "Scriptural *Proof*" of God's gift to us in Christ of deliverance from all sin. So I must let it stand as merely a Scriptural *Illustration* of the blessedness of the life when Christ has been accepted for this deliverance.

Walking with God.

"Enoch *walked with God*: and he was not; for God took him" (Gen. v. 24).

"Before his translation he had this testimony, that *he pleased God*" (Heb. xi. 5).

"The Lord appeared to Abram, and said unto him, I am the Almighty God; *walk before me, and be thou perfect*" (Gen. xvii. 1).

"*The Kingdom of Heaven.*"

We who are living in this dispensation are, if we will but by faith enter into the position of blessing God has given us in our Lord Jesus Christ, greater than either Enoch or Abraham.

For John the Baptist was at least as great as either of them, as our Lord said of him: "*Among them that are born of women there hath not risen a greater than John the Baptist.*" But He added, "*Notwithstanding he that is least in the kingdom of heaven is greater than he*" (Matt. xi. 11).

And we may all, if we will, be in this "kingdom of heaven." For it is that of which He said a little while afterwards, "There be some of them that stand here, which shall not taste of death, till they have seen *the kingdom of God come with power*" (Mark ix. 1): and it did accordingly "come with power" on the day of Pentecost, and has continued to be here in power ever since, for all who will believe in it, and in Him for their entrance into, and continuance in it.

If, then, Enoch so "walked with God" as to "please" Him, and if Abraham could so "walk before" Him as to "be perfect"—as it must have been possible for him to do, or God would not have given him the commandment to do it—surely it must be possible for every one of us, in this so much higher and "better" (Heb. xi. 40) dispensation, so to "walk worthy of the vocation wherewith" we "are called" (Eph. iv. 1); so to "walk worthy of God who hath called" us "unto his kingdom and glory" (1 Thess. ii. 12); so, having "received Christ Jesus the Lord," to "*walk in him*" (Col. ii. 6), that we also shall "*please God*," and "*be perfect before*" Him.

Christ in us as well as for us.

For we are all agreed that *no other "walk" than a blameless one can be pleasing to Him*; those who contend the most strenuously for the impossibility of our so walking, and who yet believe that He is pleased with us, doing so on the ground *that He does not look at all either at our walk, or at ourselves*—our walk, according to their view, being necessarily so full of failure, and ourselves so utterly and irretrievably bad—but on *Christ for us*; and, that seeing us pure and spotless and every way perfect *in Him*, He is pleased with us *for his sake*.

And that He does thus see us in Him, and is pleased with us for his sake, we who believe in deliverance from all sin fully and rejoicingly agree; but delight to believe also that He sees Christ *in* us down here as well as *for* us up there, and just as perfect in the one place as the other, and that so He is doubly pleased with us in seeing Him in this double relation to us.

And we trust in Him as entirely for the rightness of our walk as for the absolving us from our guilt (Isa. xlv. 24; 1 Cor. i. 30, 31): delighting as much in "*I will go in the strength of the Lord God*" as in "I will make mention of thy righteousness, even of thine only" (Ps. lxxi. 16).

"Remission" or "Forgiveness of Sins."

A word in the original which is often translated "forgiveness" or "remission" frequently has a far wider meaning than that which we generally attach to these words, and especially to "forgiveness." Along with pardon it includes deliverance from sin.

This is seen in the use made of it by our Lord in the opening of his ministry at Nazareth:—

Deliverance and Setting at Liberty.

"The Spirit of the Lord is upon me, because he hath anointed me to preach the Gospel to the poor; he hath sent me to heal the broken-hearted, to preach *deliverance* to the captives, and recovering of sight to the blind, to *set at liberty* them that are bruised" (Luke iv. 18).

Here there is the same word in the original for both "*deliverance*" and "*setting at liberty*;" and it is the original word in many passages in which "*remission*" or "*forgiveness*" appears in our translation; as, for instance, in that passage in Ephesians, in which St. Paul, after naming our Lord Jesus Christ, says "In whom we have redemption through his blood, the *forgiveness* of sins" (Eph. i. 7).

Dean Alford in his Greek Testament says of the meaning of the word as there used by St. Paul, "*not to be limited, but extending to all riddance from the practice and consequences of our transgressions:*" of which consequences surely the very worst is *the propensity to continue to transgress*, or, in other words, indwelling sin inclining us to sin again.

So we see here again, that in our redemption through the blood of Christ we have, if we will believe for it, deliverance from all indwelling sin.

"*Loosed us from our Sins.*"

In the opening of the Book of the Revelation there is another word used to express our deliverance from sin by the blood of our Lord. It is translated in the revised version :—
"Unto him that loveth us, and *loosed* us from our sins by his blood" (Rev. i. 5).

And if "loosed," how much? surely as entirely —to use the figures He has given us in his Word— as the liberated "prisoner" from his cell (Ps. cxlvi. 7), or the "escaped" "bird out of the snare of the fowlers" (Ps. cxxiv. 7).

Surely nothing short of this would be a fulfilment of his word, "If the Son therefore shall make you free, ye shall be *free indeed*" (John viii. 36).

"*He hath done all Things Well.*"

The people cried out on seeing the miracles of bodily healing of our dear Lord, "*He hath done all things well*" (Mark vii. 37); and these were, as we have already considered above, true pictures of the Father's work of healing upon our souls (John v. 19; xiv. 9), by Him.

But there were two things which, to enable our Lord to do his miracles, He required of those on whom they were to be done; namely, *to believe in his power to heal, and to be willing that He should exercise it upon them*. And these same things God needs now to enable Him to apply to our souls that perfect healing which He has indeed wrought out for them in and by Him.

"*Won't let Him.*"

There is an account by the American missionary, William Taylor, the earnest and successful advocate of "self-supporting missions," of a conversation which he had with "a small African boy."

"'George, don't you think God wants to save you from your sins?'

"'Yes, sir.'

"'If God wants to save you why doesn't He do it? He is the Almighty, why doesn't He do whatever He wants to do?'

"After a little reflection the boy slowly and seriously replied: 'Mr. Taylor, it is because *I won't let Him.*'"

We read that in one place our Lord "*could there do no mighty work, save that he laid his hands on a few sick folk and healed them. And he marvelled because of their unbelief*" (Mark vi. 5, 6).

And this was the place in which—it being that in which He had been brought up—He ought to have been the best known (John xiv. 9), and, therefore, the most fully believed in.

And so we often find now among those by whom He ought to be the best known and the most fully believed in, the most determined unbelief in his power perfectly to save, and therefore the most entire shutting of themselves out from his exercising it upon them.

He wants to save them to the uttermost.

He is almighty to save them to the uttermost.

But they "*won't let Him.*"

"The Law of the Spirit of Life."

St. Paul, in the seventh chapter of the Epistle to the Romans, describes the extent to which sin may still prevail in us even after we have been brought on so far in the spiritual life as to "delight in the law of God after the inward man."

And having brought up his terrible picture to the point of "O wretched man that I am, who shall deliver me from the body of this death?" he then, in the eighth chapter, sets forth God's glorious deliverance of us from that miserable bondage to "the law of sin and death" by bringing us under the power of another and opposite "law," the "law of the Spirit of life in Christ Jesus."

Here is his account of the dreadful power over us of the first of these two "laws," until the deliverance comes to us by the blessed power of the other.

Power of Evil over us.

"We know that the law is spiritual: but *I am carnal, sold under sin.* For that which I do I allow not: for *what I would, that do I not; but what I hate, that do I.* If then I do that which I would not, I consent unto the law that it is good. Now then it is no more I that do it, but sin that dwelleth in me. For I know that *in me (that is, in my flesh), dwelleth no good thing:* for to will is present with me; but *how to perform that which is good I find not.* For *the good that I would I do not:* but *the evil which I would not, that I do.* Now if I do that I would not, it is no more I that do it, but sin that dwelleth in me.

"I find then a law, that, *when I would do good, evil is present with me.* For I delight in the law of God after the inward man: *but I see another law in my members, warring against the law of my mind, and bringing me into captivity to the law of sin which is in my members.* O *wretched man that I am! who shall deliver me from the body of this death?*

I thank God through Jesus Christ our Lord. So then with the mind I myself serve the law of God; but *with the flesh the law of sin* " (Rom. vii. 14-25).

The blessed Deliverance.

And here is the perfect deliverance:

" There is therefore now no condemnation to them which are in Christ Jesus, who walk not after the flesh, but after the Spirit. For *the law of the Spirit of life in Christ Jesus hath made me free from the law of sin and death.* For what the law could not do, in that it was weak through the flesh, God sending his own Son in the likeness of sinful flesh, and for sin, condemned sin in the flesh: *that the righteousness of the law might be fulfilled in us, who walk not after the flesh, but after the Spirit*" (Rom. viii. 1-4).

Under the first of these two " laws " he shows himself to have been no more able to resist the power of evil upon him, than a withered leaf to resist the force of the wind; according to that word in Isaiah, " *We all do fade as a leaf*; *and our iniquities, like the wind, have taken us away*" (Isa. lxiv. 6).

Yet even in that sad state there was that which was good in him, which, though so powerless against the evil, yet continued to struggle against it.

Grace here again abounding.

But in the sweet power of that other law it was not merely that the good got the upper hand; but the evil had now no place. The " law of the Spirit of life in Christ Jesus " made him "*free* from the law of sin and death," " that the righteousness of the law might be fulfilled in " him in his walking " not after the flesh, but after the Spirit." And where the righteousness of the law is *fulfilled* there is no room for evil; for where any, even the least degree of evil is, there the righteousness of the law is *not* "fulfilled."

Is not, then, that word in the eighth of Romans about the law of the Spirit of life in Christ Jesus making us free from the law of sin and death, and the righteousness of the law being fulfilled in us in our walking not after the flesh, but after the Spirit, another "Scriptural Proof" that our heavenly Father has given us in our Lord Jesus Christ, and in the blessed Spirit in and through Him, entire deliverance from sin?

Christ declaring the Father's Name.

" He hath looked down from the height of his sanctuary; from heaven did the Lord behold the earth; to hear the groaning of the prisoner; to loose those who are appointed to death; to *declare the name of the Lord in Zion, and his praise in Jerusalem*" (Ps. cii. 19–21).

However blessed a fulfilment of this passage there is to be hereafter to God's earthly Israel, certainly a most glorious fulfilment of it has taken place already in the incarnation, and birth, and life, and death, and resurrection, and ascension, and intercession of our Lord Jesus Christ, and in the gift of the Holy Ghost through Him to his Church.

God had said, " *In all places where I record my name* I will come unto thee, and I will bless thee" (Exod. xx. 24): and the Lord Jesus Christ is the place in which his name is indeed recorded: the true Temple (John ii. 19): the real meeting place of God with man: and "*the angel of his presence*" (Isa. lxiii. 9), *in whom his name is* ("Behold, I send an Angel before thee, to keep thee in the way, and to bring thee into the place which I have prepared ... *my name is in him*," Exod. xxiii. 21). And God has indeed come to us and "blessed us with all spiritual blessings in heavenly places" in Him (Eph. i. 3); blessings that eye had not seen, nor ear heard, neither had entered into the heart of man (1 Cor. ii. 9); blessings unspeakable and full of glory (2 Cor. ix. 15; 1 Pet. i. 8).

All blessings through the Father's Name.

And all these blessings are fulfilled in us by his *declaring the Father's name* to us. "I have," He said, "declared unto them thy name, and will declare it: that the love wherewith thou hast loved me may be in them, and I in them" (John xvii. 26). These are the last words of the prayer which He made aloud in the presence of the disciples the evening before his crucifixion, that they might have his joy fulfilled in themselves; and not they only, but we also who believe on Him through their word. And as they are the last words, so may we not also say that they are the crowning words? Can we think of any greater "breadth, and length, and depth, and height" (Eph. iii. 18) of blessedness, than that the very love with which the Father loves Him should be in us, and He Himself in us?

Does God say we must have Sin in us?

Now, if God had told us that He leaves us under the necessity of still having sin dwelling in us, along with this love with which He loves our Lord, and along with our Lord Himself, sin which He by his grace has made us to hate with intense hatred, and which He says is the "*abominable thing*" which He "*hates*" (Jer. xliv. 4)—and we are sure with a hatred infinitely greater than any which we can feel towards it because of his holiness being infinitely greater than any with which He can endow us—there would of course have been nothing for us but to submit our ignorance to his infinite wisdom, and wait till we "know even as we are known" for the clearing up of such an inscrutable "mystery of iniquity" (2 Thess. ii. 7) as this must surely have appeared to us.

But even then I think it would have behoved us to cry earnestly to Him to show us *how much* sin He thus still left us under the necessity of enduring; in order that we might seek to Him to rid us by his grace of *every particle up to that point*, whatever it might be.

Dare any of us say this?

But can any of us deliberately declare before Him that He really has told us that after all He has done to "redeem" us "from all evil" (Gen. xlviii. 16 : Titus ii. 14), He has yet left us under any such compulsion either to sin *at all,* or to have *any* sin still in us?

If any of my brothers in Christ tell me that they can declare this, it is of course not for me to judge them in their so reading his Word. But *it is* for me to say that, if they *can* see such things in it, *I cannot,* but must declare that if I sin now at this moment, or have any sin in me at this moment, or ever sin again, or ever have any sin in me again, it is not, so far as I can see, through any compulsion that He has left me under of doing so or having it so, but in the teeth of his holy revealed will, so far as I am enabled by the blessed Spirit to understand it, and in spite of abundant (Rom. v. 20) "righteousness and strength" (Isa. xlv. 24) provided for me in the gift of his Son as my Almighty Deliverer from all the power of the evil one over me and from all his works in me.

And as for anything contrary to this in his holy Word, I cannot see even *one* passage in it which, carefully considered, can be made out to be so; while the passages positively declaring or clearly implying entire deliverance from all sin, and which cannot by any amount of consideration be made even to appear to say anything else, seem to me to shine out of it by, to say the least, *hundreds*.

Trusting in the Name of the Lord.

Even under the Old Testament, our Lord so far declared the Father's name to the prophets by his Spirit " which was in them " (1 Peter i. 11), that they could say:—

" They that *know thy name* will put their trust in thee: for thou, Lord, hast not forsaken them that seek thee" (Ps. ix. 10).

" Our heart shall rejoice in him, because we have trusted in *his holy name* " (Ps. xxxiii. 21).

" It shall come to pass, that whosoever shall call on *the name of the Lord* shall be delivered: for in Mount Zion and in Jerusalem shall be deliverance, as the Lord hath said " (Joel ii. 32).

" *Deliverance* " from what and from whom? Surely from all enemies and from all their oppression: in our case, from the devil and all his works, all sin in whatsoever shape.

"*The name of the Lord* is a strong tower: the righteous runneth into it, and is safe " (Prov. xviii. 10).

"*Safe*" from whom? Surely, here again, from all enemies (Luke i. 71, 74). Surely it would be strange indeed if we were under compulsion to bring the worst of them—for if there be sin in us it will be admitted on all hands to be a much worse enemy than any outside of us can be—along with us inside the tower, when running into it as God's own declared place of safety from them all.

"O Lord, my Strength."

I do not like to leave this triumphing over all enemies in the "Name of the Lord," without bringing in some verses, in addition to those already quoted a little way back, from:—

"A psalm of David, the servant of the Lord, who spake unto the Lord the words of this song in the day that the Lord delivered him from the hand of all his enemies, and from the hand of Saul: And he said:—

"I will love thee, O Lord, my strength. The Lord is my rock, and my fortress, and my deliverer; my God, my strength, in whom I will trust; my buckler, and the horn of my salvation, and my high tower. I will call upon the Lord, who is worthy to be praised: so shall I be saved from mine enemies."

"He sent from above, he took me, he drew me out of many waters. He delivered me from my strong enemy, and from them which hated me: for they were too strong for me."

"For by thee I have run through a troop; and by my God have I leaped over a wall. As for God, his way is perfect: the word of the Lord is tried: he is a buckler to all those that trust in him. For who is God save the Lord? or who is a rock save our God?

"It is God that girdeth me with strength, and maketh my way perfect. He maketh my feet like hinds' feet, and setteth me upon my high places. He teacheth my hands to war, so that a bow of steel is broken by mine arms. Thou hast also given me the shield of thy salvation: and thy right hand hath holden me up, and thy gentleness hath made me great. Thou hast enlarged my steps under me, that my feet did not slip.

"I have pursued mine enemies, and overtaken them: neither did I turn again till they were consumed. I have wounded them that they were not able to rise: they are fallen under my feet. For thou hast girded me with strength unto the battle: thou hast subdued under me those that rose up against me. Thou hast also given me the necks of mine enemies; that I might destroy them that hate me. They cried, but there was none to save them: even unto the Lord, but he answered them not. Then did I beat them small as the dust before the wind: I did cast them out as the dirt in the streets."

"The Lord liveth: and blessed be my rock; and let the God of my salvation be exalted" (Ps. xviii).

Could David have used words to express more complete triumph over all his enemies?

His name, the Hebrew scholars tell us, means "the beloved one," and we know he is a type of Him who is in an infinitely higher sense God's Beloved One, and of whom He says to us, "I will make an everlasting covenant with you, even *the sure mercies of David.* Behold, I have given him for a witness to the people, a leader and commander to the people " (Isa. lv. 3, 4).

Have we in Him a less perfect victory over our spiritual enemies than that which God gave to his earthly Israel by their earthly David over their earthly ones?

"Deliver us from Evil."

Taking this petition of "the Lord's Prayer," "*Deliver us from evil*" (Matt. vi. 13), or, as in the revised version, "*from the evil one,*" which He has given us to pray without limitation or qualification, and applying to it his words already so often quoted. "What things soever ye desire, when ye pray, believe that ye receive" (revised version, "*have received*"), "them, and ye shall have them" (Mark xi. 24), have we not here again a positive assurance of deliverance from all sin, outward or inward, if we believe for it? For is not all sin, outward or inward, both "evil" and the work of "the evil one?"

I say "*if we believe for it*," for otherwise doubtless it would be with us according to that word of St. James respecting those who "ask" otherwise than "in faith, nothing wavering," "He that wavereth is like a wave of the sea driven with the wind and tossed. For let not that man think that he shall receive anything of the Lord" (James i. 6, 7). So that any who do not really believe that God has the deliverance to give, and that He is ready to give it, and does give it to all who believingly ask it (Matt. vii. 11), shut themselves out from receiving it.

"That which he requested."

"And Jabez called on the God of Israel, saying, Oh that thou wouldest bless me indeed, and enlarge my coast, and that thine hand might be with me, and that thou wouldest keep me from evil, that it may not grieve me! And God granted him that which he requested" (1 Chron. iv. 10).

Is it not very sweet, this form in which the answer to his prayer is recorded? "God granted him"—not *all these blessings*, but—"*that which he requested*;" as if the only limit to the grant was the extent of his request: so that if there had been more in his heart to pray for, he would equally have had it; as it would still doubtless have been "God granted him *that which he requested.*"

It is like "Open thy mouth wide, and I will fill it" (Ps. lxxxi. 10; and "Be it unto thee even as thou wilt" (Matt. xv. 28); and "He will rise and give him *as many as he needeth*" (Luke xi. 8); and "*Whatsoever ye shall ask* in my name, that will I do" (John xiv. 13); and "*All things, whatsoever ye shall ask* in prayer, believing, ye shall receive" (Matt. xxi. 22); and "If ye abide in me, and my words abide in you, *ye shall ask what ye will, and it shall be done unto you*" (John xv. 7): and like God's continued granting of Abraham's requests as long as he continued to urge them (Gen. xviii. 23—33): and like the teaching of many Old Testament types—such as "King Solomon gave unto the queen of Sheba *all her desire, whatsoever she asked*, beside that which Solomon gave her of his royal bounty" (1 Kings x. 13); and "What wilt thou, queen Esther? and what is thy request? it shall be even given thee to the half of the kingdom" (Esther v. 3); and the oil not "staying" till the empty vessels, "not a few," which the poor widow borrowed of all her neighbours, were every one filled (2 Kings iv. 3, 6); and the King of Israel smiting Syria as often as he had smitten with the arrows upon the ground (2 Kings xiii. 18, 19); and Israel being victorious over Amalek all the time the hands of Moses were held up (Exod. xvii. 11, 12): the asking being in every case the only limit of the receiving.

If then we can find it in our heart by God's grace to take that prayer of Jabez, "*that thou wouldest keep me from evil, that it may not grieve me,*" —which probably he prayed with reference to earthly evil—and in the name of our Lord Jesus Christ pray it believingly with respect to all spiritual evil, does not all that God shows Himself to be as the answerer of prayer, warrant our believing undoubtingly that He "grants" us just this which we "request," preservation from all sin outward or inward?

"Hath cast out thine enemy."

"Sing, O daughter of Zion; shout, O Israel; be glad and rejoice with all the heart, O daughter of Jerusalem. The Lord hath taken away thy judgments, he *hath cast out thine enemy*: the king of Israel, even the Lord, is in the midst of thee: *thou shalt not see evil any more.* In that day it shall be said to Jerusalem, Fear thou not: and to Zion, Let not thine hands be slack. The Lord thy God in the midst of thee is mighty; he will save, he will rejoice over thee with joy; he will rest in his love, he will joy over thee with singing" (Zeph. iii. 14–17).

Surely this is all for us—for I have answered already from the Word of God in the beginning of this book, the sad teaching which would hand over all such glorious promises exclusively to the Jews in the next dispensation—and yet, surely, there is no room here for sin outward or inward.

What meaning could we attach to the words, "*He hath cast out thine enemy*," if after their fulfilment to us, there were still to be sin in us? And so also of the words, "*Thou shalt not see evil any more.*" And then all those expressions of God's exceeding joy over us, "*He will rejoice over thee with joy, he will rest in his love, he will joy over thee with singing;*" how can they be made to agree with sin still in us? Can He who is "of purer eyes than to behold evil," and who cannot "look on iniquity" (Hab. i. 13), so feel towards us if through unbelief we will not let Him (Mark vi. 5, 6) deliver us from the existence of sin in us, as well as from its guilt upon us? (John xiv. 23: xv. 10).

And if it be said that the words do indeed imply the absence of sin, but that they refer to a future time of glory, not to that of our warfare down here; the answer is that such encouragements as "Fear thou not;" "let not thine hands be slack. The Lord thy God in the midst of thee is mighty, he will save," must surely apply to us while yet in our militant state here, and not after we have entered into our eternal rest.

"I the Lord do keep it."

"In that day sing ye unto her, A vineyard of red wine. I the Lord do keep it; I will water it every moment: lest any hurt it, I will keep it night and day" (Isa. xxvii. 2, 3).

Keep it with what sort of keeping? Surely, perfect! (Ps. cxxi. 3–5). And if so, how can any sin be there? For the reason for the keeping is "lest any hurt it;" and sin is a hurtful thing, and as much so in the shape of indwelling as of outbreaking sin: indeed often more so; for outbreaking sin is manifest to us, and drives us to repentance, and to seek and find forgiveness for it; but merely indwelling sin may be working its mischief in us unperceived.

And if it be said that God means his whole Church when speaking of his vineyard, and that evidently there is sin there, and that He says so; then the answer is, that this is because the Church does not believe for the fulfilment of the Word. "But what if some did not believe? shall their unbelief make the faith of God without effect? God forbid!" (Rom. iii. 3, 4). He is faithful to his word to every individual member of the Church who will believe in Him to enable Him to be so.

And accordingly, every such fully believing one is kept "night and day" safe from the hurtful thing in any shape whatever.

"Judgment" for the "Oppressed."

"The Lord executeth righteousness and judgment for all that are oppressed" (Ps. ciii. 6).

Our Lord Jesus Christ has expounded this to us in the Gospel according to St. Luke:—

"There was in a city a judge, which feared not God, neither regarded man: and there was a widow in that city; and she came unto him, saying, Avenge me of mine adversary.

"And he would not for a while: but afterward he said within himself, Though I fear not God, nor regard man; yet because this widow troubleth me, I will avenge her, lest by her continual coming she weary me.

"And the Lord saith, Hear what the unjust judge saith. And shall not God avenge his own elect, which cry day and night unto him, though he bear long with them? I tell you that he will avenge them speedily. Nevertheless when the Son of man cometh, shall he find faith on the earth?" (Luke xviii. 2–8.)

How much?

Now *how much* "righteousness and judgment" does our Lord here lead us to believe were executed by that unjust judge for that poor one oppressed by her adversary?

Can we in reading the account conceive of them as anything otherwise than complete? Would not any other idea be inconsistent with the plain meaning of his words?

And has not the righteous "judge of all the earth" "executed" equally perfect "righteousness and judgment" for us in our much more powerful adversary's much more grievous oppression upon us, if we will but believe for it; believe, that is, in Him in and by whom He has done it?

And, so believing, are we not then free from sin? For is it not entirely of sin and its consequences that the oppression consists?

"Shall He find faith?"

"Nevertheless when the Son of man cometh, shall he find faith in the earth?" What an illustration of the prophetic truthfulness of these words of our Lord in the end of the above parable is afforded by the way in which He is received by so many of us his people, on his "coming" to us continually by his Word, with his "exceeding great and precious promises" of full salvation!

Is it not with many of us as it was with his disciples in his time on earth, when:—

"He took unto him the twelve, and said unto them, Behold, we go up to Jerusalem, and all things that are written by the prophets concerning the Son of man shall be accomplished. For he shall be delivered unto the Gentiles, and shall be mocked, and spitefully entreated, and spitted on: and they shall scourge him, and put him to death: and the third day he shall rise again. *And they understood none of these things: and this saying was hid from them, neither knew they the things which were spoken*" (Luke xviii. 31-34)?

And yet what plainer words could He have used to tell them of his coming sufferings and death? And what plainer words could He use now than those by which He tells us of the deliverance from all sin which his sufferings and death have purchased for us?

And though He has a "cloud of witnesses" (Heb. xii. 1) to the fulfilment of his promises of deliverance, the reception of their testimony by too many is still:—"*Their words seemed to them as idle tales, and they believed them not*" (Luke xxiv. 11).

God and his People of old.

Here is God's charge to his people of old, and their consecration of themselves to Him, and his acceptance of them and blessing upon them:—

" This day the Lord thy God hath commanded thee to do these statutes and judgments: thou shalt therefore keep and do them with all thine heart, and with all thy soul.

" *Thou hast avouched the Lord this day to be thy God,* and to walk in his ways, and to keep his statutes, and his commandments, and his judgments, and to hearken unto his voice:

" *And the Lord hath avouched thee this day to be his peculiar people, as he hath promised thee,* and that thou shouldest keep all his commandments; and to make thee high above all nations which he hath made, in praise, and in name, and in honour; and that thou mayest be a holy people unto the Lord thy God, as he hath spoken " (Deut. xxvi. 16–19).

Their short time of obedience and blessing.

" And Israel served the Lord all the days of Joshua, and all the days of the elders that overlived Joshua, and which had known all the works of the Lord, that he had done for Israel " (Josh. xxiv. 31).

" And the Lord gave unto Israel all the land which he sware to give unto their fathers; and they possessed it, and dwelt therein. And the Lord gave them rest round about, according to all that he sware unto their fathers: and there stood not a man of all their enemies before them; the Lord delivered all their enemies into their hand. There failed not ought of any good thing which the Lord had spoken unto the house of Israel; all came to pass" (Josh. xxi. 43–45).

We have " a better hope."

" *All the days of Joshua, and all the days of the elders that over-lived Joshua.*" And then they ceased to be faithful, and God was no longer able to fulfil to them his promises of blessing, but could only hear and answer from time to time their cry of distress in the wretchedness which they brought upon themselves by their unfaithfulness.

But that was under "the law" which "made nothing perfect, but the bringing in of a better hope did; by the which we draw nigh unto God" (Heb. vii. 19). And we are living now in the realisation of this " better hope," the reality and substance of the " good things " of which the law was " the shadow " (Heb. x. 1).

In our ever-living Joshua.

Moreover, our Joshua is not only our " leader and commander" (Isa. lv. 4) to *bring us into* the promised land of fulness of spiritual blessing (Eph. i. 3), as the earthly Joshua brought the Israelites into Canaan; but unlike the earthly Joshua whose " days " came to an end, He " *continueth ever* " (Heb. vii. 24) as "the mediator" (Heb. viii. 6) of the " new " and " better covenant," and as our great " High Priest " (Heb. iii. 1), " able also to save " us " to the uttermost " coming unto God by Him (Heb. vii. 25), to *keep us always in it.*

Shall not, then, all that blessedness fulfilled for that little while to the earthly Israel, be always perfectly fulfilled to us, of our *walking in God's ways, keeping his statutes and his commandments, and his judgments, and hearkening to his voice, and being a holy people unto the Lord our God as He has spoken*?

And *not one of our enemies standing before us but all delivered of the Lord into our hand*, all our sins, that is, of every sort outward or inward, what of sin remains on us or in us?

"Holiness and Righteousness before Him."

"Blessed be the Lord God of Israel; for He hath visited and redeemed his people, and hath raised up an horn of salvation for us in the house of his servant David; as he spake by the mouth of his holy prophets, which have been since the world began: that we should be saved from our enemies, and from the hand of all that hate us; to perform the mercy promised to our fathers, and to remember his holy covenant; the oath which he sware to our father Abraham, that he would grant unto us, that we being delivered out of the hand of our enemies might serve him without fear, in holiness and righteousness before him, all the days of our life" (Luke i. 68–75).

A heading to St. Luke's Gospel.

These are some of the words spoken by Zacharias when, after the birth of John the Baptist, he had recovered his speech and "was filled with the Holy Ghost and prophesied." And standing as they do at the very beginning of St. Luke's "declaration" of the Gospel (Luke i. 1), may we not take them as a sort of descriptive heading to its contents; a statement, in a concise form, of its substance?

And do they not express entire deliverance from all sin? What lower meaning than this can we attach to:—

"That we *being delivered out of the hand of our enemies might serve him, without fear, in holiness and righteousness before him, all the days of our life*"?

For present fulfilment in us.

And does not the fact that it is "*all the days of our life,*" that we are thus to "serve him without fear, in holiness and righteousness before him," show the deliverance to be a present thing, not to be waited for till death or the coming again of our Lord?

And is not then this one passage by itself a conclusive "Scriptural Proof" that God does offer us in our Lord Jesus Christ entire deliverance now from all sin, inward as well as outward?

Is not indeed this deliverance and the service to Him resulting from it, declared here to be the very object for which He has "visited and redeemed" us by our Lord Jesus Christ?

"To the Uttermost."

"They truly were many priests, because they were not suffered to continue by reason of death: but this man, because he continueth ever, hath an unchangeable priesthood. Wherefore he is able also to save them to the uttermost that come unto God by him, seeing he ever liveth to make intercession for them' (Heb. vii. 23–25).

This passage has been referred to above again and again, but only incidentally in connection with other passages. I wish now to take it up by itself.

What is " the uttermost" ?

" Able also to save them *to the uttermost* that come unto God by him."

Now would it not be the merest perversion of language to make salvation " to the uttermost " in the matter of deliverance from sin mean anything short of entire deliverance? And have we not then here another in itself sufficient " Scriptural proof" that God does give us in our Lord Jesus Christ this perfect deliverance, if we will but by faith accept Him for it—accept Him as our High Priest (Heb. iii. 1), whose all-prevailing intercession founded upon Himself as the perfect Sacrifice, procures it to us, and accept Him as " that eternal life which was with the Father and was manifested unto us " (1 John i. 2) so to be in us and we in Him (John xv. 4) that we may have no life apart from Him (Gal. ii. 20; Col. iii. 3, 4; Rom. vi. 6), and therefore no sin on us or in us (1 John iii. 5, 6).

The Land of Blessing.

It was " a good land and a large" (Exod. iii. 8); " a land that " God " had espied for them, flowing with milk and honey, which is the glory of all lands " (Ezek. xx. 6); " a land of brooks of water, of fountains, and depths that spring out of valleys and hills; a land of wheat, and barley, and vines, and fig trees, and pomegranates; a land of oil olive, and honey; a land wherein thou shalt eat bread without scarceness, thou shalt not lack anything in it; a land whose stones are iron, and out of whose hills thou mayest dig brass" (Deut. viii. 7–9).

God's care over it.

"For the land, whither thou goest in to possess it, is not as the land of Egypt, from whence ye came out, where thou sowedst thy seed, and wateredst it with thy foot as a garden of herbs: but the land, whither ye go to possess it, is a land of hills and valleys, and drinketh water of the rain of heaven: a land which the Lord thy God careth for: the eyes of the Lord thy God are always upon it, from the beginning of the year even unto the end of the year" (Deut. xi. 10–12).

And their great blessedness in it.

And God promised them if faithful to Him when in the land; "Then I will give you rain in due season, and the land shall yield her increase, and the trees of the field shall yield their fruit, And your threshing shall reach unto the vintage, and the vintage shall reach unto the sowing time:

"And ye shall eat your bread to the full, and dwell in your land safely. And I will give peace in the land, and ye shall lie down, and none shall make you afraid: and I will rid evil beasts out of the land, neither shall the sword go through your land. And ye shall chase your enemies, and they shall fall before you by the sword. And five of you shall chase an hundred, and an hundred of you shall put ten thousand to flight: and your enemies shall fall before you by the sword" (Lev. xxvi. 3–8).

"The Lord shall cause thine enemies that rise

up against thee to be smitten before thy face: they shall come out against thee one way, and flee before thee seven ways" (Deut. xxviii. 7).

The spiritual fulfilment to us.

All these things are among the "whatsoever things were written aforetime," "for our learning, that we through patience and comfort of the scriptures might have hope" (Rom. xv. 4).

They are a picture of perfect earthly peace and fruitfulness, and every other earthly blessing, including entire riddance of all evil beasts, and triumph over and destruction of all enemies. And if we so believe in our Lord Jesus Christ as to have in Him all the spiritual blessedness here foreshadowed, including the riddance out of us of all the *spiritual* "evil beasts," the triumph over and destruction of all the *spiritual* "enemies," what will there remain of sin in our lives or in our hearts?

"Righteousness and Strength."

"Surely, shall one say, in the Lord have 1 righteousness and strength" (Isa. xlv. 24).

We are all agreed in saying "*In the Lord have I righteousness,*" in the fullest meaning of the words as regards our justification from the charges of the law of God against us (Matt. v. 25, 26): why not so say it also as regards the "fulfilment" of "the righteousness of the law" "*in us*" (Rom. viii. 4)?

And why not all be agreed also to say in their fullest meaning, the further words "*and strength*"? strength "over all the power of the enemy" (Luke

x. 19). And then what will there be left in us of him or his works, what sin in heart or life?

Will it not—in accordance with "As he is, so are we in this world" (1 John iv. 17)—be with us as it was with our Lord, that "the prince of this world cometh, and hath nothing in" us (John xiv. 30)?

"From all Iniquity."

"The grace of God that bringeth salvation hath appeared to all men, teaching us that, denying ungodliness and worldly lusts, we should live soberly, righteously, and godly, in this present world; looking for that blessed hope, and the glorious appearing of the great God and our Saviour Jesus Christ; who gave himself for us, that he might redeem us from all iniquity, and purify unto himself a peculiar people" (revised version, "*a people for his own possession*"), "zealous of good works" (Titus ii. 11–14).

To be fulfilled in our hearts now.

"Gave himself for us *that he might redeem us from all iniquity.*" And we know that when God speaks of "iniquity," He means iniquity of heart at least as much as of outward life. For "the Lord seeth not as man seeth; for man looketh on the outward appearance, but *the Lord looketh on the heart*" (1 Sam. xvi. 7). And this redeeming us from all iniquity, and purifying us to Himself as a people for his own possession is a present thing, as it is in order to our being "zealous of good works," to be done now and not at death or at the coming of the Lord.

But if we do not believe for this entire present redemption, of course it is not fulfilled to us (Heb. iv. 2).

"A New Creature."

"If any man be in Christ, he is a new creature: old things are passed away; behold all things are become new" (revised version, "*the old things are past away, behold they have become new*") (2 Cor. v. 17).

Are not all the things of our hearts and lives altogether evil till we come to Christ and are in Him? And does not "*The old things are past away, behold they have become new,*" express that they are all now the opposite of what they were; good, that is, instead of evil: and if so, then, here again, where is the room for sin in life or heart?

But if we believe for only a partial making of the old things new, that is all that we have.

"Taketh away all his Armour."

"When a strong man armed keepeth his palace, his goods are in peace: but when a stronger than he shall come upon him, and overcome him, he taketh from him all his armour wherein he trusted, and divideth his spoils" (Luke xi. 21, 22).

What is the "*armour* wherein he trusted" but our ignorance, self-conceit, pride, hardness of heart, evil habits of thought and feeling, aversion to God and all belonging to Him, inclination to all evil; or, in other words, what is it but *indwelling sin* in its various shapes? And if "*all*" is taken away, is there any left?

But here again we must believe for it, or all will not be taken away; but that will be left for the taking away of which we have failed to believe.

"Fear not."

"*God expostulateth with his people about his mercies to the church, about his promises, and about the vanity of idols.*"

"Fear thou not; for I am with thee: be not dismayed for I am thy God: I will strengthen thee; yea, I will help thee; yea, I will uphold thee with the right hand of my righteousness.

"Behold, all they that were incensed against thee shall be ashamed and confounded: they shall be as nothing; and they that strive with thee shall perish. Thou shalt seek them, and shalt not find them, even them that contended with thee: they that war against thee shall be as nothing, and as a thing of nought. For I the Lord thy God will hold thy right hand, saying unto thee, Fear not; I will help thee.

"Fear not, thou worm Jacob, and ye men of Israel; I will help thee, saith the Lord, and thy redeemer, the Holy One of Israel. Behold, I will make thee a new sharp threshing instrument having teeth: thou shalt thresh the mountains, and beat them small, and shalt make the hills as chaff. Thou shalt fan them, and the wind shall carry them away, and the whirlwind shall scatter them: and thou shalt rejoice in the Lord, and shalt glory in the Holy One of Israel.

"When the poor and needy seek water, and there is none, and their tongue faileth for thirst. I the Lord will hear them, I the God of Israel will not forsake them. I will open rivers in high places, and fountains in the midst of the valleys: I will make the wilderness a pool of water, and the dry land springs of water. I will plant in the wilderness the cedar, the shittah tree, and the myrtle and the oil tree; I will set in the desert the fir tree, and the pine, and the box tree together: that they may see, and know, and consider, and understand together, that the hand of the Lord hath done this, and the Holy One of Israel hath created it" (Isa. xli. title and 10-20).

Call to us to trust for entire deliverance.

Surely, the again and again repeated charge, "Fear thou not; for I am with thee: be not dismayed, for I am thy God." "Fear not, I will help thee." "Fear not, thou worm Jacob, and ye men of Israel, I will help thee, saith the Lord," is a call to us from God to put perfect confidence in Him for entire deliverance and entire subsequent preservation from every enemy, sin of every sort or shape, outward or inward.

And surely the accompanying words of encouragement—"I am with thee," "I am thy God, I will strengthen thee; yea, I will uphold thee with the right hand of my righteousness," "I the Lord thy God will hold thy right hand," "I will help thee, saith the Lord, and thy Redeemer the Holy One of Israel—" express his absolute engagement thus to deliver and preserve us, if we will trust Him to do it.

And what less than this is contained in the declaration concerning our enemies, that they "shall be as nothing" and "shall perish," and that we "shall seek them and shall not find them," and they "shall be as nothing and as a thing of nought," and we shall "thresh them" and "beat them small," and "make" them "as chaff," and "shall fan them and the wind shall carry them away, and the whirlwind shall scatter them"? Surely, all these are to us just multiplied promises of the entire casting out and destruction of all evil, all sin inward or outward.

Blessedness following upon it.

And what a blessed state of spiritual power and enjoyment follows upon this!—the " rivers " opened " in high places, and fountains in the midst of the valleys," the " wilderness " made " a pool of water, and the dry land springs of water," and " the cedar, the shittah tree, and the myrtle and the oil tree," " planted " by God Himself " in the wilderness," and " the fir tree and the pine, and the box tree together," " set " by Him " in the desert."

Surely the entire passage is just a sweet picture of entire santification first, and then blessed fruitfulness following upon it, and both alike wrought by the almighty power of God. And surely it is all put before us for its realisation in ourselves, and its realisation in us *now*.

"Delivered." "Translated."

" For this cause we also, since the day we heard it" (namely, their "faith in Christ Jesus," and "love in the Spirit"), "do not cease to pray for you, and to desire that ye might be filled with the knowledge of his will in all wisdom and spiritual understanding; that ye might walk worthy of the

Lord unto all pleasing, being fruitful in every good work, and increasing in the knowledge of God; strengthened with all might, according to his glorious power, unto all patience and long suffering with joyfulness; giving thanks unto the Father, which hath made us meet to be partakers of the inheritance of the saints in light: who hath delivered us from the power of darkness, and hath translated us into the kingdom of his dear Son" (Col. i. 9–13).

Agrees with Prayers in Ephesians.

This most blessed prayer is in exact accordance with those two in the Epistle to the Ephesians, considered a little time back, with respect to the absence of any petition in it for their deliverance from sin; it being assumed apparently that from "the day" they "heard" "the word of the truth of the gospel," "and knew the grace of God in truth" as declared to them by "Epaphras," who was for them "a faithful minister of Christ" (verses 5–7), they understood that they had already entire deliverance from it in the death and burial, and resurrection of our Lord Jesus Christ ("I delivered unto you first of all that which I also received, how that Christ *died for our sins* according to the scriptures; and that he *was buried*, and that he *rose again* the third day, according to the scriptures" 1 Cor. xv. 3, 4).

But I introduce it here for the sake of those words at its close, "*who hath delivered us from the power of darkness, and hath translated us into the kingdom of his dear Son.*"

Christ's finished Work.

Here, as in so many similar cases, the tenses of

the verbs are corrected in the revised version. It is not there "*hath* delivered," but simply "delivered," and not "*hath* translated," but simply "translated," both the verbs being in the "Aorist" tense spoken of some time back, expressing that the deliverance and translation were completed once for all; the reference being doubtless to the finished work of our redemption by our Lord Jesus Christ, but into the power and blessedness of which, as a matter of fact in our own selves, we only enter when, and so far as, we believe in Him for it.

" Delivered" and " translated," how much?

But the questions I wish to ask here, as in so many similar cases above, are; "delivered," *how much?* "translated," *how much?* Surely, if St. Paul had meant anything but completely, he must have put in some qualifying words to show that he did not mean an entire deliverance, and an entire translation. And if he did mean entire deliverance from the power of darkness, and entire translation into the kingdom of God's dear Son, surely, then, we have here a declaration that there is in Christ's finished work for us—if we will but accept Him for the fulfilment of it also in us—entire salvation from all sin.

And, surely, it is ours the moment we believe in Him for it; as shown by the very wording of the invitation to it "Come; for *all things* are *now* ready" (Luke xiv. 17).

"Having no part Dark."

"The light of the body is the eye: therefore

when thine eye is single, thy whole body also is full of light; but when thine eye is evil, thy body also is full of darkness. Take heed therefore that the light which is in thee be not darkness. If thy whole body therefore be full of light, having no part dark, the whole shall be full of light as when the bright shining of a candle doth give thee light" (Luke xi. 34–36).

Full of light.

"*If thy whole body, therefore, be full of light having no part dark, the whole shall be full of light.*" Is it conceivable that our Lord is here putting an impossible case? Must it not be that He is telling us what He requires each of us to be, and what He is able and desirous to make us, if we will only, by putting away our unbelief, let Him?

And if indeed the whole of our spiritual being —for it is that of course of which He is speaking— is full of light having no part dark, where is the room for sin? Is not this, taken along with "God is light, and *in him is no darkness at all*" (1 John i. 5), just a fulfilment in us of "Be ye holy; *for I am holy*" (1 Peter i. 16), and of "Every man that hath this hope in him purifieth himself, *even as he is pure*" (1 John iii. 3), and of "*As he is,* so are we in this world" (1 John iv. 17)?

"Ask of Me."

"Yet have I set my king upon my holy hill of Zion. I will declare the decree: the Lord hath said unto me, Thou art my Son; this day have I begotten thee. Ask of me, and I shall give thee the heathen for thine inheritance, and the uttermost parts of the earth for thy possession. Thou shalt break them with a rod of iron; thou shalt dash them in pieces like a potter's vessel" (Ps. ii. 6–9).

To be fulfilled to Him in us.

"Because ye are sons, God hath sent forth the Spirit of his Son into your hearts, crying, " ' Abba, Father ' " (Gal. iv. 6). And if we by this " Spirit of Christ " in us (Rom. viii. 9) cry believingly to God, to give Him all that is heathenish in us for his inheritance, and all in us that is far away as " the uttermost parts of the earth " from Him for his possession, will not this be *his* asking it of God? And will not God, on his so " asking," fulfil to Him the promise, and indeed " give " Him all these things? And will not He then really " break them with a rod of iron," and " dash them in pieces like a potter's vessel "?

And does not this mean the absolute subjection to Him of all in us that can become subject to Him; all our mere natural appetites and desires, so that they shall no more be occasions to us of sin, but be yielded to God " as instruments of righteousness," "servants to righteousness unto holiness " (Rom. vi. 13, 19); and the utter destruction of all in us incapable of being thus used in his service; all the " carnal mind," all *indwelling sin?*

This application of the passage to ourselves of course in no way clashes with the wider sense in which doubtless it is to be fulfilled hereafter in the whole earth.

The Potter and the Clay.

"The word which came to Jeremiah from the Lord, saying, Arise, and go down to the potter's house, and there will I cause thee to hear my words.

"Then I went down to the potter's house, and, behold, he wrought a work on the wheels. And the vessel that he made of clay was marred in the hand of the potter: so he made it again another vessel, as seemed good to the potter to make it.

"Then the word of the Lord came to me, saying, O house of Israel, cannot I do with you as this potter? saith the Lord. Behold, as the clay is in the potter's hand, so are ye in mine hand, O house of Israel" (Jer. xviii. 1–6).

The vessel entirely remade.

When "the clay was marred in the hand of the potter," and "so he made it again another vessel as seemed good to the potter to make it," did he leave in it, or reproduce in it, any of those things for which he had been obliged to condemn the first vessel? or did he not indeed "make it again" an entirely new vessel?

And when God tells us that as remade by Him in Christ "we are his workmanship, created in Christ Jesus unto good works, which God hath before ordained that we should walk in them" (Eph. ii. 10); and that "If any man be in Christ, he is a new creature: old things are passed away; behold, all things are become new" (2 Cor. v. 17); does He not mean us to understand that He has remade us in Him, if we will but believe in Him for it, as completely as Jeremiah saw the potter remake the marred vessel?

Our "marred" state and our hope in it.

Here is our "marred" state in his hand:—

"We are all as an unclean thing, and all our righteousness are as filthy rags: and we all do fade as a leaf; and our iniquities, like the wind, have taken us away. And there is none that calleth upon thy name, that stirreth himself up to take hold of thee: for thou hast hid thy face from us, and hast consumed us, because of our iniquities."

But here is our hope in this our utterly ruined condition:—

"But now, O Lord, thou art our father; we are the clay, and thou our potter; and we all are the work of thy hand" (Isa. lxiv. 6–8).

Let us all then, in simple faith, yield ourselves entirely up to Him in Christ, really as clay in the hands of the potter, indeed to remake us "as seems good" to Him: and He will remake us, does now remake us, has already remade us, if we will believe in Christ for it, not with sin in us or on us—for *that* we are sure by his Word never "seems good" to Him—but "a vessel unto honour, sanctified, and meet for the master's use, and prepared unto every good work" (2 Tim. ii. 21); because entirely freed from sin (Rom. vi. 18, 22).

"The Son of God manifested."

"For this purpose the Son of God was manifested, that he might destroy the works of the devil" (1 John iii. 8).

And "this purpose" for which He was 'manifested" He certainly has not failed to accomplish.

And we have the benefit of his accomplishment of it just when and to the extent to which we believe in Him and give ourselves up to Him for its fulfilment in us. So if we fully thus believe in Him and give ourselves up to Him *now* (2 Cor. vi. 2), all the devil's works in us are *now* as a matter of fact destroyed. Or, in other words, we are delivered from all sin outward or inward.

One healthy one against the world.

And if only one in all the world should thus believe, and then be a witness for the Lord Jesus that He had dealt with him according to his faith (Matt ix. 29) and destroyed all the devil's works out of him; and all the rest of the world should unite in declaring that it was not so with them, and in therefore denying that it was ever so with anyone, all their united testimony would not in the least discredit his single testimony on the other side; just as, if there were only one healthy man, and all the rest of the world, being sickly, were to unite in declaring that there was no such thing as health, their united testimony would not in the least discredit his single testimony that there was such a thing, seeing that he himself was well.

"These Abominations."

"Will ye steal, murder, and commit adultery, and swear falsely, and burn incense unto Baal, and walk after other gods whom ye know not; and come and stand before me in this house, which is called by my name, and say, We are delivered to do all these abominations?" (Jer. vii. 10.)

In a meeting of a number of men and boys, a man stood up and spoke in a lively way on the blessedness of being a Christian. One, who, though not present at the time, was responsible for the right ordering of the meeting, remonstrated with him afterwards for what he had done, as he was known by many in the meeting to be from time to time "the worse for drink."

He answered that it was not often that he was so, and that we all make slips now and then, "for 'in many things we offend all.'" Notwithstanding such occasional failings in his "walk," he thought it was as right for him as for any other professed disciple of Christ to stand up and bear testimony for Him. All had their failings, some way or other, and this was his way.

When confronted with that passage "Nor thieves, nor covetous, nor *drunkards*, nor revilers, nor extortioners, shall inherit the kingdom of God" (1 Cor. vi. 10), he answered that he was not a drunkard in the sense there intended; but only made a slip occasionally in the matter of drink, as other Christians did in other ways—shortness of temper, perhaps, or something of that sort—not so disreputable, it may be, in the sight of man, but perhaps equally wicked in the sight of God.

Where is the line?

This wretched man's case seems an almost exact carrying out, in the profession of Christianity, of the wickedness charged in the text above against God's people of old, of their committing the grossest sins and then coming and standing before Him in the house which was called by his name, and saying, "We are delivered to do these abominations." And yet *if his general principle had been admitted that all must and do sin*, without any rule as to the nature and amount of the sin thus included in the normal state of a Christian, would there not have been some difficulty in refuting his claim to profess publicly his discipleship to Christ, although thus occasionally getting drunk?

None of my brothers and sisters in Christ likely to read this book would intentionally countenance even in the remotest degree any such "turning the grace of our God into lasciviousness" (Jude 4): but I would earnestly ask those of them who deny that God has given us in the Gospel entire deliverance from sin, to consider whether their doctrine does not involve in it the *principle* of which the conduct of such evil doers is the working out in so gross a form.

Are we " delivered to do " any sin ?

For are not all sins, from the most glaring outward acts of profligacy to the least inward wrong feelings or desires—I mean wrong feelings or desires *really our own*, not any mere *temptations* to them, however strong, nor any thoughts, however wicked, put into our minds by the evil one, but rejected with hatred by us—alike "abominations," though of very different degrees of enormity, it may be, in the sight of our holy Lord God? And can I, in the light of his Word, come and stand before Him, and truthfully say of *any*, even the very smallest of them, "I am delivered to do these abominations"?

And if I am not really "delivered to do" them,

but on the contrary He has given me in his Son deliverance from all necessity of doing them, would it not be a dreadfully wicked thing in me not to accept Him for this deliverance, and by the power of the Holy Ghost exerted in me through Him to live free from them?

Preventing others accepting deliverance.

And would it not be a further and yet much more dreadfully wicked thing in me—if I really knew what I was doing—if to my non-acceptance of Him myself for the deliverance, I added my endeavours to prevent my fellow-Christians from accepting Him for it? Should I not then be coming frightfully near to his terrible word, "Ye shut up the kingdom of heaven against men: for ye neither go in yourselves, neither suffer ye them that are entering to go in" (Matt. xxiii. 13)?

And yet is not this the very thing that many dear children of God are at this moment doing—and that in the idea of doing God service?

"Let God arise."

"Let God arise, let his enemies be scattered: let them also that hate him flee before him. As smoke is driven away, so drive them away: as wax melteth before the fire, so let the wicked perish at the presence of God" (Ps. lxviii. 1, 2).

Does not God mean this to be fulfilled in our souls? And if He does indeed arise in them and scatter his enemies; and all in them that hates Him has to flee before Him, driven away as smoke is driven away; and if as wax melteth before the fire, so all the wicked things in us, the indwelling sin of every sort, perishes at his presence; are we not then in a state of entire freedom from sin whether of life or heart?

"He shall preserve thy soul."

"I will lift up mine eyes unto the hills, from whence cometh my help. My help cometh from the Lord, which made heaven and earth. He will not suffer thy foot to be moved: he that keepeth thee will not slumber. Behold, he that keepeth Israel shall neither slumber nor sleep.

"The Lord is thy keeper: the Lord is thy shade upon thy right hand. The sun shall not smite thee by day, nor the moon by night. The Lord shall preserve thee from all evil: he shall preserve thy soul. The Lord shall preserve thy going out and thy coming in from this time forth, and even for evermore" (Ps. cxxi.).

The idea the translators had of this psalm is shown by the title which they have put to it:—

"*The great safety of the godly who put their trust in God's protection.*"

Promise of deliverance from all sin.

Is it possible in the light of the New Testament to read it through in the child-like spirit in which God tells us to receive his Word (1 Pet. ii. 2), and not see in it a promise of entire preservation from all sin?

What short of this can be meant by "*The Lord shall preserve thee from all evil: he shall preserve thy soul*"? And are not all the other clauses just varied forms of this blessed promise?

And of course entire *preservation* from sin implies previous entire *deliverance* from it. We cannot be perfectly *preserved* from it if we have any of it in us or on us. It is first, " The very God of peace *sanctify you wholly*," and then " Your whole spirit and soul and body be *preserved blameless* " (1 Thes. v. 23).

So is not this psalm in itself another perfect "Scriptural Proof" that God does indeed give us, if we will take it, that is, believe in our Lord Jesus Christ as the fulfilment in us of his promise of it, entire deliverance from all sin, outward or inward?

"In the Strength of the Lord God."

" I will go in the strength of the Lord God: I will make mention of thy righteousness, even of thine only " (Ps. lxxi. 16).

" *In the strength of the Lord God.*" To us, in the light of the New Testament, *Christ* (1 Cor. i. 24) is " the strength of the Lord God." And we " *go* in the strength of the Lord God" when we so " walk " " in him " (Col. ii. 6) that we can truthfully say " To me to live is Christ" (Phil. i. 21), and " I live; yet not I, but Christ liveth in me " (Gal. ii. 20).

Which is the stronger, Christ or sin?

And if we can thus indeed, in this sense of having Christ in us as our life, " go in the strength of the Lord God," does not the question of whether we can or cannot live free from sin depend upon this—which is the stronger, Christ or sin?

Bless God, we are all agreed in the answer. Then why not all agree also that, in Christ as "the strength of the Lord God" we "will go"—that is, live continually—free from sin, making "mention of" his "righteousness, even of" his "only"; and in saying it believingly, find it, by the power of the Holy Ghost, blessedly fulfilled in us (Eph. iii. 20)?

"Free indeed."

"If ye continue in my word, then are ye my disciples indeed; and ye shall know the truth, and the truth shall make you free" (John viii. 31, 32).

"If the Son therefore shall make you free ye shall be free indeed" (John viii. 36).

We have already, in looking into the extent of present deliverance from sin given to us by God in our Lord Jesus Christ, considered the words "Healed," "Delivered," "Ransomed," "Redeemed," "Saved," and "Translated," as used by Him in his Word without hint of his intending us to take them in any other than their plain ordinary meaning of perfect healing, perfect deliverance, perfect ransoming, perfect redemption, perfect salvation, and perfect translation.

In our Lord's words above, "The truth shall make you free," we have a similar unqualified use of the word "Free." And in his further declaration "Ye shall be *free indeed*" we have not only this mere absence of expression of limit to the freedom: but in addition to this, the *positive exclusion* of any idea of limit to it.

And we know what it is that He meant from

which we are to be "free indeed" by his words just before, "Verily, verily, I say unto you, *Whosoever committeth sin is the servant of sin.*"

Have we not here then his promise that continuing in his word, and so being his disciples indeed, and knowing the truth, we shall be perfectly free from the commission of sin?

From indwelling sin.

And, as we have already seen in a previous section, that God looks upon sin in the heart as already committed (1 Sam. xvi. 7; 1 John iii. 15; Matt. v. 28; Heb. iv. 12, 13; Ps. cxxxix. 2), does not the promise of entire freedom from *committing* sin involve in it, *in his sense of it*, that of entire freedom also from *indwelling* sin?

And so are not those words of our Lord, "If the Son therefore shall make you free, ye shall be free indeed," the declaration of a state of things— into which He offers if we are willing, to bring each one of us—in which there is entire deliverance from all sin, whether of life or heart?

"Thy Light and Thy Truth."

" O send out thy light and thy truth: let them lead me, let them bring me unto thy holy hill, and to thy tabernacles. Then will I go unto the altar of God, unto God my exceeding joy: yea, upon the harp will I praise thee, O God my God" (Ps. xliii. 3, 4).

" *O send out thy light and thy truth!* Has not God answered this prayer by *sending* (John vi. 29,

38, 39, &c.) Christ to us as "the Light" (John i. 4, 5, 7, 9) and "the Truth" (John xiv. 6)? And does not Christ bring all who are so yielded up to Him as to enable Him to do it to God's "holy hill and to" his "tabernacles"? For is it not written "*Ye are come unto mount Sion, and to the city of the living God*" (Heb. xii. 22)? "*Are* come" now already in our lifetime here on earth, while waiting for the yet much more blessed sense in which the words are doubtless to be fulfilled to us and in us in the glory above.

"*Who shall ascend into the hill of the Lord?*"

And if we are indeed brought there by Him, what sin can remain upon us or in us? for "Who shall ascend into the hill of the Lord? or who shall stand in his holy place? *He that hath clean hands, and a pure heart*" (Ps. xxiv. 3, 4). "Clean hands," freedom from *outward*, "a pure heart," freedom from *inward*, sin.

Is not, then, that cry of God's people of old, with his answer to it in his gift of Christ to us, another "Scriptural Proof" that He does in Him, if we will but believe in Him for it, give us entire deliverance from all sin outward and inward?

And thus believing, and continuing to believe in Him, the rest of that very blessed passage is fulfilled in us, in God being, in a sense in which He never was before, our "*exceeding joy*," and in our being able to *praise* Him with a fulness of thanksgiving such as we never knew before, as indeed, to each one of us individually, "God, MY God."

"Behold, I make a Covenant."

"And he said, Behold, I make a covenant: before all thy people I will do marvels, such as have not been done in all the earth, nor in any nation: and all the people among which thou art shall see the work of the Lord: for it is a terrible thing that I will do with thee. Observe thou that which I command thee this day: behold, I drive out before thee the Amorite, and the Canaanite, and the Hittite, and the Perizzite, and the Hivite, and the Jebusite" (Ex. xxxiv. 10, 11).

What to us are "the Amorite and the Canaanite, and the Hittite, and the Perizzite, and the Hivite, and the Jebusite" but evil in its various forms which would dispute our entrance into and possession of the promised land of perfect blessedness in Christ (Isa. xxvi. 3)?

Unbelief shuts out from the blessing.

And what was it but unbelief that prevented the fulfilment of the "covenant" of God with his earthly Israel to "drive out before" them all those earthly enemies of Himself and of them?

And what is it but unbelief that prevents now to any of us his spiritual Israel the fulfilment of his covenant with us in Christ (Isa. lv. 3) of "driving out before" us all the spiritual enemies of Himself and of us, and so enabling us to live a life "before" Him of "perfect" (Gen. xvii. 1; James i. 25; Phil. iii. 15) freedom from sin outward or inward (Luke i. 74, 75)?

I may seem to return again and again to the implied promise to us of full salvation from all sin contained in his promises to his people of old of deliverance from all their earthly enemies, and in his fulfilment of these promises to them whenever they believed in Him for their fulfilment. But this is only because He Himself presses upon us for "our examples" (1 Cor. x. 6; Heb. iv. 11) in so many ways in his Word his dealings with them and theirs with Him.

"The Lord thy God is with thee."

"When thou goest out to battle against thine enemies, and seest horses, and chariots, and a people more than thou, be not afraid of them: for the Lord thy God is with thee, which brought thee up out of the land of Egypt. And it shall be, when ye are come nigh unto the battle, that the priest shall approach and speak unto the people, and shall say unto them, Hear, O Israel, ye approach this day unto battle against your enemies: let not your hearts faint, fear not, and do not tremble, neither be ye terrified because of them; for the Lord your God is he that goeth with you, to fight for you against your enemies, to save you" (Deut. xx. 1–4).

If that word of promise in their warfare with their earthly enemies, "*The Lord thy God is with thee,*" secured to them, if they believed it, perfect victory over them all, what ought not Christ as "Immanuel," "*God with us,*" (Matt. i. 23) the fulfilment of all the promises (2 Cor. i. 20), to be to us in our spiritual warfare?

Ought not our victory to be, if it were possible, even more perfect than that which God promised to them on their believing in Him for it?

And if in the case of any of us there is not this perfect victory, is it not from want of faith in Him for it? And does He, as we are often inclined to do, call this unbelief our misfortune or infirmity; or does He not rather call it our terrible sin (Ps. lxxviii. 21, 22; xcv. 11)?

"Mindful of His Covenant."

"He will ever be mindful of his Covenant."

"He sent redemption unto his people: he hath commanded his covenant for ever: holy and reverend is his name" (Ps. cxi. 5, 9).

Christ is the Covenant.

Doubtless "*his covenant*" includes all the "exceeding great and precious promises" made with us in Christ (2 Cor. i. 20).

For *is not Christ Himself the covenant?* Is it not written of Him "I the Lord have called thee in righteousness, and will hold thine hand, and will keep thee, and *give thee for a covenant of the people, for a light of the Gentiles*" (Isa. xlii. 6); and "Thus saith the Lord, In an acceptable time have I heard thee, and in a day of salvation have I helped thee: and I will preserve thee, and *give thee for a covenant of the people*, to establish the earth, to cause to inherit the desolate heritages" (Isa. xlix. 8)?

All the blessings, then, which we have been considering in this book, and any that we may yet consider in it, are just parts of that solemn engagement of God with us in Christ, which He declares, in one of the two passages above, He has "commanded for ever," and of which, in the other, He pledges Himself ever to "be mindful."

Our unmindfulness of the Covenant.

And if in the case of any of us these blessings have failed to be realised in our experience, is not this because of that most sad—and, except in the light of the Word of God, showing how deeply we have fallen away from Him, most unaccountable—state of things, that while He, whose part in the covenant is the giving to us all the good things contained in it, is *ever mindful* of it, we, for whom all these good things are, have been so *utterly unmindful* of it as never to have looked what is in it, or else never to have come to Him believingly to "enquire of" Him "to do" for us the things which we saw in it (Ezek. xxxvi. 37)? And this, though it is written :—

"*Remember* his marvellous works that he hath done, his wonders and the judgments of his mouth, O ye seed of Abraham his servant, ye children of Jacob, his chosen ones. He is the Lord our God; his judgments are in all the earth. BE YE MINDFUL ALWAYS OF HIS COVENANT; the word which he hath commanded to a thousand generations" (1 Chron. xvi. 12–15).

Or "*Testament.*"

The word translated "*Covenant*" in the New Testament is also sometimes translated "*Testament*" :—

"This is my blood of the *new testament*, which is shed for many for the remission of sins" (Matt. xxvi. 28).

" He is the mediator of *the new testament*, that by means of death, for the redemption of the transgressions that were under *the first testament*, they which are called might receive the promise of eternal inheritance. For where a *testament* is, there must also of necessity be the death of the testator. For a *testament* is of force after men are dead: otherwise it is of no strength at all while the testator liveth " (Heb. ix. 15–17).

I have heard the conduct of many of us in respect to the " Covenant " or " Testament," compared to that of a man who having a magnificent inheritance left to him with a house upon it, should take possession of the house and make himself comfortable there, without troubling himself to enquire about anything else.

For, are there not many dear children of God who are contented to rejoice in their conversion—to rejoice in their having, so to speak, changed their dwelling place from the ante-room to hell, which rightly describes their unsaved state, to " the house of God " and " the gate of heaven," which is the right description of their state as now being saved (Gen. xxviii. 16)— without troubling themselves to look further into the " eternal inheritance " ?

Our elder brother's will.

They show but very little, in regard to the " *new testament*," of the spirit of the good Scotch girl in persecuting times, overtaken by soldiers on her way to a secret meeting for worship with her fellow-believers, and answering their commander's demand of where she was going—" To my Father's house: *my elder brother has died: his will is to be read to-day; and* I HAVE AN INTEREST IN IT."

They do not in any believing earnestness of heart pray to "the God of our Lord Jesus Christ, the Father of glory," to "give unto" them "the spirit of wisdom and revelation in the knowledge of him: the eyes of" their "understanding being enlightened; that" they "may know *what is the hope of his calling, and what the riches of the glory of his inheritance in the saints, and what is the exceeding greatness of his power to usward who believe, according to the working of his mighty power, which he wrought in Christ, when he raised him from the dead*, and set him at his own right hand in the heavenly places, far above all principality, and power, and might, and dominion, and every name that is named, not only in this world, but also in that which is to come: and hath put all things under his feet, and gave him to be the head over all things to the church, which is his body; the fulness of him that filleth all in all" (Eph. i. 17–23).

Spiritual dwarfs.

And thus disregarding the injunction of our heavenly Father, that "leaving the principles of the doctrine of Christ" we should "go on unto perfection" (Heb. vi. 1), they remain "babes" in spiritual things ("When for the time ye ought to be teachers, ye have need that one teach you again which be the first principles of the oracles of God; and are become such as have need of milk, and not of strong meat. For every one that useth milk is unskilful in the word of righteousness: for *he is a babe*" Heb. v. 12, 13. "And I, brethren, could not speak unto you as unto spiritual, but as unto carnal, even as unto *babes in Christ*" 1 Cor. iii. 1): and as years roll on without any corresponding growth by them in the spiritual life, they find themselves—or, at any rate, are seen by their fellow-believers, and yet more clearly by the unconverted world about them, which has a wonderfully keen perception of what a child of God ought to be—miserable spiritual dwarfs, if indeed after a course of years of such a life, there can be said to be any spiritual life left in them at all.

Let us, any of us who have thus been so sadly unmindful "of his covenant," now at once accept our dear Lord by faith as our Deliverer from this wretched state, and He will delight (Jer. ix. 24; Hos. xiii. 9; Zech. ix. 12) perfectly to save (Heb. vii. 25) us out of it. And then being no more *unmindful*, but, as our heavenly Father is, *ever* "*mindful* of his covenant," shall we not, in the constant enjoyment of all its blessedness, be to Him "for a people, and for a name, and for a praise, and for a glory" (Jer. xiii. 11), in a life in which entire freedom from sin is indeed included, but in the blessedness of which even that unspeakable blessing is comparatively only a small part; only as the clearing of the ground for the building us up into a "holy temple in the Lord," "an habitation of God through the Spirit" (Eph. ii. 21, 22)?

"Shalt not turn away from me."

"I will instruct thee and teach thee in the way which thou shalt go: I will guide thee with mine eye" (Ps. xxxii. 8).

"Thou shalt call me, My father; and shalt not turn away from me" (Jer. iii. 19).

"I will give them one heart, and one way, that they may fear me for ever, for the good of them, and of their children after them. And I will make an everlasting covenant with them, that I will not turn away from them, to do them good; but I will put my fear in their hearts, that they shall not depart from me" (Jer. xxxii. 39, 40).

These are some more of the "good things" "freely given to us" by our heavenly Father (Matt. vii. 11; 1 Cor. ii. 12), and secured to us by that "covenant" of which "he will ever be mindful."

God's fear in our hearts.

"*Shalt not turn away from me*": "*Shall not depart from me.*" It is not, shalt not turn away *altogether*, and shall not depart *much* or shall not depart *permanently*, nor any other such qualifying expression according to the limitations which so many of God's children seem to put upon his promises in their hearts, though they may not with their lips; but simply and absolutely shalt *not turn away*, shall *not depart*; and as any—the very least—turning away *is* turning away, and any—the very least—departing *is* departing, surely this is an engagement on God's part if we will, by believing it and accepting Christ for it, put it into his power (Mark vi. 5) to fulfil it, that He will preserve us from ever turning away or departing from Him even in the least degree.

And the means by which He declares He will preserve us from doing so is that He will give us the Spirit of sonship—"*Thou shalt call me, My father*"—to bind us to Him ("Because ye are sons, God hath sent forth the Spirit of his Son into your hearts, crying, Abba, Father," Gal. iv. 6), and will *put his fear in our hearts*, to destroy at its source (Matt. xii. 33) the tendency to depart from Him.

"*Prone to wander.*"

Have we not most of us been obliged to mix with our thanksgivings for his grace sad confessions of much in our hearts directly opposed to it?—

"Oh! to grace how great a debtor
Daily I'm constrained to be,
Let that grace, Lord, like a fetter,
Bind *my wandering heart* to thee.

Prone to wander, Lord, I feel it,
Prone to leave the God I love.
Here's my heart, Lord, take and seal it,
Seal it for thy courts above."

But will not the fulfilment to us—through our believing for it in our Lord Jesus Christ and in the power of the Holy Ghost exerted in us through Him—of the part of the covenant which we are now considering be the answer to our prayers in that hymn, the *binding* of our wandering hearts to Him, the *sealing* them for his courts above? And shall we thenceforth any more have to speak of feeling them "prone to wander," "prone to leave the God" we "love"? Or shall we not rather now rejoice in that so much better, so much happier, so much more scriptural experience, and so much more honouring to the dear Lord who has bought us—hearts and all else—with his precious blood:— "My heart is fixed, O God, *my heart is fixed*: I will sing and give praise" (Ps. lvii. 7, cviii. 1)?

And is not a heart thus *fixed on God* and preserved by Himself from any the least "turning away," any the least "departing from" Him, necessarily a heart always free from sin?

"Satisfied."

"Oh that men would praise the Lord for his goodness, and for his wonderful works to the children of men! For *he satisfieth the longing soul, and filleth the hungry soul with goodness*" (Ps. cvii. 8, 9).

"O Naphtali, *satisfied* with favour and full with the blessing of the Lord" (Deut. xxxiii. 23).

"The meek shall eat and *be satisfied*: they shall praise the Lord that seek him: your heart shall live for ever" (Ps. xxii. 26).

"How excellent is thy loving kindness, O God! therefore the children of men put their trust under the shadow of thy wings. They shall be *abundantly satisfied* with the fatness of thy house; and thou shalt make them drink of the river of thy pleasures" (Ps. xxxvi. 7, 8).

"Because thy loving kindness is better than life, my lips shall praise thee. Thus will I bless thee while I live: I will lift up my hands in thy name. *My soul shall be satisfied as with marrow and fatness*; and my mouth shall praise thee with joyful lips" (Ps. lxiii. 3–5).

"Blessed is the man whom thou choosest, and causest to approach unto thee, that he may dwell in thy courts: we shall be *satisfied with the goodness of thy house*, even of thy holy temple" (Ps. lxv. 4).

"The fear of the Lord tendeth to life: and he

that hath it shall *abide satisfied*; he shall not be visited with evil" (Prov. xix. 23).

"I will turn their mourning into joy, and will comfort them, and make them rejoice from their sorrow. And I will satiate the soul of the priests with fatness, and *my people shall be satisfied with my goodness*, saith the Lord" (Jer. xxxi. 13, 14).

These and many other similar passages declare that God has given to us a *satisfying* salvation.

No satisfaction where sin is.

But I ask any dear child of God who may read this, but who does not yet see in the salvation He has given us in Christ entire present salvation from all sin, *Are you satisfied?*

Can you be satisfied so long as you have in you anything that is, as all sin is, rebellion against the blessed God whom you dearly love and to whose service you desire to be entirely devoted; anything which is, as all sin is, enmity against Him?

You know you cannot. You know that so long as there is sin in your life or in your heart you cannot help being just to that extent *dissatisfied* and rightly dissatisfied, and this, however clearly you may see, and however fully you may rejoice in your entire present and eternal salvation in Christ from all its guilt, and your entire *prospective* salvation in Him from its existence.

Heartfelt experience of this dissatisfaction.

I put before you here a very sweet hymn, in one part or other of which you will, I think, find a true expression of your *dissatisfaction* according to the extent that your experience of his salvation falls short of entire deliverance from sin :—

" At even ere the sun was set,
  The sick, O Lord, around Thee lay,
Oh, in what divers pains they met!
  Oh, with what joy they went away!
Once more 'tis eventide, and we
  Oppressed with various ills draw near;
What if thy form we cannot see?
  We know and feel that Thou art here.

O Saviour Christ, our woes dispel;
  For some are sick and some are sad;
And some have never loved Thee well,
  And some have lost the love they had;
And some are pressed with worldly care,
  And some are tried with sinful doubt,
And some such grievous passions tear,
  That only Thou canst cast them out.

And some have found the world is vain,
  Yet from the world they break not free,
And some have friends who give them pain,
  Yet have not sought a Friend in Thee,
And none, O Lord, have perfect rest,
  For none are wholly free from sin,
And they who fain would serve Thee best,
  Are conscious most of wrong within.

O Saviour Christ, Thou too art man,
  Thou hast been troubled, tempted, tried,
Thy kind but searching glance can scan
  The very wounds that shame would hide,
Thy touch has still its ancient power,
  No word from Thee can fruitless fall,
Hear in this solemn evening hour,
  And in thy mercy heal us all."
—Rev. H Twells, in "Hymns of Consecration and Faith."

God be praised for the sweet Gospel truth declared in the last verse,

"*O Saviour Christ. . . .
Thy touch has still its ancient power,*"

and for the sweet Gospel prayer with which it concludes:—"*In thy mercy heal us all.*"

Let us believe for perfect healing.

And praying that prayer believingly, dear brother, it will be answered—so He declares (Mark ix. 23, xi. 24; John xi. 40)—and you will in his mercy be perfectly healed, and will have no more *consciousness* "*of wrong within*" in the sense in which the word is used in the hymn, as expressing indwelling sin as distinguished from mere remaining ignorance and weakness and infirmity (2 Cor. i. 12; Heb. ix. 14; 1 Pet. ii. 24; 1 John iii. 21; &c.), and will have that "perfect rest" which the hymn so truly says "none have" who are only in the state described in it, only, that is, believers in an imperfect salvation from sin.

And then your soul will indeed, in a sense which you have never hitherto known, "be *satisfied as with marrow and fatness*," and your mouth will, to an extent to which it has never yet done, "*praise*" Him "*with joyful lips.*"

"The Travail of his Soul."

"A woman when she is in travail hath sorrow, because her hour is come: but as soon as she is delivered of the child, she remembereth no more the anguish, for joy that a man is born into the world" (John xvi. 21).

"He shall see of the travail of his soul, and shall be satisfied" (Isa. liii. 11).

The earthly type of it.

Some of us have been privileged to see the beautiful sight of a young Christian mother, who has been enabled to lift up her heart to the Lord in her time of trial, and has been brought safely through it by Him; lying in extreme weakness indeed, but the "anguish" all over, and her heart overflowing with thankfulness to her heavenly Father; and her face shining with heavenly delight as she turns it toward the newly-born child, and sees in it of the travail of her body, and is "*satisfied.*"

But what if instead of a healthy, perfect infant it had been a poor sickly, deformed, rickety little thing; just such in body as many dear brothers believe that we must all be in our souls all our time down here, to the greater glory, as they think, of our Lord Jesus Christ in saving us? Would there not, instead of that look of heavenly delight, have been on her face the expression of anguish of heart now succeeding her anguish of body, that the dear little one, though perhaps not any the less loved on account of its sickliness and deformity, should yet be so different from what she had been hoping for as the reward of all she had gone through to give it its existence?

The reward our Lord looks for.

And if God has seen fit to take the sufferings of a woman in child-birth as a type of the sufferings of our Lord Jesus Christ to bring us into existence in the heavenly life, shall we do wrong in considering that He looks for the same reward for the agony

He endured for us which the mother hopes to receive for her travail-pangs for her child: namely, that however weak, and helpless, and dependent on Him for everything, all of which only endears us to Him so much the more, yet that we should be free from deformity and disease, or, in other words, from sin outward or inward? Is it not only so that He can indeed, in us "*see of the travail of his soul, and be satisfied*"?

And at the Present Time.

And if it be said that no doubt this is to be hereafter; but that the time has not come for it yet: then I answer that the time has come for this reward to the mother the moment the child is born: and that the promise to our Lord Jesus, in that prophecy respecting Him, coming as it does *before* "by his knowledge shall my righteous servant justify many; for he shall bear their iniquities: therefore will I divide him a portion with the great," &c. (Isa. liii. 11), appears to refer in the first instance to a *present* reward to Him: and that the further and deeper delight which He is to have in his perfected image in us in glory, would seem to answer to the mother's further and deeper delight if she should see her child grow up into *maturity* of strength and wisdom and all else that her heart can desire to see in him.

I think then that in that word " He shall see of the travail of his soul and shall be satisfied," taken along with its context, we have at any rate a confirmation of the more direct " Scriptural Proofs," that God intends us even in this present life to be entirely without sin.

"All that is within me."

Does God really give us that lovely hundred and third psalm as our own, and mean us in all sincerity of heart to say, "*All that is within me bless his holy name*"?

A great difficulty.

But how then if there be *sin* in us? *That* cannot bless his holy name. And if any of our thoughts, feelings, desires, imaginations, or whatever other things are in us, are tainted with it, just to that extent it is impossible for them to bless his holy name.

What then is to be done? Are we to give up the holy and beautiful words because of the apparent impossibility of their fulfilment? or are we to use them because He has given them to us, and leave Him to deal with the impossibility? knowing that "the things which are impossible with men are possible with God" (Luke xviii. 27), "for with God all things are possible" (Matt. xix. 26).

God must deal with it.

Surely this last is the right course to take in his sight: and by his grace let us take it. Let us accept the psalm as entirely our own. Let us say those words of it in all sincerity of heart; and put our trust in Him through our Lord Jesus Christ (1 Pet. i. 21), to make them by the almighty power of his Spirit in us ("able to do exceeding abundantly above all that we ask or think *according to the power that worketh in us*") a blessed reality in the very act of our saying them.

"He will bind us up."

"Come, and let us return unto the Lord: for he hath torn, and he will heal us; he hath smitten, and he will bind us up. After two days will he revive us: in the third day he will raise us up, and we shall live in his sight. Then shall we know, if we follow on to know the Lord: his going forth is prepared as the morning; and he shall come unto us as the rain, as the latter and former rain unto the earth" (Hosea vi. 1-3).

"Moreover the light of the moon shall be as the light of the sun, and the light of the sun shall be sevenfold, as the light of seven days, in the day that the Lord bindeth up the breach of his people, and healeth the stroke of their wound" (Isa. xxx. 26).

"*He hath torn, and he will heal us: he hath smitten, and he will bind us up.*" Is there room here for any other idea than that of a perfect healing, a perfect binding up?

"After two days will he revive us: *in the third day he will raise us up*, and we shall live in his sight:" referring doubtless to the resurrection—though in the future when the words were written—of our Lord Jesus Christ on the third day from the dead, and to what his resurrection is to us.

Only as we realise our resurrection with Christ.

For it is only as we realise that God has indeed "raised us up together, and made us sit together in heavenly places in Christ Jesus" (Eph. ii. 6), above the guilt, the dominion, and, as I am here endeavouring to show, the existence in us of sin, that we do indeed "live in his sight," in that more abundant life which our Lord Jesus Christ as the Good Shepherd came to bring to his sheep (John x. 10); and only so that the blessedness declared in the latter part of the above passage is fulfilled in us, of our "following on to know the Lord," and experiencing that "his going forth is" indeed "prepared as the morning," and that He does "come unto us as the rain, as the latter and former rain unto the earth."

But, unhappily, many children of God do not see it to be their privilege to *get beyond the two days*. And so though they are "reconciled" indeed "unto God by the *death* of his Son," yet for want of attaining to *the third day*, by realising "the power of his resurrection" (Phil. iii. 10), they are not yet "saved"—in the sense of this fulness of salvation—"*by his life*" (Rom. v. 10).

And being thus themselves only partly "healed," and "bound up" from their "torn" and "smitten" state, they cannot understand the perfect healing and perfect binding up in which they see others so greatly rejoicing, but set it down as a thing of their imagination, or as a delusion of the evil one.

But can such dear souls reconcile their own only imperfect cure, and their judgment of those professing to be perfectly cured, with the unqualified promise in the sweet passage we are considering?

Blessedness of perfect healing.

And can they know anything at all fully and *continuously* of the exceeding spiritual blessedness, the "joy unspeakable and full of glory" (1 Pet. i. 8), the power to "arise" and "shine" because our "light is come, and the glory of the Lord is risen upon" us (Isa. lx. 1; Phil. ii. 15), declared in the second of the two passages above to be the consequence of the perfect "healing," the perfect "binding up"? Let us look carefully again at the words in which this is expressed:—

"*The light of the moon shall be as the light of the sun, and the light of the sun shall be sevenfold, as the light of seven days, in the day that the Lord bindeth up the breach of his people, and healeth the stroke of their wound.*"

"*As the days of heaven upon the earth.*"

It is as the very beginning of heaven—"as the days of heaven upon the earth" (Deut. xi. 21)—as shown even more clearly perhaps in another sweet passage in Isaiah, in which the blessedness of the perfect healing, the perfect binding up, is expressed in a similar and yet varied figure, corresponding to that used by St. John in the Revelation (xxi. 23; xxii. 5) in describing what he saw of the glory of heaven:—

"Thou shalt call thy walls Salvation, and thy gates Praise. The sun shall be no more thy light by day; neither for brightness shall the moon give light unto thee: but the Lord shall be unto thee an everlasting light, and thy God thy glory. *Thy sun shall no more go down; neither shall thy moon withdraw itself: for the Lord shall be thine everlasting light, and the days of thy mourning shall be ended*" (Isa. lx. 18-20).

("And the city had no need of the sun, neither of the moon, to shine in it: for the glory of God did lighten it, and the Lamb is the light thereof."

"And there shall be no night there; and they need no candle, neither light of the sun; for the Lord God giveth them light," Rev. xxi. 23; xxii. 5).

Both the passages in Isaiah are undoubtedly for spiritual fulfilment in us now, on our believing on our Lord Jesus Christ as our perfect "healing," our perfect "binding up." And both of them include, as only a preparatory part of their exceeding blessedness, entire present deliverance from all sin.

'Thy Word have I hid in mine heart."

"Thy word have I hid in mine heart, *that I might not sin against thee*" (Ps. cxix. 11).

"Concerning the works of men, *by the word of thy lips I have kept me from the paths of the destroyer*" (Ps. xvii. 4).

Do not these passages, and the many others to the same effect in the Old Testament (Ps. xix. 7–11; cxix. 9; &c.), amount to a declaration that *the Word of God as it existed at the time they were written was a sufficient preventive to sin?*

Christ dwelling in our hearts by faith.

And what shall we say, then, of our completed Bible, and of Him of whom, as we know in the light of the New Testament, the whole of it teaches us (John v. 39; Luke xxiv. 27) the *Living and Eternal* "WORD" (John i. 1), who now—if we are "strengthened with might by" God's "Spirit in the inner man," rightly to believe in Him for it—*dwells in our hearts* by faith (Eph. iii. 16, 17)?

If, in this infinitely higher sense than that probably which was in the mind of the Old Testament

"THY WORD HAVE I HID IN MINE HEART." 125

writer when the Holy Spirit prompted him to write the words, we are continually (John viii. 31) enabled by God's grace truthfully to say, "THY WORD have I hid in mine heart that I might not sin against thee," would it not be dreadfully dishonouring to Him, and to the Father whose gift He is to us, to doubt that we have in Him perfect, absolute, continual deliverance and preservation from all sin?

"Loose him and let him go."

"They took away the stone from the place where the dead was laid. And Jesus lifted up his eyes and said, Father, I thank thee that thou hast heard me. And I knew that thou hearest me always: but because of the people which stand by I said it, that they may believe that thou hast sent me.

"And when he thus had spoken, he cried with a loud voice, Lazarus, come forth. And he that was dead came forth, bound hand and foot with grave clothes: and his face was bound about with a napkin. Jesus saith unto them, Loose him and let him go" (John xi. 41–44).

"*Loose him and let him go.*" How long did it take the disciples to obey this word of our Lord? And when they had obeyed it, how much was there left of the grave clothes on Lazarus? Was he not then as free from them as if he had not had them on him at all?

Lazarus a type of ourselves.

And is he not, in that miracle of our Lord upon his body, a type of ourselves, in his miracle upon our souls, of speaking them out of death into life, according to his word, "Verily, verily, I say unto you, The hour is coming, and now is, when the dead shall hear the voice of the Son of God: and they that hear shall live" (John v. 25)?

And do we not also, many of us, see in him after he had come forth, but was still "bound hand and foot with grave clothes, and his face bound about with a napkin," a further likeness to ourselves in our bondage to "the law of sin and death" (Rom. vii. 23; viii. 2) even after we have been spoken by the voice of the Lord into spiritual life?

Are we not to be set free as he was?

And does not the Lord mean a work of spiritual deliverance to be wrought on every such raised up, but still bound, soul corresponding to that work of bodily deliverance, wrought upon the raised up but still bound, body of Lazarus? And does He not mean this to be wrought through the agency of those already walking with Him in spiritual freedom, as the work on the body of Lazarus was wrought by those already walking with Him in bodily freedom? Does He not give to these spiritually free ones, with respect to each such soul, the same command which He gave to those disciples with respect to the body of Lazarus, "Loose him and let him go"?

And does He not mean this work of loosing and letting go to be done as soon on the newly raised souls as it was done on Lazarus's newly raised body? And is it not to be done by the bringing to bear upon them the "exceeding great and precious promises" of fulness of salvation from all sin, that they, by believing in Him for their fulfilment, may be set as entirely free from all remaining adherence of sin to them as his body from its adhering grave clothes?

And have we not then, in that word, another strong confirmation of the more direct Scriptural Proofs, that He has indeed provided for us the means of our being entirely delivered from all sin, and that He intends them so to be used upon us, that we shall every one of us be, and that now at once, as a matter of fact, thus entirely delivered?

Oh, may He use what there is of his own Word, even in this little book, for the loosing and letting go of many dear souls! Dear Lord Jesus, so use it for thy name and glory's sake! Amen.

"All our works in us."

"*A song inciting to confidence in God, for his judgments, and for his favour to his people. An exhortation to wait on God.*

"In that day shall this song be sung in the land of Judah; we have a strong city; salvation will God appoint for walls and bulwarks."

"Thou wilt keep him in perfect peace, whose mind is stayed on thee: because he trusteth in thee. Trust ye in the Lord for ever: for in the Lord Jehovah is everlasting strength."

"Lord, thou wilt ordain peace for us: for thou also hast wrought all our works in us. O Lord our God, other lords beside thee have had dominion over us: but by thee only will we make mention of thy name" (Isaiah xxvi. title and 1, 3, 4, 12, 13).

"*Thou also hast wrought all our works in us.*" Does this really mean exactly what it says? And if it does, and we believe in our Lord Jesus Christ for its fulfilment in us (2 Cor. i. 20), and so have it fulfilled in us as a matter of fact, what sin can there be in us? For we know that sin can never be a work of God, and so if "all our works" in us are indeed wrought of God, there cannot in any of them be the least sin.

No peace where sin is.

And we can see that the fulfilment of this word is needed for the fulfilment of that other sweet word connected with it, " *Thou, Lord, wilt ordain peace for us.*" For perfect peace—and it is called perfect peace in one of the other verses (" Thou wilt keep him in *perfect peace*, whose mind is stayed on thee: because he trusteth in thee ")—can never be except in perfect freedom from sin. For sin is a disturbing thing. It is a wicked thing, and "There is no peace, saith my God, to the wicked" (Isa. lvii. 21). And though as God's saved ones in Christ we are no longer of the wicked in the same sense as the unsaved, yet wickedness is wickedness, as much, and indeed a great deal more, in the saved than in the unsaved, in his children than in his enemies: and just to the extent in which it is in them it must prevent their peace.

So have we not in that word, " Thou, Lord, wilt ordain peace for us: for thou also hast wrought all our works in us," another Scriptural Proof that God does give us in our Lord Jesus Christ entire deliverance from all sin, inward as well as outward?

"Hallowed be thy name."

"Our Father, which art in heaven, Hallowed be thy name. Thy kingdom come. Thy will be done in earth as it is in heaven" (Matt. vi. 9, 10).

In all the earth hereafter.

No doubt, all these three petitions are to be answered to the full extent hereafter, when "*The earth shall be full of the knowledge of the Lord, as the waters cover the sea*" (Isa. xi. 9).

But has not God now already on earth a people who *have the knowledge of Him* (John xvii. 2, 3)? And does He not expect as much honour and service now from each one of them (1 Cor. vi. 20), as He is to have hereafter from each one of those who shall then have the knowledge of Him?

And surely in us now.

Does He not, that is, expect that "this people" whom He has "formed for" Himself (Isa. xliii. 21), and *of* and *to* whom He says, "Ye are a chosen generation, a royal priesthood, an holy nation, a peculiar people; that ye should show forth the praises of him who hath called you out of darkness into his marvellous light" (1 Pet. ii. 9), should now at this present time, by their making to Him believingly the above three petitions and receiving from Him accordingly that which they desire in them (Mark xi. 24; 1 John v. 14, 15), hallow his name "in earth as it is" hallowed "in heaven," and have his kingdom set up in them "in earth as it is in heaven," and his will done in them, and by them, "in earth as it is in heaven"?

Not with the wisdom, or strength, or anything else of the angels—for *that* we may be sure He does not look for from us, any more than He looks for the angels to serve Him with his own infinite wisdom and strength—but with just that measure of wisdom and strength, and all else with which He has endowed us.

"*According to that a man hath.*"

And then we loving and serving Him with all our little heart, and mind, and soul, and strength, are no doubt as much accepted by Him as they loving and serving Him with all their great heart, and mind, and soul, and strength; " For if there be first a willing mind, it is accepted according to that a man " or an angel " hath, and not according to that he hath not " (2 Cor. viii. 12).

The widow's two mites were " more " in the sight of God than the " much " which the " many that were rich " cast into the treasury; because they were all she had, and their much was only a part of what they had (Mark xii. 41–44). And, doubtless, if they too had cast in all they had, her two mites would still have been *as much* as all their riches, as both she and they would then alike have done " what " they " could " (Mark xiv. 8); which is all that the angels can do, and all that He requires in earth or heaven.

The way provided for it.

And is not the way provided by Him for our thus doing his will on earth as it is done in heaven, in that word which we were considering in the last section, " Thou also hast wrought all our works in us"? For how could the brightest archangel serve Him better than by all his works being wrought in him by God Himself?

And we know, in the light of the New Testament, how He can thus work all our works in us; that it is by his own Almighty Spirit, given to us through our Lord Jesus Christ, and revealing Him in us as "of God made unto us wisdom and righteousness, and sanctification and redemption" (1 Cor. i. 30), and as our very life by which thus to live only to the glory of God (Gal. ii. 20; Col. iii. 4).

And with all this fulfilled in us—and surely, it is his will that it should be in every one of us: only, we must give ourselves up to Him believingly for it—what sin can there be on us or in us?

"In the presence of mine enemies."

"Thou preparest a table before me in the presence of mine enemies" (Ps. xxiii. 5).

In the earlier part of the psalm we have, "He restoreth my soul," without any qualifying word to suggest that the restoration may be otherwise than complete. And yet, surely, no soul can be said to be, in the plain simple meaning of the word, "restored" in which any sin is left. I must not, however, dwell on this point, as to do so would seem like a repetition of what has been said above on the similar unqualified use of the words "healed," "redeemed," "ransomed," "saved," "delivered," "translated," "satisfied," and "bound up."

"*Thou preparest a table before me in the presence of mine enemies.*" Do not these words express great spiritual blessedness, with the consciousness of such perfect protection from all enemies, that their very nearness in their malice only enhances our enjoyment of our rich feast, by constantly reminding us of our blessed security from their evil designs?

" *Christian* " and " *Giant Pope.* "

Do not they raise in our minds the idea of their being as powerless to carry out their wicked devices, as old " Giant Pope " when he could " do little more than sit in his cave's mouth grinning at pilgrims as they go by, and *biting his nails because he cannot get at them* "?

And as " Christian," in spite of his " You will never mend till more of you be burned," " set a good face on't, and so went by and *catched no hurt*," and then broke out in a sweet song of rejoicing; so, ought we not to use this sweet psalm and all other such parts of God's Word in all fulness of thanksgiving for entire deliverance and preservation from all the evil that our spiritual enemies have done or would seek to do to us, and in so using them, have this perfect deliverance and preservation become a fact to us and in us, and be enabled henceforth to live without sin in heart or life?

"The cup of salvation."

" And he came out, and went, as he was wont, to the Mount of Olives; and his disciples also followed him. And when he was at the place, he said unto them, Pray that ye enter not into temptation. And he was withdrawn from them about a stone's cast, and kneeled down, and prayed, saying, Father, if thou be willing, remove this cup from me: nevertheless not my will, but thine, be done. And there appeared an angel unto him from heaven, strengthening him. And being in an agony he prayed more earnestly: and his sweat was as it were great drops of blood falling down to the ground" (Luke xxii. 39–44).

"Christ hath redeemed us from the curse of the law, being made a curse for us: for it is written, Cursed is every one that hangeth on a tree: that the blessing of Abraham might come on the Gentiles through Jesus Christ; that we might receive the promise of the Spirit through faith" (Gal. iii. 13, 14).

"He was wounded for our transgressions, he was bruised for our iniquities: the chastisement of our peace was upon him; and with his stripes we are healed" (Isa. liii. 5).

"Ye know the grace of our Lord Jesus Christ, that, though he was rich, yet for your sakes he became poor, that ye through his poverty might be rich" (2 Cor. viii. 9).

"What shall I render unto the Lord for all his benefits toward me? I will take the cup of salvation, and call upon the name of the Lord" (Ps. cxvi. 12, 13).

The price and the purchase equal.

Was it not a full cup of the guilt of our sins, and of the shame and sorrow attaching to them, and of the wrath of God deserved by them, which our dear Lord saw before Him when, "being in an agony, he prayed the more earnestly, and his sweat was as it were great drops of blood falling down to the ground"?

And are we to say that by drinking it as He did to the dregs He has purchased for us a less than equally full " cup of salvation "?

Are we not raised by his having made us one with Himself, if we believe in Him for it, to a height of enrichment equal to the depth of the " poverty " into which He sank by making Himself one with us?

Is not that " blessing of Abraham " that " comes on " us Gentiles " through Jesus Christ," by our " receiving the promise of the Spirit "—the revealer to us and in us of all the " good things " " freely given to us of God " (Matt. vii. 11; 1 Cor. ii. 12); —equal in height to the depth of the " curse " which He was " made " in order to purchase this blessedness for us?

And if, varying the form of the question as often as we will, the answer must still always be that the purchased benefit for us must be according to the cost to Him at which it has been purchased, do we not in the inscrutable depth of his sufferings see that the salvation procured for us by them must be infinitely more glorious than anything which even those among us who have the most exalted ideas of it have ever yet had any conception of?

Fulness of blessing ours now.

And that this blessedness is ours at this present moment according to our capacity for receiving it is shown by that word of St. Paul, quoted more than once above, telling the Corinthians what the Gospel was which he preached:—

" Now then we are ambassadors for Christ, as though God did beseech you by us: we pray you in Christ's stead be ye reconciled to God. For he hath made him to be sin for us, who knew no sin; that we might be made the righteousness of God in him. We then, as workers together with him, beseech you also that ye receive not the grace of God in vain. *For he saith, I have heard thee in a time accepted, and in the day of salvation have I succoured thee: behold* NOW *is the accepted time; behold* NOW *is the day of salvation* " (2 Cor. v. 20—vi. 2).

And surely in this full present salvation there is included, as forming, indeed, comparatively but a small part of it—scarcely more than a mere preparation for it—the one particular blessing which we are specially considering in this book, perfect present deliverance from all sin, outward or inward.

"I will take."

" If any man thirst, let him come unto me and drink " (John vii. 37).

" Let him that is athirst come. And whosoever will, let him take of the water of life freely " (Rev. xxii. 17).

In the previous section we had " *I will take* the cup of salvation " (Ps. cxvi. 13): and here we have "whosoever will *let him take* the water of life freely; " and, in accordance with it, " If any man thirst, let him come unto me *and drink.*"

Coming but not drinking.

And is it not for want of carefully attending (" *hearken diligently* " Isa. lv. 2) to the plain meaning of such parts of the Bible and fully and perseveringly acting upon what we hear God say to us in them, that many who have had intense desires for perfect deliverance from sin in heart and life, and have brought these desires to Him in prayer again and again in the deepest earnestness of heart, have yet as a matter of fact gone on still undelivered, and have at last, perhaps, sunk into the ranks of those who declare any such deliverance impossible?

They have "thirsted" time after time, and each time have obeyed the above loving call of our dear Lord, " If any man thirst, let him come unto me and drink," as far as the first half of it, namely to "*come*;" and every time of coming have looked with intense longing at the river of the water of life flowing out of Him as the smitten Rock (1 Cor. x. 4), and have cried to Him in, it may be, almost an agony of desire, to give them to drink of it: but not obeying his word, " What things soever ye desire when ye pray, *believe that ye receive them*, and ye shall have them" (Mark xi. 24), and so not believing that He then and there "granted" them "that which" they "requested" (1 Chron. iv. 10), they have failed to obey the second half of his sweet command, namely, to "*drink*": and thus have gone away with their thirst as unsatisfied as ever, to renew again and again this process of coming and crying to Him and going away without taking and drinking—their unbelief still strengthening itself by each such fresh victory over them—till at last, perhaps, finding the uselessness and hopelessness of *so* coming, and yet not seeing any better way, they have ceased to come at all.

"*Do give me a cup of tea.*"

There is a story, well worn, but not on that account any the less useful as an illustration, of a good clergyman—whose name and that of the place in which he was exercising his ministry are given, but I need not bring them in here—one of whose flock continued week after week and month after month in great distress of soul because she could not receive as a fact—and so have it become a fact to her—that God had in Christ reconciled her to Himself, "not imputing" her "trespasses unto" her (2 Cor. v. 19).

One day she asked him to take tea with her; and he accepted the invitation in the hope that God might bless his time with her to the setting her soul at liberty.

When he saw she had the tea ready, he said, "I should so very much like a cup of tea: would you be kind enough to give me a cup of tea?"

"Yes," she said, "it is just ready; I will pour it out directly."

But again he said, "Oh do be so kind as to give me a cup of tea! I am so very much in want of a cup of tea!"

She had now filled the cup, and held it out to him. But instead of taking it he only kept on more and more earnestly begging her to give him a cup of tea, till at length—so the story goes—he went down on his knees with "O pray, pray, do give me a cup of tea! I am so very much in want of a cup of tea!"

She thought it was time now to put down the cup and make for the bell, as she did not admire being alone in the room with a madman.

But he stopped her with "Oh, no; you need not ring the bell. I am not out of my senses; but only showing you, by what I am doing to you about the cup of tea, what you have been doing all these months towards God about your salvation, praying and praying and praying for it, while He has all the while been holding it out to you in Christ, and beseeching you (2 Cor. v. 20) to accept it by accepting Him as his gift to you" (1 John v. 11).

The story goes that the practical illustration had the desired effect of leading the dear soul to accept our Lord as her salvation (Isa. xii. 2).

Do not some of us here see ourselves?

But is not that just the way so many treat God in the matter of deliverance from indwelling sin? They long for it, cry to Him for it, see his distinct promises of it, and bring them to Him, and, in words, claim of Him the fulfilment of them: and yet never obeying, with respect to their desires and prayers, the plain, simple, most blessed words which here I must once more repeat, " What things soever ye desire when ye pray, *believe that ye receive them, and ye shall have them*" (Mark xi. 24), and never taking to themselves that other sweet word, " This is the confidence that we have in him, that if we ask anything according to his will, he heareth us: and if we know that he hear us, whatsoever we ask, *we know that we have the petitions that we desired of him*" (1 John v. 14, 15), they do not seem to get an inch nearer to the object of the deep longings of their heart, namely, perfect restoration to God by the entire riddance out of them of sin, which so far as it exists in them is separation from Him.

Let us not only " come," but also " drink."

Let us, then, dear brothers and sisters in Christ, in our earnest longings after holiness, not be content with merely knowing that " there is a river the streams whereof shall make glad the city of God" (Ps. xlvi. 4); of which "beautiful" (Ps. xlviii. 2) city, if we believe in our Lord Jesus Christ for it, we are now citizens (Heb. xii. 22; Phil. iii. 20, revised version); or with merely coming to its brink and looking at, and thinking how delightful it must be to drink of the lovely living water; or, even yet further, crying ever so earnestly to the dear Lord, or to the Father in his name, to give us to drink of it: but let us obey also the second half of his loving invitation, "*and* DRINK:" or—as it is in that passage in the Revelation—being "*athirst*," "TAKE *of the water of life* FREELY."

How we drink.

This we do by pleading believingly the words of promise, and accepting by faith the fulfilment of them in our Lord Jesus Christ (2 Cor. i. 20), and receiving by faith the gift of the Holy Ghost "shed on us abundantly through" Him (Titus iii. 5, 6), to reveal Him in us and make us "know the things that are freely given to us of God" (1 Cor. ii. 12); and by being then sure that we "*have received*" (Mark xi. 24, revised version) the things declared in the promises: without waiting for any change of feeling or other "sign" (John iv. 48) of any sort; but leaving that to God to give afterwards, as He shall see best, in his own time and way, but we holding on all the while to simple faith in the bare Word itself, and in our Lord Jesus Christ as its fulfilment, and in the gift of the blessed Spirit through Him.

This is hard work, I know, to believe that all is indeed ours, without the least present change of feeling to witness in us that it is so. Yet surely it is the Scriptural way: for we are to be filled " with all joy and peace," not in order that we may believe, but " *in believing* " (Rom. xv. 13), though, of course, these blessed signs, when in God's good time and way they follow on our believing, do very sweetly confirm our faith (John iv. 53).

Undoubting faith.

"Whatever my God tell me to do, that I try to do," said the dear believing black preacher. " If my God tell me jump through stone wall, *I jump at it.* That belong to me. To get me through, that belong to God." And so, though it may seem to us, being what we are, that we are shut out, as by a stone wall, from any hope of entire holiness of heart and life, we are nevertheless to believe the word that when we ask for it we " have received" it. That is our jumping at the wall, and undoubtedly God will be faithful to his word, in bringing us through it into all the blessedness on the other side.

Another lively instance of it.

" Hard to believe that the whale swallowed Jonah!" said the dear old fully believing sister, in astonishment at a brother less firm in the faith than herself: " I would have believed at once if God had said that *Jonah swallowed the whale.*"

We need it for holiness.

It may need—it *does* need—faith like this in God and his Word to believe that He gives to such as we are freedom from all sin, outward or inward; and if any of us, earnestly desiring this deliverance and holding on to nothing that would be inconsistent with it, are yet conscious of powerlessness to exercise such faith, then let us take this difficulty to our dear Lord, our Almighty Saviour all the way through, from the first good thought till He has us safe with Himself in glory, and, with such faith in Him as we have, cry to Him like one of old, conscious of the same difficulty, " Lord, I believe; help thou mine unbelief" (Mark ix. 24). And He will strengthen us to believe in Himself for all that we can see in the blessed Word of God that God has given to us in Him; of which this deliverance from outward and inward sin is, as noticed above, but a little part: little more than our preparedness for the reception of God's further and much greater gifts waiting ready for us in Him (1 Cor. ii. 9).

" *Subdued kingdoms.*"

Some of God's believing ones of old by such a faith " subdued kingdoms, wrought righteousness, obtained promises" (Heb. xi. 33): and we by it subdue the kingdoms in us of the world, the flesh, and the devil; not only, indeed, subdue them, but have them entirely cast out of us; and receive in their stead, in all its blessed fulness, the " kingdom of God," which is " righteousness and peace and joy in the Holy Ghost" (Rom. xiv. 17); and are thus brought into a position to " work righteousness" to an extent beyond anything we could before have imagined, and to " obtain promises" which would otherwise have remained entirely " sealed" to us (Isa. xxix. 11).

"If God be for us who can be against us?"

God for us.

"If *God* be *for us*, who can be against us?" (Rom. viii. 31); that is, to do us any hurt (Isa. xxvii. 3; Luke x. 19), or to shut us out from any part of the fulness of blessing which belongs to us by the very fact of his being for us.

God with us.

And " God *for* us " has given us " God *with* us: "—" They shall call his name Emmanuel, which being interpreted is, *God with us* " (Matt. i. 23).

" The Word," which " was in the beginning with God," " and was God," " *was made flesh and dwelt among us* " (John i. 1, 2, 14).

And then He stooped lower still, to be yet much more wonderfully God with us in taking on Himself our sins and the condemnation and death due to them. " Being found in fashion as a man, he *humbled himself, and became obedient unto death, even the death of the cross* " (Phil. ii. 8). " His own self bare our sins in his own body on the tree " (1 Pet. ii. 24). God " made him " " who knew no sin " " to be sin for us " (2 Cor. v. 21).

God in us.

And because He became, in such a depth of humiliation and suffering, " God with us," we have, through Him, that further most wonderful and most blessed gift in " the mystery " (Col. i. 26) of our redemption, *God in us*: and, receiving Him, we " are the temple of the living God; as God hath said, I will dwell in them, and walk in them; and I will be their God, and they shall be my people" (2 Cor. vi. 16). And yielding ourselves up to Him and obeying Him, and, by Him in us as our power, coming out and being separate, and not touching the unclean thing, we have the sweet word fulfilled to us of God receiving us and being a Father to us, and we the sons and daughters of Him, the Lord Almighty (2 Cor. vi. 17, 18).

"*Let us cleanse ourselves.*"

The practical application which St. Paul makes of this to ourselves is, " Having therefore these promises, dearly beloved, let us cleanse ourselves from all filthiness of the flesh and spirit, perfecting holiness in the fear of God " (vii. 1).

The "*let us cleanse,*" in the original, is, as already noticed some time back, in the "*Aorist*" tense, signifying the doing it at once, at a stroke ; letting the Word, immediately on our receiving it, have its full effect upon us and in us (1 Thess. i. 5), in the power of the Holy Ghost, so that it may with truth be forthwith said of us, " Ye have *purified your souls* in obeying the truth through the Spirit" (1 Pet. i. 22).

"*Perfecting holiness.*"

But the " *perfecting holiness* " is in the *present* tense, expressing the continuing to do it, the constant growing, that is, in all active goodness, for all our lifetime down here—and we may presume to all eternity afterwards—for which that complete, once-for-all, cleansing from all filthiness of the flesh and spirit, the entire clearing away out of us of all sin, was the necessary preparation.

God in us ready to do his part.

" *God for us* " has perfectly done his work—I say it reverently—of devising for us a perfect salvation, and giving us a perfect Saviour to bring it to us and work it out for us.

" *God with us* " has perfectly done his work of bringing it to us and working it out for us.

And " *God in us* " is ready and desirous (Rom. xv. 30) in equal perfection to do his work of perfectly applying in us this perfectly devised and perfectly wrought-out salvation; by leading us to the Lord Jesus Christ; showing us our need of Him; revealing Him in us; and taking of his things and showing to us, that we may receive Him, and believe in his name, and have power from Him to become the sons of God, and know that we have eternal life in Him, and have Him dwell in our heart by faith, and love Him, and keep his words, and be loved of the Father, and have them come unto us and make their abode with us. And then we have " God in us," in the yet much more blessed way than at the first coming of the Holy Ghost to us, of all the three persons in the holy, blessed, and glorious Trinity dwelling permanently in us.

Can God and sin dwell together?

And if any dear brother tell me that along with the indwelling of the blessed Trinity in us, we must also have indwelling sin, I must yet once again repeat that unless he can show me this in the Word of God, I am utterly unable to receive it; and that I have looked through the Word with all the power to do so which God has given me, and cannot see in it a trace of any such declaration by Him.

And as for the half dozen passages or thereabouts which I know our brother would bring forward in support of his belief that God has declared the necessity of our having sin always in us—all of which passages I hope carefully to consider hereafter in the little book, "Answer to Objections," to follow this one—I cannot but think that it is because of his having been taught this doctrine beforehand, that he thinks he sees it in them; and cannot but think also that it is for the same cause that he is unable to turn his mind to the consideration of the multitude of other passages declaring, in unmistakable language, our entire deliverance from all sin, if we will receive it by believing fully in, and yielding ourselves entirely up to, GOD FOR US, GOD WITH US, AND GOD IN US.

Cleansing from all unrighteousness.

"If we say that we have no sin, we deceive ourselves, and the truth is not in us. If we confess our sins, he is faithful and just to forgive us our sins, and to cleanse us from all unrighteousness" (1 John i. 8, 9).

We must look a little at the self-deceivers who professed "to have no sin;" whose error St. John is here refuting.

Corruptions in the early Church.

St. Paul wrote to the Philippians:—

"Many walk, of whom I have told you often, and now tell you even weeping, that they are the enemies of the cross of Christ: whose end is destruction, whose God is their belly, and whose glory is in their shame, who mind earthly things" (Phil. iii. 18, 19).

And St. Peter wrote of some "false teachers among you, who privily shall bring in damnable heresies, even denying the Lord that bought them;" "chiefly them that walk after the flesh in the lust of uncleanness," who "shall utterly perish in their own corruption" (2 Pet. ii. 1, 10, 12).

Which were still to increase.

And both these Apostles foretold that these evil livers and evil workers should increase, and do more and more evil ("Evil men and seducers shall wax worse and worse, deceiving, and being deceived," 2 Tim. iii. 13: see also Acts xx. 29, 30; 2 Thess. ii. 3–12; 1 Tim. iv. 1, 2; 2 Tim. iii. 1–7; iv. 3; 2 Pet. ii. 1–3, 12, 17–22).

Much increased when St. John wrote.

And at the much later time at which St. John is believed to have written, the evils which they, in the spirit of prophecy, had spoken of as so surely to increase in the Church were, as a matter of fact, greatly increased by the growing up among the Christians of a number of heretical sects, composed of men desirous of sharing in the benefits of Christianity but having no idea of giving up their heathen lives; like the "men from Babylon, and from Cuthah, and from Ava, and from Hamath, and from Sepharvaim," whom "the king of Assyria" "placed" "in the cities of Samaria," who "*feared the Lord, and served their own gods*" (2 Kings xvii. 24–33).

CLEANSING FROM ALL UNRIGHTEOUSNESS. 147

The creed of the heretical sects.

These heretics believed in a self-existent and perfectly holy being, who had brought into existence a number of beings, like himself in holiness, who lived with him in exceeding blessedness in the place which he had prepared for them.

They believed matter to have existed from eternity, and to be altogether evil; and that up to a certain time it had only been a shapeless mass: but then one of the holy happy beings, wandering from the place of glory, came to the confused heap, and formed this world out of it; and also formed out of it men's bodies; and then by some means stole fire out of the holy happy place to animate them. And this heavenly fire became in each of them a holy soul encased in an altogether evil body.

Their views about our Lord.

In professing to embrace Christianity they believed in our Lord as one of many messengers sent from time to time by the great and holy being in the glory to comfort and strengthen the pure souls, whom he looked upon as his daughters, in their sad condition of being shut up in the evil bodies till the time should come for their release to return to him in the glory.

But they could by no means allow Him to have had a material body, as that would be to suppose Him to be connected with evil. They held that He had only the *appearance* of a human body.

Nor did they believe in any atonement made by Him for sin: for they looked upon our souls alone as being ourselves, and these being, according to their belief, always and unalterably holy, they considered that even if wallowing in evil with our bodies, we ourselves were, and ever had been, and ever should be, perfectly sinless, so that there was nothing and never could be anything in us to be atoned for.

St. John's antidote to their poison.

That St. John wrote to counteract evil teachings of some sort, is shown by his words: "These things have I written unto you *concerning them which seduce you*" (ii. 26). And that the *seductions* were of the nature here described is shown by the pains with which he enforces the opposite truths to these particular false doctrines.

As to our Lord's human body.

For the epistle opens with a reiterated most emphatic declaration that our Lord had indeed a real and undeniably material body.

"That which was from the beginning, *which we have heard, which we have seen with our eyes, which we have looked upon, and* OUR HANDS HAVE HANDLED, of the Word of life" (i. 1).

As to fellowship with God while in sin.

And then follows his denunciation of the deadly doctrine that we can be right with God when living in evil:—

"This then is the message which we have heard of him, and declare unto you, that God is light, and in him is no darkness at all. *If we say that we have fellowship with him, and walk in darkness, we lie, and do not the truth*" (i. 5, 6).

And then he declares the real Christian life in contrast to this falsehood, and the real way to be right with Him:—

"But if we walk in the light, as he is in the light, we have fellowship one with another, and the blood of Jesus Christ his Son cleanseth us from all sin" (i. 7).

Their professed inherent sinlessness.

And then he declares the falsity of any pretensions to goodness of our own, on account of which to "say that we have no sin;" instead of confessing our sins, that we may be pardoned by God for them, and cleansed by Him from them:—

"*If we say that we have no sin*, we deceive ourselves, and the truth is not in us" (i. 8).

And then he shows the only true way to be indeed rid of sin:—

"If we *confess our sins*, he is faithful and just to forgive us our sins, and to *cleanse us from all unrighteousness*" (i. 9).

And then he denounces in another form the error of those heretics of our supposed always inherent sinlessness from the beginning:—

"*If we say that we have not sinned*, we make him a liar, and his word is not in us" (i. 10).

All his writing clear and consistent.

Keeping, then, in mind those words, "These things have I written unto you concerning them that seduce you," and looking into the teaching of these "seducers," all his writing in this beginning of his epistle is seen to be perfectly consistent with itself, and with all the rest of the epistle, and all the rest of the Bible.

But read carelessly, may be misunderstood.

But leaving out of notice that declaration of the object for which he was writing, and the nature of the seductions of those heretics, and taking those words, "If we say that we have no sin, we deceive ourselves, and the truth is not in us," as applying to himself and to all his fellow-believers at the time at which he was writing—though they had confessed their sins and God had been "faithful and just to forgive" them their "sins and to *cleanse*" them "*from all unrighteousness,*" so that they now had no sin because He had cleansed it off from them and out of them—many dear souls have got themselves into inextricable confusion; making him seem directly to contradict the teaching of the other apostolical epistles, and of the Acts of the Apostles, and of the Gospels, and of all the rest of the Bible; including most emphatically his own teaching in the rest of this epistle, in which he makes declarations of the entire freedom from sin provided for us by our heavenly Father, perhaps more positive, varied, and multiplied than are to be found in any other part of the Bible of only the same length; declarations to the utter and absolute exclusion of the idea of there being sin in believers really believing and living as God would have them to believe and live.

Those two passages above sufficient.

Those two very blessed passages above, "If we walk in the light as he is in the light," "the blood of Jesus Christ his Son *cleanseth us from all sin,*" and "If we confess our sins, he is faithful and just to forgive us our sins, and to *cleanse us from all unrighteousness*," would alone, one would think, prevent any thought arising in minds unbiassed by previous contrary teaching, that those words, "If we say that we have no sin, we deceive ourselves, and the truth is not in us," could apply to himself and the faithful ones among his fellow-believers in their already, by the blood of our Lord Jesus Christ, and the power of the Holy Ghost applying it to their souls, perfectly cleansed state. But here are some of the many other passages in the epistle in which also entire deliverance from sin is either expressed or implied:—

His further testimony to freedom from sin.

" My little children, these things I write unto you, *that ye sin not*" (ii. 1).

" Hereby we do know that we know him, *if we keep his commandments.* He that saith I know him, and *keepeth not his commandments*, is a liar, and the truth is not in him" (ii. 3, 4).

" But whoso *keepeth his word*, in him verily is the love of God perfected: hereby know we that we are in him" (ii. 5).

" I have written unto you, young men, because ye are strong, and the word of God abideth in you, and ye *have overcome the wicked one*" (ii. 14).

" Every man that hath this hope in him *purifieth himself, even as he is pure*" (iii. 3).

" Ye know that he was manifested to take away our sins; and in him is no sin. *Whosoever abideth in him sinneth not: whosoever sinneth hath not seen him, neither known him.* Little children, let no man deceive you: he that doeth righteousness is righteous, even as he is righteous. *He that committeth sin is of the devil*; for the devil sinneth from the beginning. For this purpose the Son of God was manifested, *that he might destroy the works of the devil.* Whosoever is born of God *doth not commit sin;* for his seed remaineth in him: and he *cannot sin,* because he is born of God. In this the children of God are manifest, and the children of the devil: whosoever *doeth not righteousness* is not of God" (iii. 5–10).

"Beloved, if our heart condemn us not, then have we confidence toward God. And whatsoever we ask, we receive of him, *because we keep his commandments, and do those things that are pleasing in his sight*" (iii. 21, 22).

"And he that *keepeth his commandments* dwelleth in him, and he in him" (iii. 24).

"Herein is our love made perfect, that we may have boldness in the day of judgment: because *as he is, so are we in this world*" (iv. 17).

"By this we know that we love the children of God, when we *love God, and keep his commandments.* For this is the love of God *that we keep his commandments*" (v. 2, 3).

"For whatsoever is born of God overcometh the world: and this is the victory that overcometh the world, even our faith" (v. 4).

"We know that whosoever is born of God *sinneth not;* but he that is begotten of God keepeth himself, and *that wicked one toucheth him not*" (v. 18).

Attempted answer to these passages.

Many dear souls try to save themselves from being shown by these passages not yet to be believers in our Lord according to St. John's idea of a believer in Him, by saying that all such declarations of freedom from sin apply only to our new nature in Him, which is, of course, altogether sinless; but that we have, and that God knows we have, and makes allowance for it, the old sinning nature as well; so that while these declarations are fulfilled in us as regards our new nature, we still have sin in us, and still do sin, as regards the old.

But the attempt vain.

But it is vain to attempt to give such an answer to some of the passages, as for instance such as this:—

"He that saith, I know him, and keepeth not his commandments, is a liar, and the truth is not in him."

For the "he" here must include the man's whole being, with both his natures, if he has two. And so the declaration is positive that any man saying he knows God, who does not, in his entirety, of however many natures he may be composed, keep his commandments, "is a liar, and the truth is not in him." St. John does not say that God may not have him in hand to save him, so that he may presently be brought on to the knowledge of God: but he does say positively that he does not in his present state know Him, and that if he says that he does, "he is a liar, and the truth is not in him."

The old nature dead in full believers.

But indeed to attempt to give that answer about the two natures to any of the passages, is to declare ourselves not yet fully Christ's. For that old nature, which is thus made the excuse for our sinning and for our having sin in us, is "*the flesh*"; of which it is written in a passage already quoted above, "They that are Christ's *have crucified the flesh* with the affections and lusts" (Gal. v. 24): and it is also "the old man"; of which it is written, "Knowing this, that *our old man is crucified with him*, that the body of sin might be destroyed, that henceforth we should not serve sin. For he that is dead is freed from sin" (Rom. vi. 6, 7): so that to such believers in Christ—and He calls upon us all to be such believers in Him—there are no more two natures: for that old sinning one is now dead and gone, and there is only that one new one left which is Christ dwelling in our heart by faith (Eph. iii. 17; Gal. ii. 20), by which, or, rather, by *Whom*, we can indeed have all those glorious words of St. John declaring such absolute freedom from sin always and perfectly fulfilled to us and in us.

"The desires of thine heart."

"Delight thyself also in the Lord; and he shall give thee the desires of thine heart" (Ps. xxxvii. 4).

It is certain that if we delight ourselves in the Lord we shall have an earnest desire in our heart to be rid of everything displeasing to Him—all sin, that is, of every sort.

But here we have the positive promise that if we delight ourselves in Him, He will give us the desires of our heart, and therefore this desire of our heart, the being rid of all sin.

God, therefore, gives us here an infallible means of being delivered from all sin of every sort: and all we have to do is to make sure of being in the state to which the promise is attached; namely, that of delighting ourselves in the Lord.

And the way to attain to this state is, we know, in the light of the New Testament, to believe on our Lord Jesus and accept Him as the Father's gift to us, and have in and by Him the eternal life of knowing the only true God and Him whom He has sent (John xvii. 3 ; 1 John v. 11), and have the love of God shed abroad in our hearts by the Holy Ghost given to us (Rom. v. 5), and so be able to say, " We also *joy in God* through our Lord Jesus Christ, by whom we have now received the atonement " (Rom. v. 11).

Doing this and then *pleading believingly, and receiving by unreasoning and undoubting faith* the fulfilment of the promise, " Delight thyself also in the Lord, and he shall give thee the desires of thine heart," we have from Him, then and there, this desire of our heart, the entire deliverance from all sin.

"Sweet Water and Bitter."

" Doth a fountain send forth at the same place sweet water and bitter ? Can the fig tree, my brethren, bear olive berries ? either a vine, figs ? so can no fountain both yield salt water and fresh " (James iii. 11, 12).

These words form part of St. James's rebuke of the misuse of the tongue, respecting which he had just before said, " Out of the same mouth proceedeth blessing and cursing. My brethren, these things ought not so to be." But they have an equally strong bearing upon evil in any other form in the lives of those professing to belong to God.

In trying to make those to whom he was writing see the wrongness of their inconsistent conduct by pointing them to the trees bearing each one only its own fruit, and to the fresh springs sending forth only fresh water, he was anticipating our own good Bishop Butler, in showing "The analogy of religion" "to the constitution and course of nature."

Of ourselves judging what is right.

And he was following the example of our Lord in his words of reproof to the people:—

"When ye see a cloud rise out of the west, straightway ye say, There cometh a shower, and so it is. And when ye see the south wind blow, ye say, There will be heat, and it cometh to pass. Ye hypocrites, ye can discern the face of the sky and of the earth; but how is it that ye do not discern this time? Yea, and why even of yourselves judge ye not what is right?" (Luke xii. 54–57.)

"*Yea, and why even of yourselves judge ye not what is right?*" Should we any of us in acting upon this word of our Lord, and beginning of ourselves to judge what is right, be able to judge it right that sin should remain in a child of God? Should we not say, "*My brethren, these things ought not so to be.* Doth a fountain send forth at the same place sweet water and bitter? Can the fig-tree, my brethren, bear olive berries? either a vine, figs?"

And yet is not this sending forth at the same place sweet water and bitter, this bearing by the same tree of two different sorts of fruit, the very thing asserted, on the theory of it being impossible for us to live without sin, to be the normal state of the hearts and lives of the children of God?

But our Lord says:—

"A good tree cannot bring forth evil fruit,

neither can a corrupt tree bring forth good fruit" (Matt. vii. 18). "Either make the tree good, and his fruit good; or else make the tree corrupt, and his fruit corrupt" (Matt. xii. 33).

And again He says by the Apostle Paul:—

Works of the Flesh.

"Now the works of the flesh are manifest, which are these; adultery, fornication, uncleanness, lasciviousness, idolatry, witchcraft, hatred, variance, emulations, wrath, strife, seditions, heresies, envyings, murders, drunkenness, revellings, and such like: of the which I tell you before, as I have also told you in time past, that they which do such things shall not inherit the kingdom of God."

Fruit of the Spirit.

"But the fruit of the Spirit is love, joy, peace, long-suffering, gentleness, goodness, faith, meekness, temperance: against such there is no law. And *they that are Christ's have crucified the flesh with the affections and lusts*" (Gal. v. 22-24).

"An horrible pit."

"He brought me up also out of an horrible pit, out of the miry clay" (Ps. xl. 2).

We are all agreed that sin is the "horrible pit," "the miry clay;" and that if we are believers in the Lord Jesus we have been "brought up out" of it; and that if we are such believers in Him as to have received the Holy Ghost from and through Him we have Him in us as "a well of water, springing up into everlasting life" (John iv. 14).

But on the theory of the necessity of our always having sin in us, we have brought up some of the contents of the "horrible pit" with us and in us on our being brought up out of it: and these constitute in themselves a little "horrible pit" in each of us; so that though we are no more in the pit, we have it in us.

And so we have the fountain of the sweet water of life in Christ Jesus and the horrible pit with its filthy contents, side by side—or in whatever other way they may co-exist—in the narrow compass of our hearts.

Pollution of the living water.

And all the "living water" that springs up in us "into everlasting life" to ourselves, and to overflow out of us as "rivers of living water" (John vii. 38), in glory to God and blessing to man, is polluted with the filth of the pit.

This the holders of the theory appear to accept as its logical consequence: for they declare distinctly and positively that there is nothing even in our most holy things that is not mixed with sin.

As I have already said in substance above, if God had told us this in the Bible, we could only have bowed our heads in unquestioning submission; however unable to understand such an incomplete destruction of the "works of the devil" (1 John iii. 8) in us. But many of us, I rejoice to repeat, though trying to "hearken diligently" (Isa. lv. 2) to all that He there says to us, are thankfully unable to hear Him speak any such word.

"Instead of—"

"Instead of the thorn shall come up the fir tree, and instead of the brier shall come up the myrtle tree: and it shall be to the Lord for a name, for an everlasting sign that shall not be cut off" (Isa. lv. 13).

"*Instead of,*" not alongside of; nor a tree partly a thorn and partly a fir, or partly a briar and partly a myrtle, as there would be on the theory of sin always remaining in us; but a fir and a myrtle alone: so that of the thorn and of the briar it must now be said " The wind "—the blessed Spirit who blows upon the flesh and it withers away (Isa. xl. 6–8)—" passeth over it and it is gone, and the place thereof shall know it no more " (Ps. ciii. 16).

This was the prophecy of old of what was to be in the Gospel times. And the fulfilment in the New Testament is declared in that word more than once referred to above, " Therefore if any man be in Christ, he is a new creature: *old things are passed away; behold, all things are become new* " (2 Cor. v. 17).

And we have already above looked at the *old things* as being only sinful, and at the *new things* as entirely free from sin.

"Sanctify you Wholly."

" I know whom I have believed, and *am persuaded that he is able to keep that which I have committed unto him against that day* " (2 Tim. i. 12).

What was it that St. Paul had thus *committed* to our Lord, or to the Father in his name? and what was the extent of *keeping* he expected to be exercised over it?

We may find an answer to both these questions in his words to the Thessalonians, telling them of the extent to which he committed them to the keeping of God, and of his confidence in Him that He would so keep them:—

"The very God of peace *sanctify you wholly*; and I pray God your *whole spirit and soul and body be preserved blameless unto the coming of our Lord Jesus Christ. Faithful is he that calleth you, who also will do it*" (1 Thess. v. 23, 24).

Expectation of not sinning any more.

If his *committing* of himself to the keeping of the Father and of the Lord Jesus Christ was, as we cannot doubt it was, in the same fulness and strength of trust that he exercised for these converts, must it not have been his confident expectation that there would *never again be any sin in him*?

For did not his "body, soul, and spirit" make up the whole of him? And if all three were to be "preserved blameless to the coming of our Lord Jesus Christ"—after which we are all alike agreed that there would be no more question of sin in him —do not his words express full trust of freedom from sin inward and outward for ever?

"Christ liveth in me."

In the last section we looked at the *confident hope* apparently entertained by St. Paul of being always kept free from sin. But there are several passages in his writings which seem to amount to a declaration that he was so kept as a matter of fact.

One of the strongest of these, perhaps, is that word to the Galatians frequently referred to above: "I am crucified with Christ: nevertheless I live; yet not I, but Christ liveth in me: and the life which I now live in the flesh I live by the faith of the Son of God, who loved me, and gave himself for me" (Gal. ii. 20).

Or, as it is in the revised version:—

"I have been crucified with Christ; yet I live; and yet no longer I, but Christ liveth in me: and that life which I now live in the flesh I live in the faith, the faith which is in the Son of God, who loved me, and gave himself up for me."

Surely, if it was not he that was living but Christ in him, he was living a life absolutely without sin. For if there were any, the least, sin of any sort in his life, it would manifestly to that extent be he that lived, and not Christ that lived in him.

In what capacity did he speak?

Now it is of deep importance to us to know whether he spoke the words of himself as an Apostle, with an experience above that of ordinary Christians —such as when, whether in the body he could not tell, or whether out of the body he could not tell, but only God knew, he was caught up into the third heaven and heard unspeakable words, such as it was not lawful for a man to utter (2 Cor. xii. 1-4) —or whether he spoke them merely as a saved sinner, so that we also may look to be enabled to speak them of ourselves

Only as a saved sinner.

There needs only a glance at the context to decide this; for there, after " the life which I now live in the flesh, I live by the faith of the Son of God," he adds, " *who loved me, and gave himself for me;* " and it was certainly not as an Apostle, but as a sinner, that Christ loved him and gave Himself for him. For " Christ Jesus came into the world *to save sinners* " (1 Tim. i. 15). And " God commendeth his love toward us, in that, *while we were yet sinners,* Christ died for us " (Rom. v. 8); " for his great love wherewith he loved us, *even when we were dead in sins* " (Eph. ii. 4, 5).

And assuredly also He loves every one of us with just the same love. " For God *so loved the world,* that he gave his only begotten Son, that whosoever believeth in him should not perish, but have everlasting life " (John iii. 16). And " We see Jesus, who was made a little lower than the angels for the suffering of death, crowned with glory and honour; *that he, by the grace of God, should taste death for every man* " (Heb. ii. 9).

And so He " gave himself for " every one of us as much as for St. Paul, and thereby purchased for every one of us the same salvation from sin as for him.

It only needs, then, that each one of us should give himself up to Christ as entirely as he did, and believe in Him for the same extent of salvation as that for which he believed in Him, to have the same entire deliverance from sin which he had, and to live thenceforth the life of entire freedom from it which we see here that he lived.

" *None of Self and all of Thee.*"

Pastor Monod has gone the length of the above

statement of St. Paul in the last verse of his sweet hymn:—

> "Oh the bitter shame and sorrow
> That a time could ever be,
> When I proudly said to Jesus,
> 'All of self and none of Thee!
>   None of Thee, none of Thee,
>   All of self and none of Thee!'
>
> "Yet He found me, I beheld Him
> Bleeding on th' accursed tree,
> And my wistful heart said faintly,
> 'Some of self and some of Thee!
>   Some of self and some of Thee,
>   Some of self and some of Thee!'
>
> "Day by day his tender mercy,
> Healing, helping, full and free,
> Brought me lower, while I whispered,
> 'Less of self and more of Thee!
>   More of Thee, more of Thee,
>   Less of self and more of Thee!'
>
> "Higher than the highest heaven,
> Deeper than the deepest sea,
> Lord, thy love at last has conquered:
> '*None of self and all of Thee!*
>   *None of self and all of Thee,*
>   *None of self and all of Thee.*'"

And when that happy stage is reached—and God calls us all to come to it by faith now at once—then "As he is so are we in this world" (1 John iv. 17). And we know that He is without sin.

Several Texts excluding Sin.

I copy out a few more passages from St. Paul, seeming directly to express or clearly to imply that he lived a life free from sin, and that he looked to the converts to whom he wrote to live such a life.

"*To me to live is Christ.*"

"According to my earnest expectation, and my hope, that in nothing I shall be ashamed, but that with all boldness, as always, so now also Christ shall be magnified in my body, whether it be by life, or by death. For to me to live is Christ, and to die is gain" (Phil. i. 20, 21).

"To me to live *is Christ.*" This seems almost a repetition in different words of his statement which we considered above: "I live, yet not I, but Christ liveth in me." Could there be any sin in his life so long as he could truly describe it simply as "*Christ*"? Must he not either have used too strong an expression when he wrote that—which surely none of us will venture to suppose—or else have been living at the time a life without sin?

"*Holiness and godly sincerity.*"

"Our rejoicing is this, the testimony of our conscience, that in simplicity" (revised version, "holiness") "and godly sincerity, not with fleshly wisdom, but by the grace of God, we have had our conversation in the world, and more abundantly to you-ward" (2 Cor. i. 12).

"*Have had:*" so this life of *holiness* and *godly sincerity* which they rejoiced to be living was one they had entered upon some time ago. They were not waiting for death or the coming of the Lord to bring them into it. And is there any sin in such a life?

"*Holily, righteously, and unblamably.*"

"Ye are witnesses, and God also, how holily and justly" (revised version, "righteously") "and unblamably we behaved ourselves among you that believe" (1 Thess. ii. 10).

"*Behaved*," showing here again that it was a thing begun some time since. And does not "*holy*," "*righteous*," and "*unblamable*" "behaviour" exclude the idea of sin; and could it be the fruit of a heart in which there was sin?

"*Children of God without blemish.*"

"That ye may be blameless and harmless, the sons of God, without rebuke" (revised version, "children of God without blemish"), "in the midst of a crooked and perverse nation, among whom ye shine as lights in the world" (Phil. ii. 15).

"*Blameless and harmless*," "*children of God without blemish*," shining "*as lights in the world.*" And that it was so with the Philippians, or might be so, and was intended by God to be so, is shown by his exhorting them to let it be so. And yet, where in such a life shall we find room for sin?

"*Without blemish, before Him in love.*"

"Blessed be the God and Father of our Lord Jesus Christ, who hath blessed us with all spiritual blessings in heavenly places in Christ: according as he hath chosen us in him before the foundation of the world, that we should be holy and without blame" (revised version, "without blemish") "before him in love" (Eph. i. 3, 4).

"*Holy* and *without blemish before him in love:*" in our own personal selves down here as being in Christ and He in us: and not *only* as included in Him up there in the presence of God for us.

Surely such words cannot be true of any in whom there is sin. And the other texts above, referring to the same state, show that it is a matter of this present time, and not to take place at death or at the coming of the Lord.

"*Preserved blameless.*"

I must insert again here in this connection a passage already commented on above:—

"The very God of peace *sanctify you wholly; and I pray God your whole spirit and soul and body be preserved blameless unto the coming of our Lord Jesus Christ. Faithful is he that calleth you, who also will do it*" (1 Thess. v. 23, 24).

It is not that "your whole spirit, soul, and body" *be* "blameless" *at* the coming of our Lord Jesus Christ—which might be consistent with perfect sanctification only at death or at our Lord's coming—but "be *preserved* blameless *unto* the coming of our Lord Jesus Christ;" showing that the previous prayer that the very God of peace might sanctify them wholly was one for present fulfilment; this further prayer being that God would keep them in the state of blessedness into which He had thus brought them.

Take all the above together.

If entire sanctification be not expressed in each of the above passages—and of course yet much more strongly in all of them taken together— and as given to us now without waiting for death or the coming of the Lord, what words could express this?

"Without spot, unrebukable."

"Fight the good fight of faith, lay hold on eternal life, whereunto thou art also called, and hast professed a good profession before many witnesses. I give thee charge in the sight of God, who quickeneth all things, and before Christ Jesus, who before Pontius Pilate witnessed a good confession; that thou keep this commandment without spot, unrebukable, until the appearing of our Lord Jesus Christ" (1 Tim. vi. 12–14).

The words "This commandment," or, in the revised version, "*The* commandment," are shown by the context to be here used by St. Paul, as Dean Alford says in his Greek Testament, "not to designate any special command just given, but as a general compendium of the rule of the Gospel after which our lives and thoughts must be regulated."

And we know that "the rule of the Gospel" includes all the ten commandments (Matt. v. 19), and one more (John xiii. 34), the blessed law of love, the "shalt" of the New Testament added to all the "shalt nots" of the Old.

This injunction by him to Timothy to "keep the commandment without spot, unrebukeable," is, then, very similar to that to the Philippians considered above, that they should be "blameless and harmless, the children of God without blemish."

But how if this is impossible?

But on the theory of the necessity of our always

having sin in us, it was an impossibility that Timothy should obey the injunction. Indeed, on that theory, as declaring what is the will and appointment of God for us all our time down here, any expectation and desire fully to obey it would surely have been wrong: for must it not, under any circumstances, be wrong in us to be seeking and striving after that which we know is not the will of God for us?

I have written the last paragraph as an introduction to a passage from Dr. Mahan's "Christian Perfection" on this injunction of St. Paul to Timothy. But first I copy again the words of his solemn charge:

"*I give thee charge in the sight of God*, who quickeneth all things, *and before Jesus Christ*, who before Pontius Pilate witnessed a good confession; *that thou keep this commandment without spot, unrebukeable, until the appearing of our Lord Jesus Christ.*"

Extract from Dr. Mahan.

"The command here referred to, as any one will see who will read the context, includes everything required of Christians.

"Let us suppose that Timothy had answered this epistle, informing Paul that he had read his charge with solemn interest, and that by the grace of God he expected to keep it.

"What should we think if in Paul's second epistle such a rejoinder as this were found:

"' Timothy, your letter to me has filled me with amazement and sorrow of heart. You have become a wild fanatic, a *Perfectionist*. How could you have misunderstood me so much as to suppose that I ever dreamed that you could expect to keep that awful charge?'

"Why should we be shocked at such a reply? Simply because we cannot believe that such a charge could be dictated by the Spirit of God, not only in the absence of all expectation that it would be kept, but with the intention of impressing the subject with the opposite belief."—*Christian Perfection*, by *Asa Mahan, D.D.*

"Dead unto Sin."

"Knowing this, that *our old man is*" (revised version, "*was*") "*crucified with him, that the body of sin might be destroyed*" (revised version, "*done away*"), "*that henceforth we should not serve sin*" (Rom. vi. 6).

"*I am*" (revised version, "*have been*") "*crucified with Christ*: nevertheless I live; yet not I, but *Christ liveth in me*: and the life which I now live in the flesh I live by the faith of the Son of God, who loved me, and gave himself for me" (Gal. ii. 20).

"They that are Christ's have *crucified the flesh with the affections and lusts*" (Gal. v. 24).

If St. Paul in these three passages—each of which has been partly looked at above, but I wish to take the three together here—did not mean the making an end of the old wicked nature entirely—the nature itself, not merely its workings—I cannot even form the least guess of what he did mean.

The two Natures.

A sister in the Lord holding the necessity of sin always remaining in us, speaking with a friend advocating the opposite view, asked him, as if settling the matter her way at a stroke: "But tell me now, have we, or have we not, if we really belong to God as his children, two natures; the old irredeemably bad one, that can do nothing but sin, and the new one, born of God, incapable of sinning? Have we or have we not these two natures?"

Till one of them is dead.

To which he answered and—looking at the matter in the light of the three above quoted, and other such texts—it seems to me scripturally, as I have already partly said above in considering, "If we say we have no sin:"—

"Yes, we have, if really children of God, two natures as you say, the one perfectly evil, nothing but evil, and the other perfectly good, nothing but good; until we are enlightened to see in the Word of God that the old wicked one died with our Lord Jesus Christ on the cross: and then—and so long as we really live the life of faith in Him, so that it is not we that live but He in us—we have no more two natures, but only one, the new one, free from sin, as He is free from it" (2 Cor. v. 17; 1 John iv. 17).

Could any life less perfectly holy than this fulfil those two sayings of St. Paul above quoted, "*To me to live is Christ,*" and "I live, yet *not I, but Christ liveth in me*"? or that declaration of St. John, "*As he is so are we in this world*"? (1 John iv. 17.)

"Reckoning" Ourselves Dead to Sin.

"In that he died he died unto sin once: but in that he liveth, he liveth unto God. Likewise reckon ye also yourselves to be dead indeed unto sin, but alive unto God through Jesus Christ our Lord" (Rom. vi. 10, 11). To me it is really awful —though I know they do not mean anything wrong before God, but only what they, under the teaching of their theological system, believe to be his truth and for his glory—the use to which the dear brethren who believe it impossible that sin can be taken out of us in this life, put this text; actually making it one of their strongholds against the admission of real death to sin.

They say, "'*reckon*;' that's it, you see. We are not so at all as a fact; and never can be while in the body: for as long as we are in it, sin will always be alive in us and we alive to it: but, you see, God tells us that we are, notwithstanding this, to '*reckon*' ourselves dead to it." As if the blessed God, who in Jesus has made Himself known to us as "*The Truth*," could command me to tell a dreadful untruth; which it surely would be in my mouth, to say that I reckoned myself dead to sin if I did not believe in the possibility of being so.

God says we have died.

God tells us that we *are* dead to sin ("We thus judge, that if one died for all, then were all dead;" or in the revised version, "that *one died for all, therefore all died*" 2 Cor. v. 14; see also Col. iii. 3); and, if we believe it, it becomes a fact to us. And it is only in this way of reckoning that real which God did for us by the death of his Son, and so having it become real also to us—*a fact in us*— that He can possibly tell us thus to "*reckon*" it.

We are indeed to "reckon" it true *before we have any consciousness* of its fulfilment in us: but only because this is God's appointed way of its being thus fulfilled ("All things whatsoever ye pray and ask for, *believe that ye have received them, and ye shall have them*" Mark xi. 24, revised version); so that it becomes a fact to us in the very act of our believing it to be so.

It is like the man with the withered hand, who rightly understood our Lord's command, "Stretch forth thine hand," as a command to "*reckon*" it indeed "restored, whole like as the other;" and so he stretched it forth, which he could only do because of his belief in its being restored as a fact in the very act of his obeying the command. And it was restored accordingly.

And I believe it.

And so we, if we obey the command to "reckon" ourselves "to be dead indeed unto sin," become so indeed: and continuing so to reckon ourselves, that it may continue to be a fact in us, sin is no more to us than — as has been well said — the turmoil of the street to one lying in a burial-ground alongside.

Surely this is not going a hair's-breadth beyond the words "Reckon ye also yourselves *dead indeed unto sin.*" And therefore, surely, if any of my brothers and sisters in Christ object to what I have here said, they are objecting to obedience to a positive commandment of God to us by his Apostle.

But all, I again say, wholly and solely, by abiding union with our Lord Jesus Christ by constant faith in Him; He Himself keeping us in this faith by the almighty power of the Spirit exerted continually on us and in us.

"To the law and to the testimony."

"To the law and to the testimony: if they speak not according to this word, it is because there is no light in them" (Isa. viii. 20).

"Ye shall not add unto the word which I command you, neither shall ye diminish aught from it" (Deut. iv. 2).

"Every word of God is pure . . . . Add thou not unto his words, lest he reprove thee, and thou be found a liar" (Prov. xxx. 5, 6).

"I testify unto every man that heareth the words of the prophecy of this book, If any man shall add unto these things, God shall add unto him the plagues that are written in this book: and if any man shall take away from the words of the book of this prophecy, God shall take away his part out of the book of life, and out of the holy city, and from the things which are written in this book" (Rev. xxii. 18, 19).

Not to "make a Man an Offender for a Word."

We are not to "make a man an offender for a word" (Isa. xxix. 21); and so I do not say that any one who tries to explain away a text here and a text there to make it suit a theological view which he has adopted, believing it to be of God—but into which, somehow or other, it seems impossible to make the text fit itself in its plain simple meaning—falls under the terrible condemnation of the above last-quoted passage; which, placed as it is at the extreme end of the Word of God, seems set as a safeguard to the whole of it.

But must not alter the Word of God.

But I do say that a system requiring *a multitude of texts* to be *positively altered*, by the taking away of something from them or the adding of something to them, would not, in the light of the above and other such passages (Deut. xii. 32; Ecc. iii. 14; Matt. xv. 3; &c.), appear to be one that God would wish us to adopt, or to continue in a moment longer even though bred and born in it.

And yet those systems which involve the necessity of sinning, or if not the necessity of sinning as an act, yet the necessity of the continued existence of sin in us, would really seem to be just of this character.

I speak here of that of which I have had abundant practical illustration: for again and again I have found dear Christian friends holding this doctrine, compelled to add something to or take something away from passage upon passage of God's Word, repeated to them, as their only way of bringing about any appearance of consistency between their creed and these passages.

I can only here notice some of these passages very shortly, as to do more would be to go over again too much of the ground already traversed above.

Explaining away " Healing."

" *Healeth all thy diseases* ; " here, as regards any present healing of the diseases of the soul, the dear brethren holding the necessity of the continuance of sin in us say in substance, "*healeth*, but only partially now, and not perfectly till death, or the coming again of our Lord ; " though the Word is not " *will heal* " but " *healeth.*"

"The Sun of righteousness" arising "with *healing in his wings:*" this they similarly make only a partial present healing of the soul; though of course gladly admitting that the healing was instantaneously perfect when exercised upon men's bodies.

And Redemption "*from all iniquity.*"

"Gave himself for us, that he might *redeem us from all iniquity, and purify* to himself a peculiar people, zealous of good works;" the "redemption" and "purification" to take place now, as they are preparatory to our being "zealous of *good works*" to be done now, and not at or after death or the coming of the Lord: on which they say in substance not full "*redemption*" yet; but only from the guilt and power, not from the existence of sin; nor perfect "*purification*" yet; but only so that the defilement shall be covered over in God's sight by the precious blood of Christ, and shall also not expose itself to the sight of men; but it must still exist in us.

So, in this view, the Word would seem to need altering to "redeem us *to a great extent* from iniquity, and purify *to a great extent;* with the prospect of perfect redemption and perfect purification at death or at his coming again."

Asserted Benefit of Remaining Sin.

And here they add that the continued existence of sin in us keeps us humble, and watchful, and dependent on God to prevent its breaking out again openly: so that He is glorified by its continuance in us. But happily they do not follow out this idea to what would appear its logical consequence, that as we are to be more to his glory in heaven than here, so we must have more there than here of indwelling sin.

Explaining away " Salvation."

Another text needing to be thus qualified by them is that gloriously simple one partly noticed above, "*Look unto me, and be ye saved,* all the ends of the earth: for I am God, and there is none else" (Isa. xlv. 22).

Here they have in substance to say, not wholly saved just now at the time of our *looking unto* Him, but only to a great extent; with the sure hope of being saved "to the uttermost" hereafter at death, or at the coming of the Lord. And so of that word by St. Peter, "receiving the end of your faith, even the *salvation of your souls*" (1 Peter i. 9): which to make this view consistent with it would seem to need altering to "*in great part* receiving the end of your faith, even the salvation of your souls, and being sure to receive all the rest hereafter."

And so also of all other unqualified promises or declarations of salvation; especially that very blessed one referred to just now, and more fully a little way back, "He is able also to *save them to the uttermost* that come unto God by Him" (Heb. vii. 25): which on this view would seem to need altering to "able also to save them now to a great extent that come unto God by him; and to the uttermost hereafter."

And " Plenteous Redemption."

" Let Israel trust in the Lord, for with the Lord there is mercy, and with him is *plenteous redemption,* and he shall redeem Israel from *all his iniquities*" (Ps. cxxx. 7, 8).

Here they have in substance to say, "Yes, but not *so plenteous* as to be quite *complete* just yet: from *all iniquities* indeed in the way of outward acts, but not from all workings of evil within."

And "Ransomed."

"The Lord hath redeemed Jacob, and *ransomed him from the hand of him that was stronger than he*" (Jer. xxxi. 11).

They are here compelled in substance to say, "Yes, but not so but that the stronger than he has still some part in him:" so that it is not, in that view, the perfect deliverance which we usually mean by "*ransoming.*"

Objection and Answer.

But it may be asked, "Are we not, however great the present salvation, yet constantly told to look for *full* redemption and *full* salvation only at the coming again of our Lord, as, for instance, in such passages as these:—" When these things begin to come to pass, then look up, and lift up your heads; for *your redemption draweth nigh*" (Luke xxi. 28); "Unto them that look for him shall he appear the second time without sin *unto salvation*" (Heb. ix. 28); "And it shall be said in that day, Lo, this is our God; we have waited for him, and *he will save us*: this is the Lord; we have waited for him, we will be glad and rejoice in his *salvation*" (Isa. xxv. 9).

Yes: but as we have seen in an earlier part of this book, only from evils outside of our own souls;

never from sin in us, of which alone it is a question here.

And " *The Strong Man Armed.*"

"When a strong man armed keepeth his palace his goods are in peace: but when a stronger than he shall come upon him, and overcome him, he taketh from him all his armour wherein he trusted, and divideth his spoils" (Luke xi. 21, 22).

On the theory of sin of necessity always remaining in us, the "armour" is not really "*all*" taken away from "the strong man;" nor he himself altogether turned out of his palace.

And " *A New Creature.*"

"If any man be in Christ, he is a *new creature: old things are passed away; behold all things are become new*" (2 Cor. v. 17).

Here they are obliged in substance to say, "As yet only to a very great extent a new creature; some of the old creation of necessity remaining until death or the coming of the Lord." So, in this view, not quite "*all*" old things are yet "passed away;" not quite "*all*" things have yet "become new."

"*Holiness and Righteousness before Him.*"

"Blessed be the Lord God of Israel; for he hath visited and redeemed his people, and hath raised up an horn of salvation for us in the house of his servant David; .... *that we being delivered out of the hand of our enemies, might serve him without fear, in holiness and righteousness before him, all the days of our life*" (Luke i. 68–75).

They have not, I think, anything whatever to

answer to this passage—expressing, as it surely does, perfect deliverance as unmistakably as words can express it—except that according to *their* view of "*Dispensational Truth*,"—which I endeavoured in the beginning of this book to answer from the Word of God—all such passages, even though occurring as in this case in "the Gospel of Jesus Christ" (Mark i. 1), belong only to the Jews in the next dispensation: a view which I do not think likely to be shared by any reader of this book.

"*The Serpent in the Wilderness.*"

In answer to the promise implied in the perfect cure of the Israelites from the bite of the fiery serpents on their looking at the serpent of brass, that our spiritual cure on our looking by faith on our Lord Jesus Christ lifted up for us on the cross, shall be equally perfect, I have heard nothing from the objectors to full present salvation, but "*Oh, you can never learn a doctrine from a type:*" which, even if it were accepted as a correct statement, would not weaken the *confirmation*, as in this case, by a type, of a doctrine shown to be directly stated elsewhere.

I am glad, however, to say that in the case of more than one or two earnest workers for God well known to me, who had not before seen present salvation from the existence as well as from the guilt and power of sin, their being led carefully to consider the immediately perfect cure of the Israelites has been the means, under the teaching of the Spirit, of their beginning to see this full present spiritual salvation. Indeed, I have known no part of God's Word seemingly more blessed of the Spirit in this respect of opening the eyes of his children to the extent of deliverance from sin given by Him to us in his gift of his Son, with his name of Jesus, because He should "save his people from their sins," than this little bit of his own teaching to the earnest Jewish ruler coming by night to inquire of Him.

The Twelve Spies.

"And the Lord spake unto Moses, saying, Send thou men, that they may search the land of Canaan, which I give unto the children of Israel: of every tribe of their fathers shall ye send a man, every one a ruler among them.

"And Moses by the commandment of the Lord sent them from the wilderness of Paran: all those men were heads of the children of Israel."

"So they went up, and searched the land from the wilderness of Zin unto Rehob."

"And they came unto the brook of Eshcol, and cut down from thence a branch with one cluster of grapes, and they bare it between two upon a staff; and they brought of the pomegranates, and of the figs."

"And they returned from searching of the land after forty days."

Their good and evil Report.

"And they went and came to Moses, and to Aaron, and to all the congregation of the children of Israel, unto the wilderness of Paran, to Kadesh; and brought back word unto them, and unto all the congregation, and showed them the fruit of the land.

"And they told him, and said, We came unto the land whither thou sentest us, and surely it floweth with milk and honey; and this is the fruit of it. Nevertheless the people be strong that dwell in the land, and the cities are walled, and very great: and moreover we saw the children of Anak there. The Amalekites dwell in the land of the south: and the Hittites, and the Jebusites, and the Amorites, dwell in the mountains: and the Canaanites dwell by the sea, and by the coast of Jordan.

"And Caleb stilled the people before Moses, and said, Let us go up at once, and possess it; for we are well able to overcome it."

Ten of them dishearten the People.

"But the men that went up with him said, We be not able to go up against the people; for they are stronger than we. And they brought up an evil report of the land which they had searched unto the children of Israel, saying, The land, through which we have gone to search it, is a land that eateth up the inhabitants thereof; and all the people that we saw in it are men of a great stature. And there we saw the giants, the sons of Anak, which come of the giants: and we were in our own sight as grasshoppers, and so we were in their sight.

"And all the congregation lifted up their voice, and cried; and the people wept that night.

Joshua and Caleb urge them to go up.

"And Joshua the son of Nun, and Caleb the son of Jephunneh, which were of them that searched the land, rent their clothes: and they spake unto all the company of the children of Israel, saying, The land, which we passed through to search it, is an exceeding good land. If the Lord delight in us, then he will bring us into this land, and give it us; a land which floweth with milk and honey. Only rebel not ye against the Lord, neither fear ye the people of the land; for they are bread for us: their defence is departed from them, and the Lord is with us: fear them not.

"But all the congregation bade stone them with stones."

God's Anger because they will not.

"And the Lord spake unto Moses and unto Aaron, saying, How long shall I bear with this evil congregation, which murmur against me?"

"Say unto them, As truly as I live, saith the Lord, as ye have spoken in mine ears, so will I do to you: your carcases shall fall in this wilderness; and all that were numbered of you, according to your whole number, from twenty years old and upward, which have murmured against me, doubtless ye shall not come into the land, concerning which I sware to make you dwell therein, save Caleb the son of Jephunneh, and Joshua the son of Nun.

"But your little ones, which ye said should be a prey, them will I bring in, and they shall know the land which ye have despised. But as for you, your carcases, they shall fall in the wilderness. And your children shall wander in the wilderness forty years, and bear your whoredoms, until your carcases be wasted in the wilderness."

"I the Lord have said, I will surely do it unto all this evil congregation, that are gathered together against me: in this wilderness they shall be consumed, and there they shall die.

THE TWELVE SPIES. 183

"And the men, which Moses sent to search the land, who returned, and made all the congregation to murmur against him, by bringing up a slander upon the land, even those men that did bring up the evil report upon the land, died by the plague before the Lord.

"But Joshua the son of Nun, and Caleb the son of Jephunneh, which were of the men that went to search the land, lived still" (Numb. xiii. and xiv.).

Much of this repeated now.

Is not very much of this reproduced among ourselves?

As all those twelve " rulers " and " heads of the children of Israel," believing and unbelieving alike, were agreed in the exceeding goodness of the land —all of them evidently, when showing the cluster of grapes borne between two on a staff, and the pomegranates and the figs, concurring in the report, " *Surely it floweth with milk and honey, and this is the fruit of it*"—so are not all our leaders and instructors in the things of God, when they speak to us of *our* good land, the salvation God has provided for us in our Lord Jesus Christ, entirely agreed as to its exceeding goodness? Do not they all, when telling us of it as it is in itself, and without reference to our power to possess it, vie with each other in declaring its perfection of blessedness?

The few Joshuas and Calebs.

And do not some few of them, looking away, like Joshua and Caleb, from the " giants " that stand in the way of our possession of it, and the " cities " " walled and very great," and the " Amalekites" and the "Hittites" and the "Jebusites," and the "Amorites" and the "Canaanites," to the almighty power of God who has told us to go up and possess it—say, "Let us go up at once and possess it, for we are well able to overcome it." "If the Lord delight in us, then he will bring us into this land, and give it us; a land which floweth with milk and honey. Only rebel not ye against the Lord, neither fear ye the people of the land; for they are bread for us: their defence is departed from them, and the Lord is with us: fear them not"?

The great majority of the other spies.

But do not a majority of them, on the contrary, greater, it is to be feared, than even that of ten to two in the case of those spies, looking at the strength of the cities to be taken, and the "great stature" of the inhabitants to be overcome and destroyed—our fallen nature, indwelling sin, bad habits, peculiar temperaments and besetments, unfavourable surroundings, and all the rest—and seeing us but "as grasshoppers in their sight," and leaving God's promises and his almighty power to fulfil them out of the account, say that all that glory of salvation is not for us in this life; that, however "exceeding great" the blessedness of the land, we cannot go up and possess it?

" The congregation."

And do not the bulk of the "congregation" now, following the example of that congregation of old and yielding themselves to the guidance of these disbelieving and disheartening instructors, not only refuse to go up themselves, but also reward the faithfulness of the believing few urging them to do so, much as those Israelites rewarded faithful Caleb and Joshua with their cry to "stone them with stones"?

And is there not great cause to fear that God may say of these present unbelievers, as He did to those others of old, "*As ye have spoken in mine ears, so will I do unto you;*" "*doubtless ye shall not come into the land*"?

The Children entering in.

But even if ever so large a number of the present generation should thus not be able to enter in because of unbelief (Heb. iii. 19), there are not wanting signs in the Church of so great a revival of the primitive faith of full salvation, that their children whom, as in the case of those Israelites, they condemned to be shut out along with themselves, shall nevertheless enter in. "*Your little ones, which ye said should be a prey, them will I bring in, and they shall know the land which ye have despised.*"

But if this happily should be so, yet as it was then so it may be now, that because of the unbelief of the parents the poor children may have a long time to wander in the wilderness before entering in.

"*Bade stone them with Stones.*"

In connection with the cry of "all the congregation" to "stone" Joshua and Caleb "with stones," and its parallel among ourselves now, I copy here a short piece out of Dr. Steele's "Milestone Papers," not, indeed, written by him with reference to this, but nevertheless bearing directly upon it.

Extract from "Milestone Papers."

"It is not by accident that in every age those who have fully consecrated themselves to Christ, and have been entirely sanctified by the Holy Spirit, and have proclaimed this as the privilege and duty of all Christians have been under a cloud of reproach. Christ has set reproach and persecution as two cherubim at the gate of the Eden of perfect love, to test the consecration, courage, and confidence of all who seek to enter. They who lack any one of these qualities must be excluded from this paradise.

"Dear seeker of soul-rest, are you willing to have your name cast out as evil, meekly to bear opprobrious nicknames, to be accounted as the filth and off-scouring of all things for your testimony to Christ as a perfect Saviour able to save unto the uttermost?

"But say you, Is this the indispensable condition? In this age of enlightenment and religious liberty, has not the offence of the cross ceased?

"Nay, verily, except to a world-conforming sort of Christians who keep up a state of peace with the world and a truce with the devil by declaring that they consciously sin every day, and that there is no efficacy in the blood of Christ to cleanse the heart of its depravity, and no power in the Holy Spirit to keep the trusting soul from sinning.

"Jesus wishes that all who propose to follow Him fully should count the cost and not shrink back in disappointment when they find that He has not where—in worldly honours—to lay his head. Hence total and irreversible self-abandonment is the indispensable condition of that oneness with Christ, that harmony with God, which in scriptural phrase is called perfect love."

David and Goliath.

"Now the Philistines gathered together their armies to battle. . . . And Saul and the men of Israel were gathered together, and pitched by the valley of Elah, and set the battle in array against the Philistines.

"And the Philistines stood on a mountain on the one side, and Israel stood on a mountain on the other side: and there was a valley between them."

Goliath's Challenge.

"And there went out a champion out of the camp of the Philistines named Goliath of Gath, whose height was six cubits and a span. And he had an helmet of brass upon his head, and he was armed with a coat of mail; and the weight of the coat was five thousand shekels of brass. And he had greaves of brass upon his legs, and a target of brass between his shoulders. And the staff of his spear was like a weaver's beam; and his spear's head weighed six hundred shekels of iron: and one bearing a shield went before him.

"And he stood and cried unto the armies of Israel, and said unto them, Why are ye come out to set your battle in array? am not I a Philistine, and ye servants to Saul? choose you a man for you and let him come down to me. If he be able to fight with me, and to kill me, then will we be your servants: but if I prevail against him, and kill him, then shall ye be our servants, and serve us. And the Philistine said, I defy the armies of Israel this day; give me a man, that we may fight together.

"When Saul and all Israel heard those words

of the Philistine, they were dismayed, and greatly afraid."

David's inquiry about it.

" And David spake to the men that stood by him, saying, What shall be done to the man that killeth this Philistine, and taketh away the reproach from Israel? for who is this uncircumcised Philistine, that he should defy the armies of the living God?"

"And Eliab his eldest brother heard when he spake unto the men; and Eliab's anger was kindled against David, and he said, Why camest thou down hither? and with whom hast thou left those few sheep in the wilderness? I know thy pride, and the naughtiness of thine heart; for thou art come down that thou mightest see the battle. And David said, What have I now done? Is there not a cause?"

How David felt about it.

"And David said to Saul, Let no man's heart fail because of him; thy servant will go and fight with this Philistine. And Saul said to David, Thou art not able to go against this Philistine to fight with him: for thou art but a youth, and he a man of war from his youth. And David said unto Saul, Thy servant kept his father's sheep, and there came a lion, and a bear, and took a lamb out of the flock: and I went out after him, and smote him, and delivered it out of his mouth." " Thy servant slew both the lion and the bear: and this uncircumcised Philistine shall be as one of them, seeing he hath defied the armies of the living God.

" David said moreover, The Lord that delivered

me out of the paw of the lion, and out of the paw of the bear, he will deliver me out of the hand of this Philistine.

"And Saul said unto David, Go, and the Lord be with thee.

"And Saul armed David with his armour, and he put an helmet of brass upon his head; also he armed him with a coat of mail. And David girded his sword upon his armour, and he assayed to go; for he had not proved it. And David said unto Saul, I cannot go with these; for I have not proved them. And David put them off him."

David's Weapons.

"And he took his staff in his hand, and chose him five smooth stones out of the brook, and put them in a shepherd's bag which he had, even in a scrip; and his sling was in his hand: and he drew near to the Philistine.

"And the Philistine came on and drew near unto David; and the man that bare the shield went before him. And when the Philistine looked about, and saw David, he disdained him: for he was but a youth, and ruddy, and of a fair countenance. And the Philistine said unto David, Am I a dog, that thou comest to me with staves? And the Philistine cursed David by his gods. And the Philistine said to David, Come to me, and I will give thy flesh unto the fowls of the air, and to the beasts of the field."

His Answer to Goliath.

"Then said David to the Philistine, Thou comest to me with a sword, and with a spear, and with a shield: but I come to thee in the name of the Lord of hosts, the God of the armies of Israel, whom thou hast defied. This day will the Lord deliver thee into mine hand; and I will smite thee, and take thine head from thee; and I will give the carcases of the host of the Philistines this day unto the fowls of the air, and to the wild beasts of the earth; that all the earth may know that there is a God in Israel. And all this assembly shall know that the Lord saveth not with sword and spear: for the battle is the Lord's, and he will give you into our hands."

His Victory over him.

"And it came to pass, when the Philistine arose, and came and drew nigh to meet David, that David hasted, and ran toward the army to meet the Philistine. And David put his hand in his bag, and took thence a stone and slang it, and smote the Philistine in his forehead, that the stone sunk into his forehead; and he fell upon his face to the earth. So David prevailed over the Philistine with a sling and with a stone, and smote the Philistine, and slew him; but there was no sword in the hand of David. Therefore David ran, and stood upon the Philistine, and took his sword, and drew it out of the sheath thereof, and slew him, and cut off his head therewith.

"And when the Philistines saw their champion dead, they fled. And the men of Israel and of Judah arose, and shouted, and pursued the Philistines, until thou come to the valley, and to the gates of Ekron. And the wounded of the Philistines fell down by the way to Shaaraim, even unto Gath, and unto Ekron. And the children of Israel returned from chasing after the Philistines, and they spoiled their tents. And David took the head of the Philistine, and brought it to Jerusalem; but he put his armour in his tent" (1 Samuel xvii.).

We may here see ourselves.

But why introduce here at such length an account which we have most of us known almost by heart from our childhood?

Because of its wonderful exactness as a photograph, though taken so long ago, of the state of things at this moment among ourselves.

For as the Israelites and Philistines were then gathered together to battle army against army, so now all the professed people of God on the one hand, and all the powers of evil in the world on the other, are gathered together to battle against each other.

And as there was one champion of the Philistines then, the strongest of them all, before whom Israel in general were cowed down in utter hopelessness of overcoming and destroying him, so there is one champion of the powers of evil now, the strongest of them all, before whom the great body of the Church are cowed down in utter hopelessness of overcoming and destroying it—namely *indwelling sin.*

God be praised for a few full believers.

But as there was one in the camp of Israel then, who believed there was a God in Israel, and looking only at his almighty power, dared to disregard all the great strength of the " uncircumcised Philistine" who was defying his armies; and in his name went against him and overcame and slew him; so, God be thanked, there are some now, however few in proportion to the whole number of God's people, who know that, whatever may be the power of indwelling sin in comparison with their power or that of their fellow-believers, it is yet as nothing to the power of the God and Father of our Lord Jesus Christ, and our God and Father by Him (John xx. 17); and who therefore dare to go against it, trusting in Him for its conquest and destruction; with the same result in their case as in that of David in his so going against Goliath.

Eliabs still to be met with.

And as David's elder brother, a professed experienced soldier, was very indignant that such a stripling should dare to meddle with a matter so much too high for him as the question how Goliath's challenge was to be dealt with, so there are not wanting now dear elders in the Church, who are extremely impatient with any poor foolish ignorant ones, as they think them, who dare to raise the question of dealing effectually with indwelling sin.

But David can still make answer, " What have I now done? *Is there not a cause?*" and go on in his God-appointed way to fight the giant in spite of any number of Eliabs trying to stop him.

The above put into verse.

" Who is this gigantic foe
    That proudly stalks along,
Overlooks the crowd below
    In brazen armour strong?

Loudly of his strength he boasts,
 On his sword and spear relies,
Meets the God of Israel's hosts,
 And all their force defies.

Tallest of the earth-born race,
 They tremble at his power,
Flee before the monster's face,
 And own him conqueror;
Who this mighty champion is
 Nature answers from within,
It is my own wickedness,
 My own besetting sin.

In the strength of Jesu's name
 I with the monster fight;
Feeble and unarmed I am,
 But Jesus is my might;
Mindful of his mercies past,
 Still I trust the same to prove;
Still my helpless soul I cast
 On his redeeming love.

With my sling and stone I go
 To fight the Philistine;
God hath said it shall be so,
 And I shall conquer sin.
On his promise I rely,
 Trust in an almighty Lord,
Sure to win the victory,
 For He hath spoke the word.

In the strength of God I rise,
 I run to meet the foe;
Faith the word of power applies,
 And lays the giant low:

Faith in Jesu's conquering name
    Slings the sin-destroying stone,
Points the Word's unerring aim,
    And brings the monster down.

Rise ye men of Israel, rise,
    Your routed foe pursue;
Shout his praises to the skies,
    Who conquers sin for you!
Jesus doth for you appear,
    He his conquering grace affords,
Saves you, not with sword and spear,
    The battle is the Lord's!

Every day the Lord of Hosts
    His mighty power displays,
Stills the loud Philistine's boast,
    The threatening Gittite slays.
Israel's God let all below
    Conqueror over sin proclaim:
O that all the earth might know
    The power of Jesu's name!"

CHARLES WESLEY.

"In Christ."

I have spoken much above on "*Christ in us;*" but have said little, comparatively, upon that other equally blessed part of the wonderful mystery of our redemption, "*We in Him.*"

If, as He calls us to do, we so believe and continue believing (Col. i. 23) in Him as to be in Him and abide in Him as branches in the vine (John xv. 5), and "members of his body" (Eph. v. 30) then:

We have been crucified with Him (Gal. ii. 20 revised version) and buried with Him (Rom. vi. 4), and are risen with Him (Col. ii. 12), and are seated together with Him in heavenly places (Eph. ii. 6), and are a new creature or creation in Him (2 Cor. v. 17), and are made the righteousness of God in Him (2 Cor. v. 21), and are blessed with all spiritual blessings in heavenly places in Him (Eph. i. 13), and in Him are sealed with the Holy Spirit of promise (Eph. i. 13), and builded together for an habitation of God (Eph. ii. 22), and are God's workmanship, created in Him unto good works (Eph. ii. 10), and are complete in Him (Col. ii. 10), and sin not (1 John iii. 16), and bring forth much fruit to the glory of the Father (John xv. 5, 8), and in Him have boldness and access with confidence to the Father (Eph. iii. 12), and ask what we will and it shall be done to us (John xv. 7): and it is the will of God in Him concerning us that we rejoice ever more, and pray without ceasing, and in everything give thanks (1 Thess. v. 16-18).

I suppose we shall, every one of us, be perfectly agreed that it is the unspeakable privilege and also the most solemn duty of every believer to have every word that is here written fulfilled in him.

But where in such a life is any room for sin, outward or inward?

Noah in the Ark.

If we are indeed fully in Christ, we are saved in and by Him as Noah was in and by the ark.

The flood was not only God's judgment against

the sin of the world as it then was, but also, doubtless, a type of his judgment upon all sin.

And as Noah and those with him in the ark were lifted up in it, not only above the waters of judgment, but also out of and above the world whose wickedness had brought them upon it; so those who are in Christ are lifted up, if they have eyes to see it and faith to lay hold of Him for it, above not only all judgment against sin, but also all the sin itself that calls the judgment down.

And as much as the waters, or the world beneath them, could get at Noah and those with him shut in safely by God Himself in the ark; so much and no more, it seems to me, can either judgment or sin get at us if by faith we have indeed entered into Christ, and are by faith abiding in Him, and are enlightened by the Spirit to see what He is to us, and strengthened by the Spirit to lay hold of Him by faith, for all that we thus see Him to be to us, in this respect of safety from both judgment and sin.

And if it be indeed so, then we have in this type of the ark, not only up above the waters, but also up above the wicked world drowned by them, a confirmation of the many direct proofs from God's Word that He offers us in Christ entire deliverance from sin itself as well as from its punishment.

Our Hymns.

There exist together in many of us, as it seems to me, two strangely contradictory things, at which, though I have glanced at them incidentally in one or two previous sections, I wish to look more fully here.

I mean an entire theoretical belief in the unbounded goodness of God, and in his almighty power to bless, and an entire practical unbelief that He will exert this power in our own particular case.

"*Make me, keep me pure within.*"

That this is so appears, perhaps as strongly as in any other way, in the words of some of the hymns which we sing, contrasted with the real thoughts and feelings of many of us in singing them.

We all, for instance, heartily sing:—

" Plenteous grace with Thee is found,
　Grace to pardon all my sin;
　Let the healing streams abound,
　Make me, keep me pure within."

And if asked, Is that a Scriptural prayer? we should all at once say, Yes, of course it is. But if further asked, does He, as a matter of fact, "*make*" you and "*keep*" you "*pure within,*" would not the most of us answer, No; I am sorry to say He does not?

And if further asked, Do you in singing the hymn really *expect* Him to do it, must not the answer in most cases be, No; I do not?

And if the yet further question were put, If God should prolong your life, and lead you to sing that hymn yet five hundred times more, do you think that at the end of your five hundredth additional time of singing it, He will really have "made" you, and will then really be "keeping" you "pure within"? must not the answer still be No?

And all this in the face of that command of our Lord so constantly here being brought forward,

"What things soever ye desire when ye pray, *believe that ye receive them*, and ye shall have them!"

What greater contradiction can there be anywhere than this between the theoretical faith that makes us gladly sing such a hymn as certainly expressing the revealed will of God towards us, and the absolute practical unbelief in his doing for us what in singing it we profess to ask Him to do?

"A Heart to praise my God."

To take just one more case—for these two will answer the purpose for which I am bringing them in here as well as a hundred such hymns which could easily be collected together, all showing the same thing—who does not agree in heartily singing as entirely and most blessedly scriptural, Charles Wesley's sweet hymn:—

"Oh for a heart to praise my God,
   A heart from sin set free,
A heart that always feels the blood
   So freely spilt for me!

A heart resigned, submissive, meek,
   My great Redeemer's throne,
Where only Christ is heard to speak,
   Where Jesus reigns alone.

A humble, lowly, contrite heart,
   Believing, true, and clean,
Which neither life nor death can part
   From Him that dwells within.

A heart in every thought renewed,
   And full of love divine,
Perfect and right, and pure and good,
   A copy, Lord, of Thine!

Thy tender heart is still the same,
    And melts at human woe;
Jesus, for Thee distress'd I am,
    And want Thy love to know.

My heart, Thou know'st, can never rest
    Till Thou create my peace,
Till of my Eden re-possest,
    From every sin I cease.

Fruit of thy gracious lips on me
    Bestow, that peace unknown,
The hidden manna, and the tree
    Of life, and the white stone.

Thy nature, gracious Lord, impart;
    Come quickly from above;
Write thy new name upon my heart,
    Thy new, best name of love."

And yet in the case of this hymn, as in that of the other, if the question were asked of those who have sung it with delight, Has God, as a matter of fact, granted the prayer you have made to Him in the hymn—for surely it is all prayer—and given you just the heart described in it? would not the answer, in an immense majority of cases, be, No?

And if, as before, the further question were asked, Whether we should expect Him, after ever so great a number of times of singing it, really to give us such a heart, would not the answer still in general be, No?

And this still in the face of that command of our Lord, "What things soever ye desire when ye pray, believe that ye receive them and ye shall have them."

God forgive our Unbelief.

I speak here that which I painfully know: for I am sorry to say that numbers and numbers of times I have joined in singing both those hymns and scores of similar ones in simple and absolute unbelief; not having the slightest thought that God gave me what I seemed to be asking of Him in them; and yet wondering why no good came to me by singing them, no real advance in the Christian life. But how *could* any good come to me by singing them, seeing that every time I *so* sang any of them I was just the more strengthening the hold over me of the awfully evil habit of unbelief?

The prayers that I made in such hymns—and I fear the same is the case with the prayers which tens of thousands of my dear brothers and sisters in Christ make also in singing them—were in one respect sadly like that of the Pharisee who "stood and prayed thus *with himself*" (Luke xviii. 11). For as I had no belief that God so heard as to answer the prayer, it really did begin and end *with myself*. *I had my reward* (Matt. vi. 5), in the benefit, whatever it might be, of the earnest desire and happy feelings I had in singing the hymns: but with these, and that more than counterbalancing evil of hardening myself in unbelief, the whole matter began and ended.

Unbelief meetings.

And I have been in many prayer meetings in which I fear most of our direct prayers, besides those which we made in such hymns, have been sadly of the same sort; very earnest, it may be, but with the expectation of praying for the same things again and again in the future as we had so often done in the past, without any real thought of God giving to us the things which we were with our lips so earnestly asking or seeming to ask Him to give to us.

And yet we called them "good meetings" because of their lively earnestness; whereas, looked at in the light of that command of our Lord, "What things soever ye desire when ye pray, *believe that ye receive them, and ye shall have them*," they really would not seem to deserve the name of "*Prayer meetings*" at all, either good or bad, but rather to be labelled " *Unbelief Meetings.*"

What shall we do with the Hymns?

But now I would ask, What is our right course with reference to such hymns?

Shall we sing them as I have said that I have done, and that I believe so many others have also—without believing that God gives us what we ask in them? No: that will not do, for it would be directly contrary to that command of our Lord, and to all the many other injunctions to us in God's Word to believe in Him for all we ask in Him according to his will.

Shall we, then, not use such hymns at all, because of their asking so much, and it being so difficult to believe for it all? No: that will not do any better: for it would be only distrust in God in another shape, and breaking another set of his commandments, namely, those which tell us to ask great things of Him—"Open thy mouth wide, and I will fill it" (Ps. lxxxi. 10). "Call upon me, and I will answer thee, and show thee great and mighty things which thou knowest not" (Jer. xxxiii. 3). "I am the Lord, the God of all flesh; is there anything too hard for me?" (Jer. xxxii. 27), &c.

The only right Course.

Then there remains only one other course, and that manifestly the right one, to use the hymns all the more on account of their asking such great things, as that makes them just so much the more blessedly scriptural; and, in doing so, fully to obey our Lord's command, and believe undoubtingly that *what things soever* we desire in the prayers we make in them we receive; and so enter into the power and blessedness of these things. The Lord strengthen us all by his Spirit to take this only right course, and to be, by means of it, more and more to his glory in our own advance in the heavenly life, and in helping our fellow-believers to advance in it, and in being faithful witnesses of its blessedness to our fellow-sinners, not yet believers, that they also may accept Him as their way (John xiv. 6) into it!

And it is manifest that such a course will cause us to lead a life free from sin outward or inward. For this is contained in the very words, "*Make me, keep me, pure within.*" "*A heart from sin set free;*" "*My Great Redeemer's throne, where only Christ is heard to speak, where Jesus reigns alone;*" "*A heart in every thought renewed, and full of love divine, perfect and right, and pure and good, a copy Lord of Thine.*"

Let none of us continue in unbelief.

While it is so very strange and so very sad that so many of us should in the past so often have used such words, not doubting them to be scriptural, and yet without the least thought that our heavenly Father, through our dear Lord, and by the power of his Spirit, would really give us what we seemed to be asking in them, would it not be yet much more strange and much more sad, if any of us, if He now opens our eyes to see this our past unbelief and something of the blessedness of which it has deprived us, should still remain in any measure its slaves, instead of at once accepting our dear Lord as our blessed deliverance from it, as from all other works of the devil upon us or in us?

"Who is this that cometh—?"

"*Christ sheweth who he is, what his victory over his enemies, and what his mercy toward his church.*"

"Who is this that cometh from Edom, with dyed garments from Bozrah? this that is glorious in his apparel, travelling in the greatness of his strength?"

"I that speak in righteousness, mighty to save."

"Wherefore art thou red in thy apparel, and thy garments like him that treadeth in the winefat?"

"I have trodden the winepress alone; and of the people there was none with me: for I will tread them in mine anger, and trample them in my fury; and their blood shall be sprinkled upon my garments, and I will stain all my raiment. For the day of vengeance is in mine hand, and the year of my redeemed is come. And I looked, and there was none to help; and I wondered that there was none to uphold: therefore mine own arm brought salvation unto me, and my fury, it upheld me. And I will tread down the people in mine anger, and make them drunk in my fury, and I will bring down their strength to the earth.

Song of rejoicing in the Lord.

"I will mention the lovingkindnesses of the Lord, and the praises of the Lord, according to all that the Lord hath bestowed on us, and the great goodness toward the house of Israel, which he hath bestowed on them according to his mercies, and according to the multitude of his lovingkindnesses" (Isa. lxiii. 1–7).

Powerlessness of evil to resist Christ.

We have considered a little, in a previous section, "For this purpose the Son of God was manifested, that he might destroy the works of the devil" (1 John iii. 8).

In the present passage we have the power of ripe grapes to resist the man treading them in the winepress put before us as the measure of the power of evil to prevent Christ carrying out this his purpose of destroying it.

If then we rejoicingly accept Him for this purpose, throwing open every corner of our life and heart to Him that He may indeed destroy all the work of the devil that He with his infinite ability to search it out (John ii. 25; Ps. cxxxix.; Heb. iv. 13) can discover anywhere in them, does it not follow that after He has done this—has thus thoroughly purged his floor (Matt. iii. 12)—no sin of any sort can be left in either our life or our heart?

He wants to destroy it in us.

And is He not ready and delighted (Jer. ix. 24) to do this at once (2 Cor. vi. 2) in every one of us—if we will but by thus entirely yielding ourselves up to Him make the way clear for Him to do it?

And, having so destroyed all evil in us, the way is then clear for Him to lead us on into all that further fulness of spiritual blessing which there is in Him for us (Eph. i. 3); and so to make the glorious song of rejoicing with which the prophecy concludes just the expression of the constant state of our hearts:—

"*I will mention the lovingkindnesses of the Lord, and the praises of the Lord, according to all that the Lord hath bestowed on us, and the great goodness toward the house of Israel, which he hath bestowed on them according to his mercies, and according to the multitude of his lovingkindnesses.*"

"A peaceable habitation."

"Upon the land of my people shall come up thorns and briers; yea, upon all the houses of joy in the joyous city: because the palaces shall be forsaken; the multitude of the city shall be left; the forts and towers shall be for dens for ever, a joy of wild asses, a pasture of flocks; until the spirit be poured upon us from on high, and the wilderness be a fruitful field, and the fruitful field be counted for a forest.

"Then judgment shall dwell in the wilderness, and righteousness remain in the fruitful field. And the work of righteousness shall be peace; and the effect of righteousness quietness and assurance for ever.

"And my people shall dwell in a peaceable habitation, and in sure dwellings, and in quiet resting places; when it shall hail, coming down on the forest; and the city shall be low in a low place. Blessed are ye that sow beside all waters, that send forth thither the feet of the ox and the ass" (Isa. xxxii. 13–20).

The desolation and its remedy.

The state of desolation described in the beginning of this prophecy, "thorns and briers" coming up "upon the land," "yea, upon all the houses of joy in the joyous city;" "the palaces" "forsaken;" "the forts and towers" turned into "dens for ever, a joy of wild asses, a pasture of flocks," was to last "*until the Spirit*" was "*poured upon*" God's people "*from on high:*" and then "the wilderness" was "to be a fruitful field, and the fruitful field be counted for a forest:" and all the further fulness of blessing which the prophecy goes on to describe, was to be fulfilled in their experience in the state in which they would be under the power of that blessed Spirit.

And the Spirit was abundantly "*poured upon us from on high*" on the day of Pentecost.

For St. Peter said, of the coming down of the Holy Ghost on that day, "This is that which was spoken by the prophet Joel; And it shall come to pass in the last days, saith God, *I will pour out of my Spirit upon all flesh*" (Acts ii. 16, 17).

And St. Paul wrote to Titus:—

"After that the kindness and love of God our Saviour toward man appeared, not by works of righteousness which we have done, but according to his mercy he saved us, by the washing of regeneration, and renewing of *the Holy Ghost; which he shed on us abundantly* through Jesus Christ our Saviour; that being justified by his grace, we should be made heirs according to the hope of eternal life" (Titus iii. 4-7).

How the remedy is applied in us.

But we individually enter into the benefit of his being thus "poured upon us from on high" when we believe in our Lord Jesus Christ, not merely for the pardon of our sins, but also for this gift of the Holy Ghost through Him to us as the purchase of his sufferings for us, according to that word already quoted above:

"Christ hath redeemed us from the curse of the law, being made a curse for us: for it is written, Cursed is every one that hangeth on a tree: that the blessing of Abraham might come upon the Gentiles through Jesus Christ, *that we might receive the promise of the Spirit through faith*" (Gal. iii. 13, 14).

And then the word is fulfilled in our hearts and lives of their being turned from a "wilderness" into a "fruitful field" and into "a forest," in which "judgment shall dwell" and "righteousness shall remain," "and the work of righteousness shall be peace, and the effect of righteousness quietness and assurance for ever." And we "dwell" as his "people," "in a peaceable habitation, and in sure dwellings, and in quiet resting-places."

Is there any place for sin here?

And is not all this blessedness of "*righteousness*" and "*peace*" and "*quietness and assurance for ever"* "in a *peaceable habitation,* and in *sure dwellings,* and in *quiet resting-places,*" altogether inconsistent with the idea of the disquieting, disturbing, peace-destroying thing sin—the "enemy of all righteousness"—having any place there; any place in our life or our heart, when by faith in our dear Lord for it we have been brought into that blessed state? And is He not—to ask once more a question already asked again and again above—ready to bring every one of us into it if we will only believe in Him for it, and give ourselves up to Him to enable Him to bring us into it?

"One of these least Commandments."

"Think not that I am come to destroy the law, or the prophets: I am not come to destroy, but to fulfil. For verily I say unto you, Till heaven and earth pass, one jot or one tittle shall in no wise pass from the law, till all be fulfilled.

"Whosoever therefore shall break one of these least commandments, and shall teach men so, he shall be called the least in the kingdom of heaven: but whosoever shall do and teach them, the same shall be called great in the kingdom of heaven.

"For I say unto you, That except your righteousness shall exceed the righteousness of the scribes and Pharisees, ye shall in no case enter into the kingdom of heaven" (Matt. v. 17–20).

"*Except your righteousness exceed* ——"

Dean Alford, in commenting on this passage in his "Greek Testament," says that the "*righteous-*

ness" here named by our Lord is "*purity of heart and life*, as set forth by example in the " *doers*, " and by precept in the " *teachers* just spoken of by Him. And he adds, "The whole of the rest of our Lord's sermon is a comment on and illustration of the assertion in this verse."

Doing the Father's will and our Lord's sayings.

The correctness of the above view of our Lord's sermon is especially shown in this concluding part of it:—

"Not every one that saith unto me, Lord, Lord, shall enter into the kingdom of heaven; but he that *doeth the will of my Father which is in heaven.* Many will say to me in that day, Lord, Lord, have we not prophesied in thy name? and in thy name have cast out devils? and in thy name done many wonderful works? And then will I profess unto them, I never knew you: depart from me, ye that *work iniquity.*

"Therefore, whosoever heareth these sayings of mine, *and doeth them,* I will liken him unto a wise man, which built his house upon a rock: and the rain descended, and the floods came, and the winds blew, and beat upon that house; and it fell not: for it was founded upon a rock.

"And every one that heareth these sayings of mine, *and doeth them not,* shall be likened unto a foolish man, which built his house upon the sand: and the rain descended, and the floods came, and the winds blew, and beat upon that house; and it fell: and great was the fall of it " (Matt. vii. 21–27).

And further on in his ministry when, " a certain woman of the company lifted up her voice, and said unto him, Blessed is the womb that bare thee, and the paps which thou hast sucked;" "he said, Yea, rather, blessed are they that hear the word of God, *and keep it* " (Luke xi. 27, 28).

And on the night before his crucifixion He said to the disciples:—

" He that hath my commandments, *and keepeth them*, he it is that loveth me: and he that loveth me shall be loved by my Father, and I will love him, and will manifest myself to him " (John xiv. 21).

And again :—

" *If ye keep my commandments*, ye shall abide in my love; even as I have kept my Father's commandments, and abide in his love " (John xv. 10).

Obedience of St. Paul to that Word of our Lord.

How perfectly the life and ministry of St. Paul accorded with these sayings of our Lord respecting the *doing* and the *teaching* of the commandments, we have seen in many passages above; especially in that one :—

" The law of the Spirit of life in Christ Jesus hath made me free from the law of sin and death. For what the law could not do, in that it was weak through the flesh, God sending his own Son in the likeness of sinful flesh, and for sin, condemned sin in the flesh: *that the righteousness of the law might be fulfilled* in us, who walk not after the flesh, but after the Spirit " (Rom. viii. 2-4).

" Owe no man anything," he said again, " but to love one another: for he that loveth another *hath fulfilled the law*. For this, Thou shalt not commit adultery, Thou shalt not kill, Thou shalt not steal, Thou shalt not bear false witness, Thou shalt not covet; and if there be any other commandment, it is briefly comprehended in this saying, namely, Thou shalt love thy neighbour as thyself. Love worketh no ill to his neighbour: therefore love is *the fulfilling of the law*" (Rom. xiii. 8–10).

And the epistle to the Hebrews dwells much, as we saw above, upon "the New Covenant," "*I will put my laws in their mind, and write them in their hearts*" (viii. 10; x. 16); the fulfilment of which in us gives both the inclination and the power both to "*do*" and to "*teach*" the "*commandments.*"

And of St. James.

And St. James says: "*Whoso looketh into the perfect law of liberty, and continueth therein, he being not a forgetful hearer, but a doer of the work, this man shall be blessed in his deed*" (i. 25).

And again he says:—

"*If ye fulfil the royal law according to the scripture, Thou shalt love thy neighbour as thyself, ye do well*" (ii. 8).

And of St. Peter.

And we have had to look again and again above at St. Peter's words, that there "are given unto us exceeding great and precious promises: that by these" we "might be partakers of the divine nature, having escaped the corruption that is in the world through lust" (2 Pet. i. 4). And that "*divine nature*" will, we may be sure, never "*break one of these least commandments,*" nor "*teach men so;*" but will always perfectly "*do*" and earnestly "*teach them.*"

And of St. John.

We have also seen above, how full St. John is of the keeping of the commandments and teaching men so. I copy out again here just three of the many passages showing this quoted above:—

"Hereby we do know that we know him, *if we keep his commandments*. He that saith, I know him, and *keepeth not his commandments*, is a liar, and the truth is not in him" (1 John ii. 3, 4).

'Whatsoever we ask, we receive of him, because we *keep his commandments*, and do those things that are pleasing in his sight" (iii. 22).

"By this we know that we love the children of God, when we love God, *and keep his commandments*. For this is the love of God, *that we keep his commandments*" (v. 2, 3).

And of all the inspired writers.

And so, as all the rest of our Lord's sermon on the mount would, as above said by Dean Alford, seem to have for its object the confirmation of that special part of it which we are here considering, enjoining both the doing and teaching of the commandments, so also would a great part of all the rest of the New Testament.

And the same may be said also of the Old Testament; for even *there* God's object in his dealings with his people is declared to be "*That they might observe his statutes, and keep his laws*" (Ps. cv. 45); and "*that they should make them known to their children*: that the generation to come might know them, even the children which should be born; who should arise and *declare them to their children*: that they might set their hope in God, and not forget the works of God, but *keep his commandments*" (Ps. lxxviii. 5-7).

And whatever failure there may have been *then*, as regards the accomplishment of these purposes of God, because " the law was weak through the flesh," He has provided that there need be none *now* by setting up that blessed dispensation of the Spirit on the day of Pentecost; that we, in the words above quoted, may " walk not after the flesh but after the Spirit," and so have " the righteousness of the law " " fulfilled in us," or, in other words, perfectly keep the commandments.

Disobedience to it.

And all this to the utter and absolute contradiction of that teaching which has prevailed among many in modern times, that not even the almighty power of God exerted in us to the utmost to which it ever has been exerted in any since the fall of Adam, can make the fulfilment of the law in us and by us a possibility; but that every man must, as a necessity of our fallen state, whatever God may have done already for him, and may now do in him, break his holy law in thought, word, and deed every day.

How the great number of dear children of God who hold this last-named creed can reconcile their *teaching* it, and their *admitted conformity of practice to it*, with that word of our Lord, " Whosoever therefore shall *break one of these least commandments, and shall teach men so*, he shall be called the least in the kingdom of heaven," is—I say it with all respect and love to every one of them—a mystery altogether beyond my comprehension

Keeping of God's Law.

But however that may be, I cannot but claim the passage as a proof that God desires of us, and expects to see in us, perfect conformity to all his holy law: and therefore as also a proof that He has provided for us in Christ the means of our being perfectly conformed to it; for we are all of us certainly agreed that He is the extreme opposite of the "hard" and "austere" one which the "wicked and slothful servant" declared "his lord" to be, "taking up that" he "laid not down," "reaping that" he did "not sow," "and gathering where" he had "not strawed" (Matt. xxv. 24, 26; Luke xix. 21, 22).

By abiding in Christ and He in us.

But, here again, I must repeat that it is only by our being "*in Christ*" and *He in us*, that this conformity of our hearts and lives to the law is possible. Without this, that daily breaking of it in thought, word, and deed is a certainly true account of the life of every one of us. But we abiding in Him and He in us, according to his commandment to us (John xv. 4), the law is as sure of being always fulfilled in us and by us, as it is in the other case of always being broken.

In the one case, it is "the pleasure of the Lord" prospering "in *his* hand" (Isa. liii. 10): in the other, its failing to "prosper" in *ours*.

"The end of the law."

But is not Christ "*the end of the law*"?

Yes, blessed be God! "Christ *is* the end of the law *for righteousness to every one that believeth*" (Rom. x. 4).

He is its "*end*," or full accomplishment "for righteousness" to us—if we believe in Him for it—as regards our deliverance from the *guilt* of sin; and its "*end*" or full accomplishment "for righteousness to us"—if we believe in Him for it—as regards our being made *personally* in and by Him perfectly righteous; so as to be "made the righteousness of God in him" (2 Cor. v. 21), in the sense—so much fuller and higher than that of mere acquittal from guilt—of entire deliverance out of and separation from all sin, because of our being so "joined" to Him: ("He that is joined unto the Lord is *one spirit*" (1 Cor. vi. 17): that He and we "are no more twain, but one" (Matt. xix. 6; Eph. v. 29, 30).

Those who have thus fully accepted Him as "the end of the law for righteousness" to them in this double sense are able to say, as the true expression of their own present personal experience, those words which we have considered above: "To me to live is Christ" (Phil. i. 21); and "I am crucified with Christ: nevertheless I live; yet not I, but Christ liveth in me: and the life which I now live in the flesh I live by the faith of the Son of God, who loved me, and gave himself for me" (Gal. ii. 20).

Believers only in part.

But many accept Him as "the end of the law for righteousness" to them only in the one sense of delivering them from the guilt of their sins, and not in the other, of perfectly fulfilling the law in them.

And so "the life which" they "now live in the flesh," is just the opposite, in many respects, of being " by the faith of the Son of God." For it is their own natural life, which is the very reverse of the " righteousness of God." And so to this extent there is *unrighteousness* instead of righteousness in them: and, therefore, just so far Christ is *not* " the end " or full accomplishment "of the law for righteousness" to them; seeing that just so far " the righteousness of the law " fails to " be fulfilled *in* " (Rom. viii. 4) them through their failure to believe in Him for its being so; though fully believing in Him as having fulfilled it *for* them.

That word, then, of St. Paul, that " Christ is the end of the law for righteousness to every one that believeth," so far from disproving that God looks for the fulfilment of the law in us, is just an instance of the true scriptural way of *teaching* the "commandments;" as it shows the scriptural, and indeed, only possible, way of our *doing* them; namely, by Christ, dwelling in our hearts by faith (Eph. iii. 17), doing them in us.

And as *all that He does, He does perfectly*, we in this way, by Him in us, if we believe and continue always believing in Him for it, do perfectly keep them, and so live lives "*free from sin*" (Rom. vi. 18).

Not unto us, O Lord.

And yet because it is always *only by Christ in us*, it is always, " Not unto us, O Lord, not unto us, but unto thy name give glory, for thy mercy, and for thy truth's sake " (Ps. cxv. 1); " *mercy* " in giving us such a Saviour, and such a salvation in

Him, and "*truth*" to fulfil perfectly to us, and in us, all that in his mercy He has provided for us and spoken to us.

"Turned aside unto vain jangling."

But does not St. Paul speak of some " desiring to be *teachers of the law*" as having " *turned aside unto vain jangling,*" "*understanding neither what they say, nor whereof they affirm*" (1 Tim. i. 6, 7)? Yes; here are these words of his with some of their context:—

" Now the end of the commandment is charity out of a pure heart, and of a good conscience, and of faith unfeigned; from which some having swerved have turned aside unto vain jangling; desiring to be teachers of the law; understanding neither what they say, nor whereof they affirm. But we know that the law is good, if a man use it lawfully; knowing this, that the law is not made for a righteous man, but for the lawless and disobedient, for the ungodly and for sinners, for unholy and profane, &c." (1 Tim. i. 5–9).

As we saw in the passage in the preceding section that " Christ is the end " or full accomplishment " of the law for righteousness," because it is fulfilled in and by Him both *for* us and *in* us, if we are in Him and He in us; so here we have " charity out of a pure heart, and of a good conscience, and of faith unfeigned " as " the *end of the commandment,*" in the sense of being *the effect it is intended to produce.*

Instead then of there being anything in this passage against the *teaching* as well as the *doing* the commandments, it just shows, like that one above, declaring Christ to be the end of the law for righteousness, how our doing of them is to be brought about; namely, by our first having through Him "a pure heart," and "a good conscience," and "faith unfeigned;" as it is out of these that the "*charity*" which is "*the end of the commandment*"—or in those other words of St. Paul quoted a little way back, the "*love*" which is "*the fulfilling of the law*" (Rom. xiii. 10)—proceeds.

"*A pure heart, and a good conscience.*"

"*A pure heart:*" then this supposes our being cleansed from all heart sin. For a heart in which there is any sin left is not "a *pure* heart."

And next comes "*a good conscience*," or, as St. Paul expresses it elsewhere, "always a conscience void of offence toward God, and toward men" (Acts xxiv. 16); made so by being purged "from dead works" by "the blood of Christ" "to serve the living God" (Heb. ix. 14): not purged and then defiled again, and then purged again, and so on continually, but always "kept" (1 Pet. i. 5) by "the precious blood" (1 Pet. i. 19) in the perfectly purged or cleansed (1 John i. 7) state.

What was the "vain jangling"?

And the "*vain jangling*," instead of being any teaching of the law in the sense which we are considering—namely, in its purity, and spirituality, and perfection, so that no fulfilment of it in us is possible otherwise than by our being in Christ and Christ in us—must have been some gross corruption of it.

For it was to suit the state of those would-be "teachers of the law," *after they had "swerved" from the "commandment,"* with its "end," " charity out of a pure heart, and of a good conscience, and of faith unfeigned;" just as we find now that those who will not have the "holy, and just, and good" "commandment" (Rom. vii. 12), as their standard of life, believing in our dear Lord as God's power (1 Cor. i. 24) to them to walk according to it, make to themselves standards in place of it to suit their own state: the most common one being to "*live as near the mark as we can,*" in disregard of the fact that *we* can do nothing except always and certainly miss the mark, and that it is only Christ in us who can live anywhere near it, and that *He* is just as able to live *up to* it as *near* it, and indeed *cannot do anything except always live perfectly up to it;* so that if it is really not we that live, but He that lives in us, and we by continual faith in Him make this continually to be so, we shall then be continually living not "*as near as we can,*" but "*perfectly up to the mark;*" shall always, that is, be having the law perfectly fulfilled in us by Him, and so always —to come to the same conclusion again—be living free from sin.

Guarding against being misunderstood.

I would not, however, be for a moment misunderstood to confound here those dear ones living "as near the mark as they can" with the *vain janglers.* For I know that very many of them are living lives of most devoted service to God, and crying to Him with all their hearts to make them all that He would have them to be; though—with the inconsistency of which we have almost all of us, as noticed in the section headed "Our Hymns," been so guilty—not believing, though knowing that what they ask is "according to His will," that they "have the petitions" that they "desired of him" (1 John v. 14, 15).

Dean Alford upon the "vain jangling."

Dean Alford says of the *vain janglers*:—
"We may see clearly in the data furnished in these pastoral epistles, that the Apostle had in them to deal with men who corrupted the material enactments of the moral law, and founded on Judaism, not assertions of its obligation, but idle fables and allegories, letting in latitude of morals and unholiness of life. It is against this *abuse of the law* that his arguments are directed. No formal question arises of the *obligation* of the law; these men struck by their interpretation at the root of all divine law itself: and therefore at that root itself does he meet and grapple with them."

This confirms the view taken above, that *their* teaching of the law had nothing in common with that which we have been here contemplating in connection with that Word of our Lord:—

"*Whosoever, therefore, shall break one of these least commandments, and shall teach men so, he shall be called the least in the kingdom of heaven; but whosoever shall do and teach them, the same shall be called great in the kingdom of heaven*" (Matt. v. 19).

"Possible and Impossible."

I copy out, in connection with the subject of the last three sections, a paper with the above title of " Possible and Impossible," by Dr. Asa Mahan, in the number for March 1880, of " The Divine Life," a very valuable periodical for the advocacy of full Scriptural holiness, of which he is the chief editor.

Toplady on Perfection.

"'Such,' says Mr. Toplady, 'being the unrelaxing perfection which the law inflexibly requires, it necessarily follows that the supposition of possible perfection on earth is *the most fantastic dream and the most gigantic delusion which can whirl the brain of a human being.*'

Dr. Mahan's answer.

"No utterance of any 'human being' is, or could be more true, than is the above, from the stand-point from which Mr. Toplady contemplated the subject.

"Equally true was the report of the ten spies from the point of view from which they judged of what was possible to the undisciplined armies of Israel. Leaving, as they did, God out of the account, 'no fantastic dream' could be more preposterous than the idea that such a feeble host could subdue the embattled kingdoms before them.

"Of this fact Joshua and Caleb were just as fully aware as were their associates. The former in their reckoning, however, took into account a great factor which the latter wholly overlooked—the presence and power of God in their midst.

Toplady's stand-point.

" When we take into the account merely 'the unrelaxing perfection which the law inflexibly requires,' with the new commandment supperadded, on the one hand, and a human being as he is in himself on the other—the stand-point from which Mr. Toplady made his reckoning—no 'fantastic dream' more preposterous ever whirled in a human brain than is ' the supposition of possible perfection on earth.'

" Wise men and prudent sometimes forget that 'the things which are impossible with men are possible with God'—that 'with God all things are possible,' and also, that 'all things are possible to him that believeth.'

An earthly case in illustration.

" An ancient commander having at the close of a day marshalled his forces for a great battle on the morrow, desired to know the spirit of his soldiery.

" After—under orders—they had retired for the night, he walked about among the tents, and listened to the conversation. As he approached one tent, he heard a very earnest conversation among the men within. From the vast superiority of the enemy, they predicted the certain defeat of their own army.

" Stepping suddenly into their presence, the commander confronted them with the question, 'And how much do you reckon *me* for? In calculating the relative strength of these two armies, please take *me* into the account. I have fought many battles, and never yet lost one: and I expect to lead you to victory to-morrow.'

"And he did so.

"Suppose, now, that Christ had stood visibly manifested in the presence of Mr. Toplady when the latter had just finished the sentence above cited, and had addressed the writer to this effect:—

"'In calculating the possibilities of faith, Mr. Toplady, *how much do you reckon Me for*, when " of God I am made unto" the believer " wisdom, righteousness, sanctification, and redemption"?

"'You have very carefully calculated " the unrelaxing perfection which the law inflexibly requires," and human impotency in itself to render the obedience which the law demands. Have you as carefully calculated the infinitude of " the grace of God which bringeth salvation," and what is possible to a human being, a believer in Me, under the power of that grace? You have thought much, and very correctly, of your insufficiency in yourself to think anything as of yourself. Have you as carefully acquainted yourself with the all-sufficiency which exists for you in God, and what is possible for you through an unstaggering faith in that all-sufficiency?

"'In calculating the possibilities of faith always take Me into the account, and carefully acquaint yourself with your completeness not in yourself, but in Me. Then it will no more be thought " a thing incredible with you" that " the righteousness of the law should be fulfilled in those who walk not after the flesh, but after the Spirit," than it is " that God should raise the dead."'"

Letters respecting this book.

I break off here the thread of the direct "Scriptural Proofs," to go for a while into the consideration of some letters which I have received on the "First Sheets" of them, of which I sent copies to many brothers and sisters in the Lord known to me; who, in some cases, lent them to other brothers and sisters in the Lord known to them though not to me.

On the outside of the paper cover I stated that I should "be grateful for brotherly and sisterly criticisms on these first sheets to enable me to add any necessary qualifications or explanations of any part of their contents in the remaining sheets or in the introduction."

The first letter I received on the subject of the book was from a sister in the Lord unknown to me till I received it :—

The first letter.

"Dear Friend—I have read your little book lent me by a friend, and I do desire heartily to thank my God that it was put into my hands.

"Though for years I have known my Saviour's love, and experienced the incoming of the Holy Spirit in power in my soul, yet since reading '*Scriptural Proofs*' I have had a fresh revelation of what Jesus is to me in his capacity of Saviour; and I have been able to grasp Him in a fuller and more comprehensive faith as my deliverer from indwelling sin; and that on the truth of the living God as shown so clearly in your little book.

"My heart goes with every line of it. I do trust and believe it will be blessed wherever it is read: there is so little of man in it, and so much of God. Yours in the fellowship of his Spirit,———."

A sequel to the above letter.

I told our sister of the use—of which I was sure she would approve—to which I was putting her letter, of printing and circulating it, without her name or address. To this she answered:—

"Dear Friend and Brother in the Lord,—It is very gratifying to me that you considered my letter worth making use of. It certainly was the language of my heart. I am sure the little book only requires to be known to be appreciated. Since I read mine I have been sending it round amongst my friends. It seems to me that this is the only teaching that really exalts our blessed Jesus as Saviour and also produces in us lives corresponding to the truth taught. Oh how I long that I had the ability given me to proclaim this full salvation clearly and definitely. I long also for the section of the Church to which I belong——— that it was more a living experience amongst them.

"I am taking the liberty of sending you a magazine called 'The Bond of Union,' in which you will find an 'Experience' (my own of course), related by me at a drawing-room meeting held in our own house. A minister was present whom I had not known till then, but he was so impressed at hearing it that he afterwards wrote me for the statement on paper and leave to print it. It has since been taken up largely by the Temperance people and widely circulated, and I believe with good effect. It will give you a slight sketch of the way God has led me and mine. Yours in our one Lord, ———."

It is for the sake of the "Experience" spoken of here by our sister that I have introduced this second letter from her. I give it below with her own title to it.

"Rescued from the Snares.

"We lived in a flourishing town in the South Riding of Tipperary, and carried on an extensive business as wholesale and retail grocers and wine and spirit merchants. Most of the gentry in the neighbourhood were our customers; and our business, which was the principal one in the place, was looked upon as a great public convenience, and a model of respectability.

Sinning and repenting.

"For some years I—the mistress of the house—had been converted, and was most anxious to serve the Lord. I had abundant means at my disposal, and, so far as earthly things are concerned, all that might be desired to make me happy; yet I was not satisfied. My life was, on the whole, a miserable, self-pleasing thing, a perpetual alternation of sinning and repenting, of gloomy despondency, relieved by brief experiences of forgiving love.

"*From all your idols will I cleanse you.*"

"I felt that something better than this must be possible, and I longed to realise it. Casting myself upon God, and agonising with Him in prayer, I was at length led to see the need of a fuller consecration. By the help of the Holy Spirit, I was enabled, though not without a struggle, to make a full surrender of all that I had and all that I was to God. Certain costly articles of dress had long proved a snare to me. I now saw the vanity of such profuse expense, and forthwith proceeded to abolish the 'idols.' This self-denial for the Master's sake brought unspeakable gladness to my heart, and great power for service; so that at a meeting, where I related my experience, many aged sinners were melted into tears.

"*And cause you to walk in my statutes.*"

"But another surrender, and one of a much more trying kind, was soon to be made. The most profitable branch of our business, and that which seemed essential to success in the grocery department, was inseparably mixed up with much that was evil. No drink was consumed on the premises; but the demon was there. I knew what a snare it was in the houses where it went. I knew the desolation it was working in certain families: and when I thought that I was, to some extent, abetting this work of ruin, my soul got clouded. Happily, my husband shared my scruples, and became equally anxious to escape from Satan's toils. But what were we to do? If we gave up the wine and spirit business, we saw clearly that most of our customers would leave us altogether: our grocery business would be destroyed; and financial disaster would inevitably overtake us.

"Still we heard God's voice calling and saying distinctly, 'Come out from among them, and be ye separate, and *touch not the unclean thing*:' and at length we felt compelled to make our choice between disobedience to God with worldly ease, or obedience to Him and the probable forfeiture of earthly goods. None but God knows the mental anguish we endured as we weighed the alternative possibilities of the future.

An Experiment.

"Unhappily, in our extremity we thought of a compromise. We decided to give up the liquor business for a year or two; but with the mental reservation that if the experiment failed, we should commence it again.

"The experiment did fail, just as we expected: and I am sorry to confess we embarked again in what was known as our 'legitimate trade,' but what we were feeling keenly was opposed to the law of Christ. Nevertheless our heavenly Father did not leave us to ourselves; but from undreamed-of sources rained upon us trials thick and fast. Our hearts were overwhelmed with divers sorrows.

Obedience at last.

"We saw the loving hand of God in it; and at last determined to obey. With one mighty effort, through the help of His Holy Spirit, we decided to give up our business altogether, and separate ourselves for ever from the accursed thing.

"Immediately we gave the public notice that we were leaving the town, and would sell out our entire stock at an immense sacrifice. This sale was eventually effected at a loss to us of several thousand pounds. Then with aching hearts, and a sadly diminished exchequer, we said good-bye to the old homestead, hallowed by so many tender associations of bygone years; and, like Abram departing from the plains of Haran, we went forth at the call of God literally not knowing whither we went.

God's Answer to it.

"Having yielded to Him the 'obedience of faith,' He has proved Himself to us the covenant-keeping God. By a wondrous chain of Providence He led us to a place that He had prepared for us— to a most suitable business house in a leading thoroughfare in the city, which for years had *remained empty because the estate-agent refused to allow it to be used for the drink-traffic.*

"And now three years have gone by; and God has never ceased to bless us. Five pounds of the money He gives us now brings with it more real increase than 20*l.* did before; and we can say from the depth of our hearts we would not go back to the liquor traffic for the bestowal of a kingdom.

"Nor is this all. God has done for us 'exceeding abundantly above what we asked or thought.' Since we finally gave up our license my husband and children have been savingly brought to a knowledge of the truth. No longer have we to mourn over gloomy despondency and coldness of heart; but, rescued from Satan's snares, we rejoice together as a family in the perpetual sunshine of our Father's love. To Him alone be all the praise!"

"The Obedience of Faith."

I have brought in the above "experience" of our sister and her husband, because it confirms in a lively practical way the truth expressed early in this book, that, unless we are willing to be *entirely yielded up to God*, any expectation of our being "strengthened with might by his Spirit in the inner man that Christ may dwell in" our "hearts by faith" (Eph. iii. 16, 17), that we may ask (Ezek. xxxvi. 37) in his name and have the promises fulfilled in us (John xvi. 23, 24), would be expecting to obtain the "pearl of great price" without being willing to sell all to buy it (Matt. xiii. 46).

Our brother and sister saw clearly that, at any rate, *their own particular participation in the liquor trade* was, as regarded many of its results, undoubtedly evil; so that there could be no doubt that it was the will of God that they should give it up; and no doubt, either, that if they should fail to do so, they must forfeit all hope of having fellowship with Him (1 John i. 6), and walking in the light of his countenance (Ps. lxxxix. 15).

"*Do all to the Glory of God.*"

They had to decide the question of their continuing in it, or not, according to the common-sense view of the matter to which our brother Moody forced the attention of a man who asked him whether he could as a Christian continue to deal in spirits. He told him to kneel down against a cask of whisky and ask God to enable him to send it out to his glory; and if he could do that with a clear conscience, then by all means to continue in the trade.

"*If any man will do his will.*"

"If any man will do his will," our Lord Jesus Christ said—or, as it is in the revised version, "If any man *willeth* to do his will"—"he shall know of the doctrine" "whether it be of God" (John vii. 17); "shall *know of* it, in the blessed way in which God gives us to know the things of his kingdom, by having them gloriously fulfilled by the power of his Spirit in our hearts (1 Cor. ii. 12). And so our brother and sister found it.

It was with them—as our sister rightly puts it—simply a question of that of which St. Paul declared in the opening of his epistle to the Romans, that it was the very object for which he and the other apostles had "received grace and apostleship," namely, "*obedience to the faith*" (Rom. i. 5), or, as he named it again, in the close of the epistle, "*the obedience of faith*" (Rom. xvi. 26).

They had tried to serve God with money made in their business with the drink traffic still included in it: but He mercifully made them feel in their consciences the impossibility, as declared by our Lord, of any such service to two masters, and enabled them at length to "hold to the" right "one, and despise the other" (Matt. vi. 24).

Digression on "dead flies."

What shall we say then of heavy rents received for the sites of gin-palaces by the Ecclesiastical Commissioners to be applied to the support of churches and large contributions by rich brewers and distillers to the erection of churches and cathedrals? Solomon "made" "two pillars of thirty and five cubits high," and "reared up the pillars before the temple, one on the right hand and the other on the left; and called the name of that on the right hand Jachin" (margin, "He shall establish"), "and the name of that on the left Boaz" (margin, "In it is strength," 2 Chron. iii. 17): and I have heard of a cathedral with two great towers which also have names, not, indeed, given to them by the builder, but by the common talk of the country, the name of the one being " Whisky " and the name of the other " Porter," in commemoration of the source of supply of the money with which they were built.

And I know a church of which the costly coloured window was erected, according to the inscription beneath it, *" to the glory of God, and in memory of"* a great gin-distiller !

And—to avoid appearing to attack the Establishment in particular—what must we say, also, to an owner of gin-palaces being accepted, on the retirement of Wilberforce through the infirmities of age, as the representative in public life of much of the earnest Christianity of the country, and to his being looked upon as a tower of strength in the London City Mission, on his becoming its treasurer in its early days? And what must we say, also, to men directly connected with the drink traffic being admitted for their money and influence into important offices in non-conformist churches; or, to the making of money—to be used, no doubt, for Christian purposes—by the admission of the most shamelessly lying, quack advertisements into magazines and other publications, edited by preachers of great name in one or other of these churches?

Separation of faith and practice.

Are not all these and other such things, just the " dead flies " that " cause the ointment of the apothecary to send forth a stinking savour " (Ecc. x. 1) ? Are they not all painful and polluting, and destructive instances of that which dear Archer

Butler, of Dublin, used to call *the most deadly and the most generally prevailing of all heresies, the separation of faith and practice?*

"Nevertheless the foundation of God standeth sure, having this seal, The Lord knoweth them that are his. And, *let every one that nameth the name of Christ depart from iniquity*" (2 Tim. ii. 19).

The reward of obedience.

"If ye be willing and obedient, ye shall eat the good of the land" (Isa. i. 19).

"Bring ye all the tithes into the storehouse, that there may be meat in mine house, and prove me now herewith, saith the Lord of hosts, if I will not open you the windows of heaven, and pour you out a blessing, that there shall not be room enough to receive it" (Mal. iii. 10).

"We are his witnesses of these things; and so is also the Holy Ghost, whom God hath given to *them that obey him*" (Acts v. 32).

"Ye have purified your souls in *obeying the truth* through the Spirit" (1 Pet. i. 22).

"Wherefore come out from among them, and be ye separate, saith the Lord, and touch not the unclean thing; and I will receive you, and will be a Father unto you, and ye shall be my sons and daughters, saith the Lord Almighty" (2 Cor. vi. 17, 18).

The seventh of Romans.

The second letter received by me on the subject of the book was from a well-known earnest worker for the Lord, in spreading both by word of mouth and by printed publications the knowledge of our Lord Jesus Christ as a perfect Saviour both of body and soul.

Objection to what I said upon it.

He sees one passage which he thinks needs correction, namely, the following sentence in the section on " The Law of the Spirit of Life ":—

" St. Paul in the seventh chapter of the Epistle to the Romans describes the extent to which sin may prevail in us *even after we have been brought on so far in the spiritual life* as to 'delight in the law of God after the inward man.'"

On this he says:—

"Many thanks for your *Scriptural Proofs*. I have not met anything to object to but what you say page 62 bottom, 'may still prevail in us even after we have been brought on so far in the spiritual life as to "delight in the law of God after the *inward* MAN."'

" This last shows it is not a *spiritual*, but a mere *mental*, delight: it is simply of *man*. When he speaks of the Spirit he says His Spirit *in* the inner man—i.e. *in* the man, not *of* the man, nor after the 'inner *man*.'

" Then he says 'I am' (in my entirety) 'carnal sold under sin'—to the devil.

" The *will* is his natural will: but *how* is not present; for there is no Spirit power.

" A '*law*'" (of sin) " is an uninterrupted sequence of evil, which never exists where the Spirit is. Though *there is* intermittent good and evil, sinning and repenting, this is not what the Apostle describes; but a *law* of evil, or of the devil, which issues in the 'body of death' or 'body of sin' (Rom. vi. 6).

"Then he sums up (Rom. vii. 25) his whole man in *mind and flesh*; simply a *dual* man. A converted man is a *triple* being.

"Paul commences his experience in the 9th verse, 'I was alive without the law'—i.e. did not think himself a sinner liable to death. When the commandment came he died: and he never in that chapter comes to life or conversion—not till viii. 2. It is simply the workings of conscience which continually convinces the natural mind of sin (Rom. ii. 14–15).

"Nevertheless your tract is a most useful one; quite a repertory of Scripture proofs."

This chapter so much debated.

As regards our brother's criticism on that one passage, I certainly have always considered that Romans vii. 9–25 describes Christian experience: though of a painfully low type. During a sad number of years in my own life, in which it exactly described my experience, I considered myself a Christian: and there are many whose lives I can see that it exactly describes now, whom I cannot but believe to be Christians.

But I am aware that few passages in the Bible have been the subject of more difference of view as to their meaning.

I have heard of one dear child of God answering, when asked, after years of devoted service to Him, if he had got out of the seventh of Romans, "My dear brother, *I am only just beginning to get into it.*"

And yet many other dear brothers in the Lord,

like our brother whose letter we are considering, cannot entertain the idea of St. Paul expressing in the chapter Christian experience even in its lowest stage.

Alford on Seventh Romans.

Dean Alford though very far from taking the chapter as an account of advanced Christian experience—least of all as of that of St. Paul himself at the time he was writing—yet says on " I delight in the law of God after the inner man "—and hereby contradicts our brother's view above, that this was " a mere mental delight," " Not *merely the mental and reasoning part of man*: for that surely *does not* delight in the law of God: it is *absolutely necessary* to pre-suppose the *influence of the Holy Spirit*, and to place the man in *a state of grace before this assertion can be true.*" (The italics are his own.)

He admits, however, that " most of the ancients," even up to and inclusive of Augustine in the earlier part of his Christian life—in the extreme end of the fourth or just the beginning of the fifth century—did not consider that St. Paul was in the chapter describing Christian experience at all.

Correction of the sentence objected to.

And as the only purpose of introducing that seventh chapter into the section on " The Law of the Spirit of Life " was that of leading up to the freedom from the law of sin and death, declared in the eighth, I am sorry that I *unnecessarily* used an expression involving a disputed matter of interpretation; and I wish now that the words "*in the spiritual life*" should be considered as struck out of the sentence, so that it may read:—

"St. Paul in the seventh chapter of the Epistle to the Romans describes the extent to which sin may prevail in us even after we have been brought on so far as to 'delight in the law of God after the inward man.'"

This alteration, as it avoids the question of whether the *bringing on* is *in* the spiritual life or only *towards* it, will, I think, make the sentence to avoid clashing with *any* view of the disputed chapter: and it will not make it any the less to lead on to the freedom declared in the eighth.

More kind criticism invited.

And I hope my acting at once on this first " brotherly criticism " will encourage others of my brothers and sisters in Christ also to send me their brotherly and sisterly criticisms on anything they may see to need them, either in those " First " or in these further " Sheets " of this little book.

Rejoicing in full deliverance.

The third letter received by me on the subject of the book was like the first in being from a sister in the Lord previously unknown to me:—

"I have just been reading your little book, '*First Sheets of Scriptural Proofs.*'

"Oh, how I bless God whenever I read anything which tells out his 'full salvation' clearly. Thank God I can testify to a full and perfect cleansing — my husband also — which I trusted Christ for four years ago. And in spite of the great opposition I have received and still receive from the ——— to whom I belonged, 'my soul' is rejoicing 'in God my' *Perfect* '*Saviour.*'

"I am consequently shut out from ———. But that matters very little to me now.

"Holiness does not flourish here. The Christians are too learned to become as *little children.*

"May the Master use you and all his fully sanctified ones to spread the good news. Yours in true bonds, ———."

Definite Testimony needed.

I am aware that there is danger of the above letter being distasteful to some readers because of those words, "*Thank God I can testify to a full and perfect cleansing—my husband also—which I trusted Christ for four years ago,*" and those concluding words, "May the Master use *you and all his fully sanctified ones to spread the good news.*"

For there are many who will bear any strength of speaking about deliverance from all sin, inward as well as outward, as a matter of doctrine, who yet cannot endure personal testimony to the fact of being so delivered; just as many unconverted persons will bear any amount of talk about the pardon of sin and the certainty of going to heaven, and yet will take offence immediately at anyone saying that *he* is pardoned and on his way to heaven.

But I feel there is force in the following words in an article by Doctor Lowrey, the American editor of "Divine Life," in the number of that paper for November 1884:—

"General discursive preaching, though on the subject of holiness and kindred topics, cannot take the place of definiteness. There may be a great deal of talk, and good talk also, about more religion and a deeper work of grace, entire consecration, life and power of godliness, and even the baptism of the Holy Ghost; and yet all amount to nothing so far as receiving the experience of entire sanctification is concerned.

"There is an opiate in that kind of *goodish* preaching. It does not sting any man's conscience. The dead and lukewarm and worldly vie with the most spiritual in praising such glittering generalities. Such preaching places no goal before the hungry and thirsty soul; or if it does, it fixes no time when he can reach it.

Especially personal testimony.

"The most elaborate sermons on holiness have often failed to produce any practical results for the want of a connecting link between the rich theory and the heart of the speaker. The people go away feeling that a mountain crowned with snow is a grand object to look upon, but a poor thing to warm by. Let that same preacher, provided he enjoys the blessing, parenthetically throw in gems of his own experience occasionally; and he will arrest attention and melt hearts which otherwise would remain unmoved."

I am sure there is much practical wisdom in this advice; and therefore, though it would be out of place in a book of this sort to be obtruding my own experience at every turn (I had to give a good deal of that in the little book to which this is a sequel, The " Letter to the Rev. Robert Dawson, Secretary of the London City Mission "), I am glad of an opportunity like this of my receiving the above letter of our sister to introduce the personal testimony of those who have believed on our dear Lord for full deliverance from sin.

Trying to find a saved preacher.

I was told once, long ago, by a man who believed he was saved, and who I trust really was so, that he had been kept back for a long time from believing in our Lord for salvation for want of being able to find a preacher who professed that he himself was saved. It was in the country, and there were three churches within reach of his home; and he went to them in succession with an anxious wish that he might hear one or other of the ministers say that he knew he was going to heaven: for he thought that if he could hear any one of them say *that*, he would be the one to tell him what he so much wanted to know, namely, the way to get there.

But he listened and listened in vain. He could never hear any such word. I am not saying this in reflection on those preachers; for I do not know anything about them beyond what I am here stating: but I am just telling the facts as the man told them to me.

Finding one at last.

At last there came a new minister to a chapel in the neighbourhood; and the man went to hear his first sermon. And God so ordered it that he should do what the Apostle Paul was so often led to do—just tell out his "experience;" the way, namely, in which God had led him to the knowledge of salvation in believing in our Lord Jesus Christ as "the Way" (John xiv. 6) to God and heaven. And the man at once fastened on to him as one who, having found the way himself, would be able to lead him into it.

And no doubt there are dear souls seeking for entire deliverance from sin who feel a similar desire to hear those addressing them on the subject testify that they themselves are delivered from it, to that which that man felt to hear the preachers say that they were themselves in the way to heaven; and who may be as much helped by such definite personal testimony of deliverance, as he was by the personal testimony of that minister to the fact of God having mercifully brought him into the way there.

"Thou canst make me clean."

The last of the first four letters received by me on the subject of the book is from a dear brother in the Lord well known to me, and much loved by me, during many years. I give it here entire, except the name of the place from which it is written, and the name of the writer, and a very few words in the body of the letter which, *in print,* might perhaps look like a reflection upon one particular section of the Christian Church:—

"My dear Sir and brother in Jesus,—Your little book, 'First Sheets, &c.,' came some days back, and I thank you much for thinking of me and sending it.

"I have read several parts of it many times over; and I cannot doubt that it will be a great and strong help to many of God's dear children who are seeking to be clean and to have the consciousness of

Christ dwelling in them. Indeed it seems, at least to me, just the kind of book to put a solid scriptural foundation under the faith of those who are conscious of a real and godly change in heart and of an eager desire to be wholly the Lord's.

The teaching of our Lord's miracles.

"If I may take the liberty of saying what I think, however, I do not expect the minds of some Christians . . . to be easily convinced by the conclusions drawn from some of the cases given from Scripture.

"It is a common practice for believers to regard each and all of the miracles of our Lord as a setting forth of *the conversion* of the sinner. Your little book seems to go almost as exclusively to another point, and treat them all as commonly teaching a perfect deliverance from sin, inward as well as outward.

"But it has long impressed me that each of the miracles has its own distinct teaching, and deals with one, and only one, of the many consequences of the fall; and that *all* the cases taken together declare our Lord to be the Perfect Redeemer of fallen man, and his mission and death to have fully met EVERY phase and case of the consequences of sin.

Leprosy the type of indwelling sin.

"The miracle which appears to me to distinctly declare our Lord's power and willingness to meet and remove what is called 'indwelling sin,' is that of cleansing the leper, which case stands first in the great group of miracles in Matthew viii. and ix. immediately following upon the sermon on the mount.

"I suppose that all Bible readers or students would acknowledge leprosy to express inherited sin, which could be ended only in death and cleansed only by blood. And so it seems strange to me that the cleansing of the leper by our beloved Lord does not speak to all of his willingness to meet and remove inherited sin, and so cleanse the spiritual leper of his spiritual leprosy.

We come with one trouble at a time.

"One thing is noticeable in our Lord's miracles, namely, that each person was cured of one disease, and not one person cured of two diseases. And so we find in and among our dear fellow Christians that one comes with one soul-plague, and another comes with another soul-plague; and yet surely every one of us was born by nature to inherit all the sad fruits of the fall.

"'We all are blind and crook'd and dumb,
    We all are palsied, deaf, and lame;
We lie as Lazarus in the tomb;
    We burn with fever's fiery flame.'

And most surely the pure word of God convinces of all our diseases and infirmities and soul needs, and reveals our beloved Lord as God's great Saviour from all.

Because we are so slow to learn.

"But our slow minds take in so little of God's great truth; and when we feel our inability to serve Him aright, we come to Him with our withered hand; and when we find how little we see of the beauty of Christ and heavenly realities, we come to Him about our blindness; and when our hearts are broken with the consciousness of our inward filthiness and the impossibility of being clean and pure within, we at last come to Him and say, 'Lord, if thou wilt, thou canst make me clean.'

"The more I think of these things, the more I feel a tender-hearted pity and devoted love for all mankind, especially for those who, knowing Jesus as their Saviour and Lord, have never sought Him for cleansing.

"With sincere and grateful love, yours in Jesus, ———."

Note on the above letter.

I rejoice in this letter, and heartily accept the views expressed in it. Indeed, what has already been written above—especially in the section headed " Second Blessing:" " Higher Life "—about our taking God's gift of full and perfect salvation only bit by bit as we feel our need of it and as we are in a state of preparedness to receive it, though God has given it to us in Christ as a perfect whole, is in exact accordance with what our brother here writes on this point.

But I have scarcely at all brought out, as our brother does, the distinctive teaching of each of our Lord's miracles; and so I gladly adopt now what he says on this matter, as a valuable addition to and qualification of those parts of this book to which he refers.

A second proof of my readiness to accept and profit by brotherly and sisterly criticism.

Time of Cleansing.

"In the year that king Uzziah died I saw also the Lord sitting upon a throne, high and lifted up, and his train filled the temple. Above it stood the seraphims: each one had six wings; with twain he covered his face, and with twain he covered his feet, and with twain he did fly.

"And one cried unto another, and said, Holy, holy, holy, is the Lord of hosts: the whole earth is full of his glory. And the posts of the door moved at the voice of him that cried, and the house was filled with smoke.

"Then said I, Woe is me! for I am undone; because I am a man of unclean lips, and I dwell in the midst of a people of unclean lips: for mine eyes have seen the King, the Lord of hosts.

"Then flew one of the seraphims unto me, having a live coal in his hand, which he had taken with the tongs from off the altar: and he laid it upon my mouth, and said, Lo, this hath touched thy lips; and thine iniquity is taken away, and thy sin purged.

"Also I heard the voice of the Lord, saying, Whom shall I send, and who will go for us? Then said I, Here am I; send me" (Isa. vi. 1–8).

Cleansing needed for full service.

Is not the fact noticed by our brother in his letter in the last section, that the miracle of cleansing the leper "*stands first in the great group of miracles in Matthew viii. and ix.,*" some little confirmation, at any rate, of the more direct scriptural proofs brought forward in this book, that instead of salvation from indwelling sin being, as so many suppose, the *last* miracle that our Lord needs to work in us—so that we are to look for its being wrought in us only just as we are leaving this world—it is on the contrary needed at an *early* stage of our Christian experience, as a preparation for all else which He has to do in us in fitting us for that for which we are "created" anew in Him, namely, the walking in the "good works which God hath before ordained that we should walk in them" (Eph. ii. 10)?

And for the keeping of the law.

And is not this in some degree further confirmed by that other fact noticed by our brother, with reference to the position of this miracle, that it *immediately follows upon the sermon on the mount?*

Does not this suggest that as the sermon on the mount is an exposition of the holy law of God in its spirituality as "a discerner of the thoughts and intents of the heart" (Heb. iv. 12), we have this miracle made to follow immediately upon it, to show us that all our hope of being able so to keep the law must lie in our being first brought into a state of conformity of heart to it (Heb. viii. 10; Ezek. xxxvi. 26) by that cleansing of all evil out of us, typified by the cleansing of the leper?

"*Make the tree good.*"

Did not our Lord seem, by working that particular miracle just at that particular time, to be confirming the teaching in his sermon that it is vain to expect "grapes of thorns, or figs of thistles" (Matt. vii. 16); which also He further confirmed and enforced, a little later in his ministry, by his injunction, which we have already partly considered above :—

"Either *make the tree good, and his fruit good*; or else make the tree corrupt, and his fruit corrupt" (Matt. xii. 33)?

Isaiah's felt uncleanness; and his cleansing.

And have we not a yet much stronger confirmation of the view, that in God's order the entire deliverance from sin comes at the *beginning of* and as a *preparation for* effective service to Him—instead of, where it is placed in the view referred to above, at the *end* of our life of service to Him—in the case of the prophet Isaiah, as recorded by him in the passage at the head of this section?

In the light of the glory of God, he saw himself so filthy that he could only—like Peter, when, in sight of our Lord's power, he prayed, " Depart from me, for I am a sinful man, O Lord " (Luke v. 8)—cry out :—

"Woe is me! for I am undone; because *I am a man of unclean lips, and I dwell in the midst of a people of unclean lips*: for mine eyes have seen the King, the Lord of hosts." But "Then flew," he says, "one of the seraphims unto me, having a live coal in his hand, which he had taken with the tongs from off the altar: and he laid it upon my mouth, and said, Lo, this hath touched thy lips; and *thine iniquity is taken away, and thy sin purged.*"

And then his felt unfitness even to be in the presence of God, was turned into eagerness to undertake any work to which He might be pleased to call him. For he adds:—

"Also I heard the voice of the Lord, saying,

Whom shall I send, and who will go for us? Then said I, *Here am I; send me.*"

His "sin" having been thus "purged," he was now " A vessel unto honour, *sanctified, and meet for the master's use,* and prepared unto every good work " (2 Tim. ii. 21).

God's way and man's way.

In sight of the difference between God's way, that of putting the perfect cleansing at the beginning of the life to his glory, and man's way, that of postponing it till all the time so to live down here is over, may we not well thankfully call to mind God's words by this same prophet, already quoted above:—

" My thoughts are not your thoughts, neither are your ways my ways, saith the Lord. For as the heavens are higher than the earth, so are *my ways higher than your ways,* and *my thoughts than your thoughts* " (Isa. lv. 8, 9).

The things of our spiritual life very often repeat themselves. As we many of us had such difficulty on our first coming to God in accepting the forgiveness of sin, and the sense of sonship to him, as his free gift; thinking we must *do* something to obtain his blessings; or at any rate that we must pass through some course of feeling, or something else to be fitted for receiving them: so after we know we are pardoned and accepted in Christ, and have the Spirit of adoption, we fancy again that we must *do* something for the blessed second gift of perfect cleansing; or, at any rate, that God has to put us through some long course of his work in us before we can attain to such blessedness; instead of accepting it at once, as we were at last compelled to do, in the case of our pardon, as his free gift to us in Christ.

The Gospel according to Isaiah.

It has been well pointed out that doubtless there is an intimate connection between that taking away of Isaiah's iniquity and purging of his sin, and the wonderful fulness with which " the Spirit of Christ" came in to him, that, in and by him, He might testify " beforehand the sufferings of Christ and the glory that should follow" (1 Pet. i. 11).

" Why do you not let us have in print the gospel which you preach, that we may know what it really is?" said a minister to our brother Moody in a preliminary meeting which he had with ministers in the beginning of one of his visits to London. He answered rightly, " There it is in print long enough ago *in the fifty-third of Isaiah.*"

And we have seen in several passages considered in different sections above that it was the full old gospel of perfect deliverance from the *existence* of sin in us, as well as from its guilt and its overcoming power. For those whose own iniquity is perfectly taken away and their sin perfectly purged always preach a gospel of the perfect taking away of iniquity and the perfect purging of sin.

Sickness and the Gospel.

I give now extracts from some of the further letters which have come in to me on the subject of this book, since those first four quoted from above.

A dear brother in the Lord, vicar of a country parish, writes on the section headed " Sanctification at Death,"—in which " *sickness* " is named among the many evils from which deliverance is promised to us at death, or at the coming again of our Lord; though, as we have seen, no deliverance is then promised to us from *sin*, as it would appear that we are supposed to have received *that* already on our hearing and believing the Gospel:—

Relief from sickness—when?

"What *Scripture proof* would you suggest that the statement in page 24 is correct, that *sickness* is one of those things *believers* need not expect to be relieved of till death, instead of *now by redemption through faith?*"

Certainly at death or at our Lord's coming.

Certainly those children of God who have not seen that there is deliverance for us now from sickness through the redemption which we have in Christ for body as well as soul—or who, though seeing it, yet have not believed for it with the strength of faith necessary for its attainment (Mark ix. 23; xi. 22–24)—will have it at death, or at the coming of our Lord; just as those whose hearts and lives are given to God, but who, not seeing, and therefore not believing for, deliverance from indwelling sin now, do not have it now, will, we may fully trust, have it then.

But surely also now if we believe for it.

But the question being considered in that paragraph referred to by our brother was, What evils may we, according to God's word, look to be delivered from *only* then? And I feel bound now to admit that I was wrong in putting sickness in the list of these evils, instead of naming it—if I needed to name it at all—along with sin, as an evil from which we may have deliverance *now*.

I say this on the strength of the following and other such Scriptures, all of which—though some of them, in their primary meaning, referring specially to the Jews—must, as we have seen above, have a *spiritual* fulfilment now for us if we believe for it, and doubtless a *physical* fulfilment as well if we further believe for that also.

And I am thankful to say that I see many who accept this view, not merely with the intellect as true, but also with the heart as the living and life-giving Word of God (Ps. xxix. 3-9; xxxiii. 9; John vi. 63), find it gloriously fulfilled to them in the cure of sickness and infirmities humanly speaking absolutely incurable.

Scripture Proofs.

" If thou wilt diligently hearken to the voice of the Lord thy God, and wilt do that which is right in his sight, and wilt give ear to his commandments, and keep all his statutes, I will put none of these diseases upon thee, which I have brought upon the Egyptians: for *I am the Lord that healeth thee*" (Exod. xv. 26).

" I will *take sickness away* from the midst of thee " (Exod. xxiii. 25).

" The Lord *will take away from thee all sickness*, and will put none of the evil diseases of Egypt, which thou knowest, upon thee " (Deut. vii. 15).

" Bless the Lord, O my soul, and forget not all his benefits: who forgiveth all thine iniquities; who *healeth all thy diseases* " (Ps. ciii. 2, 3).

" Behold, I will bring it *health and cure*, and will

reveal unto them the abundance of peace and truth" (Jer. xxxiii. 6).

"Heal me, O Lord, and *I shall be healed*; save me, and I shall be saved: for thou art my praise" (Jer. xvii. 14).

"Unto you that fear my name shall the sun of righteousness arise with *healing* in his wings" (Mal. iv. 2).

"They brought unto Him many that were possessed with devils: and He cast out the spirits with his word, and *healed all that were sick*: that it might be fulfilled which was spoken by Esaias the prophet, saying, *Himself took our infirmities, and bare our sicknesses*" (Matt. viii. 16, 17).

"Jesus Christ, the same yesterday, *and to-day*, and for ever" (Heb. xiii. 8).

"Who went about doing good, and *healing all that were oppressed of the devil*" (Acts x. 38).

"Is any sick among you? let him call for the elders of the church; and let them pray over him, anointing him with oil in the name of the Lord: and *the prayer of faith shall save the sick, and the Lord shall raise him up*" (James v. 14, 15).

"Go ye into all the world, and preach the gospel to every creature. He that believeth and is baptised shall be saved; but he that believeth not shall be damned. And these signs shall follow them that believe; In my name shall they cast out devils; they shall speak with new tongues; they shall take up serpents; and if they drink any deadly thing, it shall not hurt them; *they shall lay hands on the sick, and they shall recover*.

"So then, after the Lord had spoken unto them, he was received up into heaven, and sat on the right hand of God. And they went forth, and preached every where, *the Lord working with them, and con-*

firming the word with signs following" (Mark xvi. 16–20).

"*These signs shall follow.*"

These "signs," by the admission of all, continued during the lifetime of the Apostles, and for an uncertain—but certainly *long*—time afterwards. Nor is there any hint in that commission of our Lord, or in its accompanying promises, of either the commission or the promises being for any limited time: but, on the contrary, his words in the end of the Gospel according to St. Matthew show that they were for the whole of the present dispensation:—

"All power is given unto me in heaven and in earth. Go ye therefore, and teach all nations, baptising them in the name of the Father, and of the Son, and of the Holy Ghost: teaching them to observe all things whatsoever I have commanded you: and, lo, *I am with you alway, even unto the end of the world*"—or, as it is in the margin of the revised version, "unto the *consummation of the age.*"—"Amen" (Matt. xxviii. 18–20).

"*Them that believe.*"

It will be observed that the "signs" of casting out devils, speaking with tongues, taking up serpents, and if drinking any deadly thing not being hurt by it, and laying hands on the sick and their recovering, were to "follow," not the Apostles in particular, but "*them that believe.*"

This might, at first sight, appear to mean *every-one* who believes, and so to be a parallel case in this respect with those two other wonderful promises of our Lord, "He that believeth on me, as the scripture hath said, out of his belly shall flow rivers of living water" (John vii. 38), and "he that believeth on me, the works that I do shall he do also; and greater works than these shall he do; because I go unto my Father" (John xiv. 12): both which promises manifestly belong to *every* believer, and yet just as manifestly are now fulfilled in scarcely one believer in fifty; because the rest, though believers for eternal salvation, have never yet so seen these or many other of the "exceeding great and precious promises" (2 Pet. i. 4), as to believe for and receive their fulfilment.

And I would remark by the way, that this self-evident fact of the exceeding rarity of the fulfilment of those two and many other glorious promises of God, simply because most of his people fail to believe for their fulfilment, is an absolute answer to all objections to faith-healing founded on the apparent —sometimes for long periods together—non-occurrence of cases of it. They do not occur at such times, doubtless because there is no faith for them.

Not necessarily every one who believes.

But those words, "*them that believe*," have not necessarily exactly the same meaning as "*he that believeth.*" They may mean that the signs are to be fulfilled *to the believers as a body*: a view which would appear to be supported by that word of St. James quoted above, that if any is sick, he is to "call for the elders of the church, and" they are to "pray over him, anointing him with oil in the name of the Lord: and the prayer of faith shall save the sick; and the Lord shall raise him up; and if he have committed sins, they shall be forgiven him." Here the power would appear to be in the Church collectively, and to be exercised through the believing prayer of the elders.

Or the words may mean that each sign was to be fulfilled to *some* among the whole body, so as *in that way* to bring about a fulfilment of them all in the whole body: a view which would appear to be supported by that word of St. Paul in the epistle to the Corinthians, where, among many other gifts to individual members of the Church for the benefit of all, he names " *gifts of healing* " (1 Cor. xii. 9).

" My words shall not pass away."

But be it as it may as regards *the particular manner* in which these " signs " are to " follow them that believe," bless his holy name! follow *they must* in some way or other, wherever there is the belief for them: for as above said, there is no limit of time even hinted at by our Lord for them; and if they are thus still in force, then, whoever or whatever may say that they are not for us now, we may answer every difficulty and every objection with, " *Heaven and earth shall pass away, but my words shall not pass away*" (Matt. xxiv. 35).

Passages at first sight on the other side.

I may have had in my mind, when putting sickness into the list of things from which we are promised deliverance only at death or at the coming of our Lord, that passage in the Revelation:—

" There shall be no more death, neither sorrow, nor crying, *neither shall there be any more pain*: for the former things are passed away" (Rev. xxi. 4).

But on looking in the lexicon at the word here translated " *pain*," I see it has nothing to do with *sickness,* but appears to mean pain caused directly or indirectly by labour, as it is derived from the verb to labour. In " Dr. Robinson's Greek Lexicon of the New Testament" it is translated "labour, toil, travail; hence sorrow, pain, anguish;" and in Taylor's translation of Dawson's "Greek-Latin Lexicon," "labour, pain, sorrow, misery;" and in Bagster's "Analytical Greek Lexicon," "labour, travail, pain, misery, anguish;" no hint being given in any one of them of its having reference to sickness, and that verse in the Revelation being referred to by each of them.

And the word is never used in connection with any of the evils from which the poor ones were suffering, who came, or were brought, to our Lord, or to the Apostles, for healing.

But I think the passage chiefly in my mind when I put *sickness* down in that list was this:—

"And the inhabitant *shall not say, I am sick*" (Isa. xxxiii. 24).

But the context shows that this is for fulfilment in this world—to the Jews hereafter, no doubt, as regards its first signification, but also, as above said of those other promises—now, *spiritually,* to all believers in our Lord Jesus Christ, and *physically* as well, if our faith is comprehensive enough to take it both ways.

So that passage, instead of showing that the deliverance from bodily sickness is to be looked for only at death or the coming again of our Lord, is another to add to the Scriptural proofs that it is for this present time for those who can find it in their hearts by faith to take it now.

A little more on Faith-healing.

In the letter quoted a little way back, from that brother in the Lord who objected to what I had written on the seventh of Romans, there was a passage about faith-healing: but I did not there copy it out, as that was not the matter then under discussion. I copy it out here on account of its bearing on the subject of the last section:—

"I may mention I have just returned from ——, where I anointed 130 for healing. All were blessed; and, with only two or three exceptions, with healing of soul and body—in these, even cases of tumours, blindness, paralysis, &c. One man threw aside his crutches, and walked home three miles."

Thank God, instances of the healing of many together, like that reported here by our brother—who is not a novice to speak rashly or mistakenly, but his name, if I were at liberty to give it, would be recognised as that of an elder well known throughout the churches—are now frequently taking place: and many individual cases are also occurring of the cure, by simple faith for it, of diseases or infirmities altogether beyond the reach of earthly power to heal.

For the uprooting of unbelief.

And this to the happy uprooting (Matt. xv. 13), we may trust, of that human tradition, so dishonouring to our dear Lord in its limitation of his mightiness to save (Isa. lxiii. 1)—which sprang up, nobody can say how or when, and has held its place with such power in the minds of so many in the Church, without their even attempting, so far as I know, to show a shadow of warrant for it in the Word of God—that the "*healing all manner of sickness and all manner of disease among the people*" (Matt. iv. 23) was something belonging peculiarly to the first two or three or a few more centuries from the time when He began to fulfil upon men's bodies the "purpose" for which, as the Son of God, He "was manifested," of destroying "the works of the devil" (1 John iii. 8).

I say "the first two or three or a few more centuries," because objectors to faith-healing now do not seem to question its continuance in the Church, in greater or less force, for, at any rate, some centuries after the death of our Lord.

Sickness a work of the devil.

If any reader should demur to sickness being here spoken of as a *work of the devil*, I would refer to the frequency with which demoniacal possession is named in the Gospels as the cause of the evils from which the poor ones were suffering who came, or were brought, to our Lord to be healed (Matt. ix. 32; xii. 22; xv. 22; xvii. 15, 18; &c.), and most especially to his own words in connection with one of his miracles as thus reported in the Gospel according to St. Luke:—

"He was teaching in one of the synagogues on the sabbath. And, behold, there was a woman which had a spirit of infirmity eighteen years, and was bowed together, and could in no wise lift up herself.

"And when Jesus saw her, he called her to him, and said unto her, Woman, thou art loosed from thine infirmity. And he laid his hands on her: and immediately she was made straight, and glorified God.

"And the ruler of the synagogue answered with indignation, because that Jesus had healed on the sabbath day, and said unto the people, There are six days in which men ought to work: in them therefore come and be healed, and not on the sabbath day.

"The Lord then answered him, and said, Thou hypocrite, doth not each one of you on the sabbath loose his ox or his ass, and lead him away to watering? And ought not this woman, being a daughter of Abraham, whom *Satan hath bound*, lo, these eighteen years, be loosed from this bond on the sabbath day?" (Luke xiii. 10-16).

And I would also refer to St. Peter's summing up, quoted above, of all our Lord's miracles of healing, namely, that He

"Went about doing good, and *healing all that were oppressed of the devil*" (Acts x. 38).

Faith-healing and entire sanctification.

I do not consider that, in writing so much upon faith-healing, I have wandered from the subject of this book, the deliverance from all sin offered to us in the Gospel. For the two things would seem to be intimately connected.

For the want of faith on the part of the Church which has been the cause of the rarity—apparently sometimes for centuries together—of cases of faith-healing, has doubtless been the result of spiritual weakness, arising from her failure to hold on to and live in the power of the full original Gospel, with its entire deliverance from indwelling sin.

There has never been any want of *prayer* for the healing of the sick, but only a want of *God's answer* to it. And is not this to be accounted for in the same way as in a similar case of old:—

"Behold, the Lord's hand is not shortened, that it cannot save; neither his ear heavy, that it cannot hear: but *your iniquities have separated between you and your God, and your sins have hid his face from you, that he will not hear*" (Isa. lix. 1, 2)?

And so may not the return of faith-healing to her in full primitive power be dependent upon her return, first, to the full primitive faith of entire salvation from all sin, inward as well as outward?

Promises of old dependent on holiness.

That it does depend upon this, appears the more probable, from the fact that the Old Testament promises of freedom from sickness—some of which were quoted in the last section among the Scripture proofs that we are right in expecting cases of faith-healing now—are almost always conditional upon entire holiness.

The promise for instance there quoted from Exodus xv. 26: "I will put none of these diseases upon thee, which I have brought upon the Egyptians: for I am the Lord that healeth thee," has as its condition that "thou wilt *diligently hearken to the voice of the Lord thy God, and wilt do that which is right in his sight, and wilt give ear to his commandments, and keep all his statutes.*"

The context of the promise in Exodus xxiii. 25, "I will take sickness away from the midst of thee," is too long to copy out here; but on referring to it the conditions attached will be seen to be quite as strong in respect to the requirement of holiness, as in the case of that other promise.

And the promise in Deut. vii. 15: "The Lord

will take away from thee all sickness, and will put none of the evil diseases of Egypt, which thou knowest, upon thee;" is prefaced by "*Thou art an holy people unto the Lord thy God: the Lord thy God hath chosen thee to be a special people unto himself, above all people that are upon the face of the earth*" .... "Thou shalt therefore keep the commandments, and the statutes, and the judgments, which I command thee this day, to do them. Wherefore it shall come to pass, *if ye hearken to these judgments, and keep, and do them*, that the Lord thy God shall keep unto thee the covenant and the mercy which he sware unto thy fathers: and he will love thee, and bless thee, ..." (verses 6, 11–13), and then follows the enumeration of the particular blessings, of which the above of freeing from sickness is one.

First, healing of soul; then, of body.

And most of those present cases of answers to believing prayer for the cure of the body, which we are here considering under the name of "faith-healing," appear to be preceded by spiritual blessing to bring the sufferer into a right state toward God. They seem to be of the type of our Lord's double miracle of healing upon the poor sick of the palsy; *first*, "Son, thy sins be forgiven thee;" and *then*, "Arise, and take up thy bed, and go thy way into thine house" (Mark ii. 3–12).

The requirement in the workers.

And that which is required in *those through whom the power is to be exerted*, is precisely the same now as in the Apostles' days, namely, entire absence of trust in anything in themselves, and absolute trust in the name of our blessed Lord.

St. Peter said to the poor lame man at the gate of the temple:—

"Silver and gold have I none; but such as I have give I thee: *In the name of Jesus Christ of Nazareth rise up and walk.*"

And again, after the miracle, when "the lame man which was healed held Peter and John," and "all the people ran together unto them in the porch which is called Solomon's, greatly wondering":—

"When Peter saw it, he answered unto the people, Ye men of Israel, why marvel ye at this? or *why look ye so earnestly on us, as though by our own power or holiness we had made this man to walk?* The God of Abraham, and of Isaac, and of Jacob, the God of our fathers, hath glorified his Son Jesus; whom ye delivered up, and denied him in the presence of Pilate, when he was determined to let him go. But ye denied the Holy One and the Just, and desired a murderer to be granted unto you; and killed the Prince of Life, whom God hath raised from the dead; whereof we are witnesses. And *his name through faith in his name hath made this man strong,* whom ye see and know: yea, *the faith which is by him hath given him this perfect soundness in the presence of you all?*" (Acts iii. 4–16).

Prominence given to faith in the original.

In the original, faith as a concurring cause in the miracle, has a more prominent position than even in this translation; the English idiom not admitting of the full prominence being given to it.

In the order of the words in the Greek—and this, the Greek scholars all say, shows where the emphasis is—*faith comes first.* It is literally, " Through " or, Dean Alford says, " better ' *on account of* ' " " faith in his name, this one whom ye see and know hath made strong his name, &c." It is as if Peter were forcing attention to the absolute necessity of faith by naming it before even the mention of our Lord's name as the power to be brought into exercise " on account of " it.

He seemed to be saying to the " greatly wondering " Jews: Though we have told you that it is by no " power or holiness " of ours, that we have " made this man to walk," yet there is one thing in us which had to do with the working of the miracle, and without which it would not have taken place— faith in the one only " name under heaven, given among men, whereby " (Acts iv. 12) any work of " salvation " can be wrought " in the earth " (Jer. ix. 24 ; Ps. lxxiv. 12).

Do not let us limit God (Ps. lxxviii. 41).

Indeed, the whole Word of God declares that undoubting faith in Him (Heb. xi.; James i. 6, 7 ; Mark xi. 22, 23 ; &c.), for the accomplishment of the cure is an indispensable requisite in the human agent through whom He is to effect it. And if any of us are conscious—as indeed, most of us must be—that *we* have no such faith for the effecting of cases of faith-healing through us, yet, surely, we ought not on that account to refuse to listen to properly authenticated reports of cases through the instrumentality of others ; as if our Lord's power could not be exerted now as of old, or as if *our* measure of faith were that also of all our fellow-believers. Surely we ought rather to be ready to welcome any sufficient testimony that He is still performing on men's bodies his miracles of mercy, through those whom He has strengthened in faith in his name up to the point needed for their being his instruments in them, though—through our own fault, it may be—He has not yet so strengthened us.

Looking only at the promise.

I give here two verses of one of Charles Wesley's hymns, written with reference to our being perfected in love, but equally applicable to our present subject of faith-healing:—

" The thing surpasses all my thought,
    But faithful is my Lord;
Through unbelief I stagger not,
    For God hath spoke the word.

Faith, mighty faith, *the promise sees,*
    And looks to that alone;
Laughs at impossibilities,
    And cries ' It shall be done.' "

" Blessed is she that believed: for there shall be a performance of those things which were told her from the Lord" (Luke i. 45).

" He staggered not at the promise of God through unbelief; but was strong in faith, giving glory to God; and being *fully persuaded that, what he had promised, he was able also to perform*" (Rom. iv. 20, 21).

Another word on 1 John i. 8.

A sister in the Lord, unknown to me till she wrote for a copy of the " First Sheets," afterwards wrote again:—

" I am very much obliged to you for " Scriptural Proofs," which I have read with great interest. They seem very conclusive. The one text which seems not in accordance is:—

" ' *If we say* that we have *no sin* we *deceive ourselves*, and the *truth is not in us*; but if we *confess our sins*,' &c., &c.

" I feel myself that the one thing that holds one back is the not being willing to let God do all He wills *in us* and *for us*—' able to do all things'— nothing too hard for Him—for His power or His love."

In answer to that difficulty about "If we say that we have no sin," I sent our sister a "proof" copy of the sheet a little way back containing the section headed "Cleansing from all unrighteousness," in which that text, and the rest of that first epistle of John, are carefully looked into with reference to the extent of deliverance from sin given to us in our Lord Jesus Christ. And she wrote again:—

" Many thanks. The proofs are, I think, very conclusive. There can be no limit to our dear Lord's power, nor surely to His *willingness* to save us from our sins. The limitation is in ourselves."

All the difficulty in ourselves.

Surely our sister is right in putting the blame of all the difficulty in the way of our full present salvation on ourselves—on our want of willingness to let God save us perfectly, or on our want of faith to accept our dear Lord for perfect salvation.

And, surely also, every system which denies the possibility of our being rid in this life of indwelling sin does practically—however unintentionally on the part of some who hold and defend it—put the difficulty, not on our own unwillingness or unbelief, but on either the inability or unwillingness of God to give us entire present deliverance.

I say "however unintentionally on the part of *some* who hold and defend it;" for there are others who maintain such views who avow distinctly their belief that we are so hopelessly ruined by the fall that not even God Himself can improve us in the least; though for Christ's sake He accepts us, and sees us spotless in Him, and exerts a power in us to make us walk to a certain extent in his ways, but with our own old evil hearts still in us, "*as black as hell can make them.*" I am here quoting the words of some reckoned thoroughly orthodox in the particular branch of the Christian Church to which I am now referring.

Difficulty of a strong intellect.

I give now a painfully interesting letter, expressing with clearness and power a difficulty which many find standing in the way of their believing for entire salvation from all sin, and so experiencing it as a glorious fact in their hearts and lives; the difficulty of *a strong intellect* preventing their becoming *altogether* "as little children" (Matt. xviii. 3), and *so* having "an entrance" "ministered unto" them "*abundantly* into the everlasting kingdom of our Lord and Saviour Jesus Christ" (2 Pet. i. 11).

The letter is from one whom I should have thought too busy for letter writing, seeing that he is almost incessantly engaged in evangelistic work; God being pleased to exert his converting power through him to the salvation of, I believe, very many souls wherever He sends him.

The first part of the letter refers to a dear brother in the Lord, who also was used of Him in the salvation of very many souls, about whom I had inquired, as I had not heard from or of him for a long time. I have to give this first part as an introduction for that which follows:—

The difficulty expressed.

"My dear Friend,—I laid dear J—— H—— in his last resting place about four years ago. I am not quite sure of the exact date. He was a splendid man, and a noble Christian.

"But he was—like myself and so many more that I meet with—much more a hungerer and thirster, an aspirant after a standard that still seemed far beyond experience, rather than a 'Naphtali *satisfied* with favour, and full with the blessing of the Lord.' It seems to me, dear Brother, as if all men of big hearts and large minds, that I know, were so. You, perhaps, may be an exception. I don't know you intellectually sufficiently well to judge. But does God affix a premium to—well, what shall I call it?—simplicity is an ambiguous word or I would use it—and incapacity or intellectual feebleness are perhaps too strong terms. Anyhow, the Apostle tells us in understanding to be *men*. How is it that the intellectual men seem to get no further than Bashan, if they get as far, and the intellectual babies go clean into Eshcol!

"Always glad to see anything you write, dear Brother, for I have you in much honour and love, though I hardly know you. Yours most faithfully in Him who has promised to satisfy the hungry soul (But when?) ———."

The blessing which was future now present.

Doubtless our dear brother's case, which is also that of, as he says, so many other *highly intellectual*, and I add, *entirely devoted* ones, is an instance of the state of soul referred to by our Lord in his sweet promise :—

"Blessed are they which do *hunger and thirst after righteousness*: for they shall be *filled*" (Matt. v. 6).

"*Shall be*," our Lord said—"for the Holy Ghost was not yet given; because that Jesus was not yet glorified" (John vii. 39). But now He *is* glorified, and the Holy Ghost *is* given. And so, surely, the answer now to our dear brother's question—"' Satisfied' But *when?*" is—"NOW."

"*Freely given to us of God.*"

For, is not that "*righteousness*," which in that state of soul we so "hunger and thirst after," just another name for "*the hidden wisdom, which God ordained before the world unto our glory*: which none of the princes of this world knew: for had they known it, they would not have crucified the Lord of glory. But as it is written, Eye hath not seen, nor ear heard, neither have entered into the heart of man, the things *which God hath prepared for them that love him*"?

And does not St. Paul, in the next following words, go on to declare the then present fulfilment of that which in the time of Isaiah—from whom he was quoting those words, " Eye hath not seen, &c."—was a matter of *distant*, and in the time of our Lord, still only of *near* prophecy:—

"But God *hath revealed them unto us by his Spirit*: for the Spirit searcheth all things, yea, the deep things of God. For what man knoweth the things of a man, save the spirit of man which is in him? even so the things of God knoweth no man, but the Spirit of God. Now *we have received*, not the spirit of the world, but the Spirit which is of God; that we might *know the things that are freely given to us of God*" (1 Cor. ii. 7–12); "*know*"—as we considered a little while back in connection with our Lord's word, " He shall *know* of the doctrine"—"*know*" in God's sense of *knowing*, in the way, that is, of blessed realisation in us.

But we must take it.

But—as we considered in the section headed " I will take"—we *must take* what He so freely *gives*; and that, as there said, by determined faith on his bare word without waiting for any feeling or other *sign* (John iv. 48) from Him; and then, with unwavering confidence, *wait* " for him" (Isa. lxiv. 4) to give to us how, and when, He pleases, the blessed *sense* that we indeed "*have*" (Mark xi. 24) the things which we desired when we prayed, and which according to his command we then, without feeling, **believed that we received.**

"*An appointed time*" *for* "*the vision.*"

For while it is written, " I have heard thee in a time accepted, and in the day of salvation have I succoured thee: behold, *now* is the accepted time; behold, *now* is the day of salvation " (2 Cor. vi. 2); it is also written, " *The vision is yet for an appointed time, but at the end it shall speak, and not lie: though it tarry, wait for it; because it will surely come, it will not tarry* " (Hab. ii. 3).

The promises to and in Christ.

That word, " I have heard thee in a time accepted, and in the day of salvation have I succoured thee," is not spoken in the first instance to *us*, but to *Christ* (Isa. xlix. 8). Is not then our way to have the benefit of it first to *accept Him* as God's gift to us, that He may " dwell in " our "hearts by faith " (Eph. iii. 17); and then to " believe in God " (1 Pet. i. 21) as fulfilling the word *to Him in us*?

" *Angels of God ascending and descending.*"

Our Lord said to Nathaniel:—

" Verily, verily, I say unto you, Hereafter ye shall see heaven open, and the angels of God ascending and descending upon the Son of Man " (John i. 51).

And has not that " Hereafter " been coming sweetly to pass, in the way of a first fulfilment at any rate, ever since the day of Pentecost when out of " heaven," which at our Lord's baptism had been " opened " (Luke iii. 21), that the Holy Ghost might come down upon Him, He came down again in his fulness, for all believers in Him? For are not all the holy and blessed things which as "the Spirit of holiness" (Rom. i. 4) He brings to us, or works in us—the love of God shed abroad in our hearts, the joy, peace, prayer without ceasing, praise at all times, rejoicing in the Lord always, in everything giving thanks, &c. (Rom. v. 5; viii. 16; Gal. v. 22, 23; Phil. iv. 4; 1 Pet. ii. 5; Heb. xiii. 15; 1 Thess. v. 16-18; &c)—just as very "*angels of God ascending*" to "*and descending*" from the opened heaven?

"*Upon the Son of Man.*"

And as it is "*upon the Son of Man*" that they "ascend and descend," are we not, here again, shown that the way to have that word of our Lord fulfilled in us, in this sense of our having all those sweet spiritual blessings coming in to fill us, is *to accept Him, to come and dwell in our hearts* (Eph. iii. 17), that *so* they may become the scene of this blessed intercourse between earth and heaven?

And surely in every heart in which its fulfilment does, as a fact, so take place, the question above of our dear brother "'*Satisfied*'—*but when?*" again receives in sweet clearness that same answer —"*Now.*"

The blessing for every one of us.

And surely our heavenly Father means it so to take place in the heart of *every one of us*: for "the promise" of that "gift of the Holy Ghost" by whom it is all brought about—and *always* brought about where He is received in his fulness—was declared by Peter to be to those who witnessed his coming down on that day of Pentecost, and to their children " and to *all that*" *were* " *afar off, even as many as the Lord our God shall call*" (Acts ii. 38, 39).

"*Christ liveth in me.*"

Oh, if we will but all take the promise as wide and as free as God speaks it to us, we shall be blessedly conscious of " a voice from heaven saying" of Christ in us, " This is my beloved Son, in whom I am well pleased" (Matt. iii. 17) ; and that it is as the " *anointed* " " *with the Holy Ghost and with power* " that He is in us, that though He has Himself left the earth, He may still be exercising his ministry in it by us—still, in us, going about " doing good, and healing all that" are " oppressed of the devil ;" because God is still " with Him " in us, as He was " with Him " in his own time on the earth, according to that word :—

" God anointed Jesus of Nazareth with the Holy Ghost and with power : who went about doing good, and healing all that were oppressed of the devil ; for *God was with him* " (Acts x. 38).

"*I in them, and thou in me.*"

" I IN THEM, AND THOU IN ME," our Lord said in his prayer the night before his crucifixion, " that they may be made perfect in one ; and that the world may know that thou hast sent me, and hast loved them, as thou hast loved me " (John xvii. 23).

And is not this fulfilled by his dwelling in our hearts by faith, as we have here been considering, and *the Father by the blessed Spirit dwelling in Him in us*, as He did in Him personally in the " days of his flesh (Heb. v. 7), when He said, " The words that

I speak unto you I speak not of myself: but *the Father that dwelleth in me*, he doeth the works" (John xiv. 10)?

Bearing on the intellectual difficulty.

In this view of all the blessedness depending upon our having Christ dwelling in our hearts by faith (Eph. iii. 17), is not the right way of treating the intellectual difficulty which we are here specially looking into, to exercise all the power of our intellect in *considering* (Heb. iii. 1) in dependence upon the promised teaching of the Spirit (John xvi. 13-15, &c.), *our Lord Jesus Christ*, and what God has made Him to be to us (1 Cor. i. 30; 2 Cor. v. 21, &c.), and what He has freely given to us in Him (Eph. i. 3, 18-23; Col. ii. 9, 10, &c.): and then in dependence on the promised strengthening of the Spirit (Eph. iii. 16, &c.), by a determined effort of will and simple unreasoning faith in what God has said, to accept Him for all that we thus see to be for us in Him?

And having done this, ought we not then to be sure, in spite of our own hearts and the devil and all else that is against us, that we indeed " have received " (Mark xi. 24, revised version) all that we have thus believed for: and then still *continuing* " in the faith grounded and settled, and not moved away from the hope of the Gospel " (Col. i. 23), to wait for *its bringing forth fruit* (Col. i. 6) in our hearts, in all holy happy feelings as God shall, as above said, be pleased to appoint, and " though it tarry wait for it " with still unwavering faith that we " have received " what God has indeed given to us, and we by his grace have indeed accepted from Him?

Illustration of "I will take."

A few years ago a meeting was being held, in a small chapel lent for the purpose, for the leading on of those who had already believed in our Lord Jesus Christ for pardon and for deliverance from the overcoming power of sin, into that further blessedness in Him, which we are specially considering in this book, the entire deliverance from its existence in the heart.

The sister conducting the meeting.

It was being conducted by a sister in the Lord ("Your sons and your *daughters* shall prophesy," Joel ii. 28; Acts ii. 17; "The Lord giveth the word: the WOMEN *that publish the tidings* are a great host," Ps. lxviii. 11, revised version), who had come to Christ as a girl, and had then for about eight years lived a life of happy, faithful service to Him, with constant preservation by Him from any manifestation of sin outwardly in her life: at the end of which time He led her to see that there was the perfect *inward* deliverance also for her; the attainment of which then became the supreme purpose of her life, and continued to be so for about two years; but without her ever seeming to get any nearer the object of her so earnest desires.

But she then saw, with wonder that she had not done so before, that this heart deliverance from all sin was just as much God's free gift to her in Christ as that pardon of her sins and deliverance from their outward power in which she had been rejoicing for now about ten years, and was so to be accepted by her without waiting for anything whatever in herself, any inward "witness of the Spirit," or happy feeling of any sort, or anything else. And she accordingly did so accept it as God's free gift to her in Christ, with the resolution by God's grace to hold on to this acceptance of it in Him; however long, even though to her dying day, she might have to wait for any "sign" from Him in the way of bright feelings, or inward sense of being cleansed, or anything else in herself.

Blessed with the knowledge of full salvation.

This was faith in the bare Word of God, and accordingly, before a week had gone by, He honoured it by saying indeed "unto" her "soul" "I am thy salvation" (Ps. xxxv. 3)—salvation in the full sense, salvation from all inward as well as from all outward sin—and filling her heart with glory ("Surely his *salvation* is nigh them that fear him; that GLORY may dwell in our land" Ps. lxxxv. 9).

She had always, as above said, been walking carefully in the fear and love of God since her conversion: but now that He had blessed her with this inward cleansing, and the happy sense of it, she felt more than ever the power of that word, "See then that ye walk circumspectly, not as fools, but as wise" (Eph. v. 15); and so went on her way with a holy, happy "fear and trembling" (Phil. ii. 12), lest she should, through inadvertence or unwatchfulness, allow evil to come in again to the sullying, to the dishonour of God and to her own deep loss, the blessed work which He had now in and through Christ by the power of the Spirit wrought in her.

" Go work to-day in my vineyard."

Presently afterwards our heavenly Father began to teach her that He does not give his good gifts to his children merely for their enjoyment, but always with a view to their being used in his service: that with each increase of the blessedness of our sonship to Him it is still, " Son, *go work* to-day in my vineyard" (Matt. xxi. 28): that " the manifestation of the Spirit is given to every man *to profit withal*" (1 Cor. xii. 7): that the " talents" which He entrusts to us must be " traded with," that at his " coming " He may receive his own " *with usury* " (Matt. xxv. 15, 16, 27). He began to make her know in her heart that it was his will that she should be *separated* " for the work " (Acts xiii. 2), of spreading in the world the knowledge of the full blessedness of salvation in Christ which she was now herself experiencing.

" Endure hardness."

There were circumstances in her case which made this a specially hard call for flesh and blood to obey. All her nature shrank from the thought of coming out in any way in public: and she knew that all her dear relatives—not indeed her father and mother, for they had both gone to be with the Lord, but all that remained to her—would be horrified at the idea of her entering on such a course as she felt our heavenly Father to be now opening out before her.

But still He pressed it upon her mind till she became quite certain that it was his will for her, so that she dared not hesitate any longer; though when she came to a positive decision about it, and felt that it was not only a *first* coming out from all, nor even a coming out *for a while*, but that it was *for all her life*, she being in her own room at the time alone with Him, screamed aloud under the wrench which it was to her flesh—though in the spirit she did not flinch from it (Matt. xxvi. 41)—to yield herself entirely up to this work all her remaining time on earth.

Diligent obedience.

But the decision once made, God has by his grace enabled her to adhere faithfully to it during the seventeen years or thereabouts which have since elapsed. She worked with much power and blessing for many years in America, where she received this special call from God; then for two or three years in various parts of England; and she has now been working between one and two years in Australia, with the prospect of not improbably going on thence to India.

In the series of meetings, in the course of which that one which I began to speak of in the beginning of this section occurred, God gave great power with the Word which He gave her to speak; and many obeyed her call to them in his name to come up to the "penitent form" or "prayer bench" in acknowledgment before all of their felt need of full inward deliverance: and a large proportion of those who did so were then and there blessed with a sense of the "supply" of all their "need according to his riches in glory by Christ Jesus" (Phil. iv. 19).

A stranger in the meeting.

On the evening in question a man with plenty of intellect in his face, after listening to her address, came up to the "penitent form," and after kneeling there for a time in prayer, returned to his seat.

A little later in the meeting the speaker called upon those who could declare that God had given them the desires of their hearts (Ps. xxxvii. 4) in entire deliverance from inward sin, and the witness of the Spirit (Rom. viii. 16; 1 John v. 10) that He had done so, to stand up and give their testimony to this to his glory, and for the encouragement of others to seek and find the same blessing.

Several obeyed this invitation, and stood up and gave lively testimony to the blessing with which God had visited them (Ps. cvi. 4); thus following the example of that one of old who said: "Come and hear, all ye that fear God, and I will declare what he hath done for my soul" (Ps. lxvi. 16); and fulfilling that other word, "with the heart man believeth unto righteousness; and *with the mouth confession is made unto salvation*" (Rom. x. 10).

His statement.

The stranger I am speaking of listened attentively to these testimonies, and then stood up and spoke to the following effect, though I cannot give *every word* exactly:—

"I have listened to what you have all been saying as to the blessing which God has given to you; which, as I understand it, is *union with Himself.* But if He had given to me what you believe He has given to you, I should speak very different words about it from such as you have been speaking. They would be *words of fire.*

"I could show you in my desk the consecration of myself and all that I am and all that I have—time, **money, talents, wife, children, and all else**— absolutely and entirely to God many years ago: and from that I have never gone back or wished to go back a hair's breadth. And three years ago I got sight of this blessing which you are speaking of; and since then the attainment to it has been the one absorbing object of my life. I have been crying to God about it with all depth of earnestness; and reading all I could lay my hands upon at all likely to help me in my search for it; and going to all the meetings I can get to likely to be helpful to me, just as I have now come to this one to-night. And I do not seem to get an inch nearer to it. Indeed I seem to myself farther from any hope of attaining to it now than I was when I started on the search for it those three years ago.

"And, almost worst of all, the converting power which God used to be pleased to exert through me in my work as a missionary seems to be passing away from me.

"And how to account for all, or for any, of this I have not the slightest idea; nor what to do now to bring about anything better than this present deplorable state of things. And, though I have felt obliged to speak as I have done, I feel that not one of you will in the least understand my case or what I am speaking about."

The cause of his failure shown to him.

One in the meeting said to him, "Brother, I understand you perfectly all the way through; for I have been over much of the same ground." And the sister in charge of the meeting pointed out to him where his failure was. She showed him that while his consecration of himself had been perfect, his perception that God had the blessing to give also perfect, and his desire for and prayer for it intensely earnest, there was wanting one all-important link in the chain of blessing, without which that which he so earnestly desired never could become his as a matter of fact, namely, *faith that God really gave it to him so that he had nothing to do but thankfully to accept it.*

But the time had now come when the chapel must be closed; and the brother who had said to him that he understood his case asked him whether it mattered what time he got home; to which he answered No; that his work sometimes kept him out till eleven or twelve o'clock, or even later, so that no one at home would be alarmed by his staying out; on which the brother said, "Then come along to my home, and let us look to God, and by his grace get the matter settled to-night."

They accordingly went off, together with the brother's wife and the sister who had been conducting the meeting, and who was staying with them.

On reaching the house, not many minutes' walk from the chapel, and going into a room with something on the table for supper, the brother said to him, "Come and take what you want of this, and then we will get into the other room with our Bibles, for whatever time may be necessary for your seeing the gift of God and believing, and being set at liberty."

Set at liberty.

But before they had been many minutes at the supper-table, God blessed a few words spoken to him by the sister who had been conducting the meeting, in the same sense as the few she had spoken to him in the chapel, to the solving of all the terrible difficulty under which he had been struggling these three years, " nothing bettered but rather " growing " worse " (Mark v. 26), and the setting his soul at liberty ; not in the way of any bright joyfulness indeed, but of real peace.

By accepting God's free gift.

He accepted all that he had been struggling for so long and so hard and so vainly, as God's free gift to him in Christ: for he saw now that it was declared in his Word to be all included in the blessedness which He has given us in Him (1 Cor. i. 30; Eph. i. 3; Col. ii. 10; &c.). And he determined—as the sister in the corresponding stage in her spiritual course had determined before him— that whatever time God might see fit to let him remain without any sensible manifestations in the way of bright emotions or otherwise, as a witness that He had indeed put him in possession of the blessing, he would by his grace hold on to his faith that He had given it because He says so, and to the fact that, he having accepted it, and always continuing to confirm his acceptance of it, it now undoubtedly, whatever might appear to the contrary, was his.

Our seal to God's truth.

Dear Archbishop Usher, in one of his grand sermons on "Our redemption by Christ," on the text " After that ye believed, *ye were sealed* with that holy Spirit of promise " (Eph. i. 13) says upon our first accepting God's gift by faith on his bare word, and *then* God coming in with his seal to the fact of our indeed *having* the " good things " (Matt.

vii. 11), "freely given to us" (1 Cor. ii. 12) by Him:—

"Now we come to speak one word of the sealing in the text. This sealing, which is a point of *feeling*, is a distinct thing of itself from faith, no part of faith. If I have faith I am sure of life, though I never have the other. There are two seals. We put to our seal to the counterpart that is drawn between God and us. The first seal is our faith.

"I have nothing but God's Word, and indeed, I have no feeling: yet, I venture my salvation, and trust God upon his bare Word. I will pawn all upon it. 'He that believeth hath set to his seal,' saith John, 'that God is true.' If men doubt, and trust God no farther than they see Him, it is not faith. But when God gives me a good word, though I am in as much distress as ever, yet I trust: though it be contrary to all sense or outward seeming, yet I put to my seal and trust Him still.

God's seal to our faith.

"Then comes God's counterpart. God being thus honoured that I believe his Word, though contrary to all sense and feeling, even his bare Word, then sets to *his* seal. And now the Word comes to *particularising*. Before, it was general: now, it comes and singles out a man; 'Say unto my soul, I am thy salvation' (Ps. xxxv. 3). That is, as I did apply the generality of God's Word unto mine own case, to bear me up against sense and feeling, then comes the Spirit of God, and not only delivers generalities, but *saith unto my soul*, I am thy salvation.

He manifests Himself to us.

"This is called in Scripture, a *manifestation*, when God manifests Himself unto us, as in Isaiah lx. 16), 'Thou shalt *know* that I the Lord am thy Saviour and thy Redeemer.' That is when we have made particular application by faith, God will put to his seal, that I shall *know* that God is my strength and my salvation. I shall *know* it. 'He that loveth me shall be loved of my Father, and I will love him, and *will manifest myself* to him' (John xiv. 21). Christ comes and draws the curtains, and looks on with the gracious aspect of his blessed countenance. When this comes, it cheers the heart; and then there are secret love tokens pass between Christ and his beloved.

As not to the world.

"'To him that overcometh will I give to eat of the hidden manna, and will give him a white stone, and in the stone *a new name written, which no man knoweth saving he that receiveth it*' (Rev. ii. 17). That is, there is a particular intimation that I shall know of myself more than any other, more than all the world besides. It is such a joy as the stranger is not made partaker of; such joy as is glorious and unspeakable; such peace as passeth all understanding. One minute of such joy overcomes all the joy in the world besides.

"Now consider; sure there is such a thing as this joy; or else do you think the Scripture would talk of it, and of the Comforter, the Holy Ghost, by whom we know the things that are freely given to us of God. There is a generation in the world that hath this joy; though you that know it not, do not, nor cannot believe it. There is a righteous generation that have it; and why dost thou not try to get it? Do as they do, and thou mayest obtain it likewise."

The two seals in the present case.

Our brother had at the supper table that night, advanced as far as the first part of what Archbishop Usher here speaks of. He had by believing God's bare word, "set to his seal that God is true."

And God soon came in to do his part of setting to his seal to our brother's faith. For when, a fortnight afterwards, he came into a little meeting which was being held in that same room in which he had thus trusted in God, he appeared to be lifted up almost as into the third heaven in blessedness, in the change in his experience, through that simple full acceptance of Christ as God's way of satisfying all the desires of his heart (Ps. ciii. 5; xxxvii. 4; lxiii. 5).

And though he has more than once since then had to pass through a very different state of soul from any of this lively joy, and to walk by bare faith without any feeling, or with the feeling all the other way; yet I believe that by God's grace shown through the sustaining power of our dear Lord (2 Cor. xii. 9) exerted in him by the blessed Spirit, he has never wavered in his faith in God as to what He did for him that night in giving him, through faith in Christ for it, that which he had been so long seeking with such intense earnestness, the entire deliverance from all sin, inward as well as outward.

I think he dates from that night a second as entire change in his spiritual experience as that first change which took place in him at his conversion many years before.

Bearing of his case on this book.

I have introduced this dear brother's case as an illustration of the matter treated of in the section headed " I will take," and of the way of overcoming intellectual difficulty to the reception of the fulness of blessing, by hard bare faith in the simple Word of God without waiting for any feelings. But it is more than this with reference to this book. For it is to the transaction which took place between God and the soul of our brother that night that the book owes its existence. For he is the missionary whose dismissal from the London City Mission—" apparently as the result of his having recently adopted higher views than he formerly held of the extent of deliverance from sin offered to us in the Gospel of our Lord Jesus Christ "—led to my Letter to the Rev. Robert Dawson, secretary of the Mission, to which these " Scriptural Proofs " are, as already incidentally mentioned, a sequel.

"Searched the Scriptures daily."

The following is from a dear brother in the Lord known to me for very many years. He is one through whom the Lord has been pleased to exert his converting power, wherever He has sent him in his work, during now more than a quarter of a century.

" My dear brother in Christ,—I rejoice greatly in the book you sent, and that God has been pleased to help you so marvellously in the writing of it. It is full of very deep Christian experience and instruction, and well calculated to stimulate an earnest desire in the hearts of the Lord's people to search the Scriptures more diligently and prayerfully, like the Bereans, ' daily, whether those things were so.' I want to read it again and again; so as to mark, learn, and inwardly digest it. Believe me, very dear brother, yours lovingly in Jesus, ———."

Some carefully testing this book by the Bible.

I have introduced this extract chiefly for that reference to *searching the Scriptures.* I am thankful to say that God has blessed those "First Sheets" to many dear souls in the way of leading them to much more thorough study of his Word than ever before, *with reference to the extent of deliverance from sin given to us by Him in our Lord Jesus Christ.* I have heard of case upon case of dear children of God going through them carefully with the Bible, and turning to *every passage* quoted in them, to study it along with its context with reference to this question.

And, as yet, I have not had from any one of such readers any expression of doubt as to whether the passages quoted are rightly brought forward in proof of God's gift to us of full deliverance from sin, inward as well as outward.

Word of strong approval.

One of the strongest words of approval which I have received of the book was from a dear brother in the Lord, an earnest student of his Word, and a diligent and successful worker in his vineyard, to whom I was giving a delightful book of Christian instruction, and to secure his interest in it, read to him a beautiful passage which I had read many times by myself with much benefit; and then I asked him, "Is not that lovely?"

"Yes," he said, "but I like your book much better, because it is all '*Thus saith the Lord*,' and that is all I care about."

And I do most gladly accept that praise for the book; and I know of no higher that I could wish it to receive.

Germ of obedience in saving faith.

The following is from a dear brother in the Lord whom I have never met, but whom I know well by repute as one who works hard to lead children of God to such a *consideration of the grounds of their faith* as may cause them to "be ready always to give an answer to every man that asketh a reason of the hope that is in" them (1 Pet. iii. 15), and may bring them to oneness of thought and feeling on matters of faith on which, for want, as he conceives, of such careful and systematic consideration, they now differ from each other.

I am glad that, reading the Bible with such critical care as our brother must have read it with, in regard to all God's statements in it with reference to the salvation given by Him to us in Christ, he should have been led so decidedly to the view of its including entire deliverance from all sin.

"Thanks for your little book. I am perfectly at one with you in your contention that 'God gives us, in our Lord Jesus Christ, perfect deliverance from *all* sin.' One of the principal hindrances to the general reception of this truth, is the confusion which exists as to the subjective conditions of the sinner's acceptance with God. The essential element of 'perfect surrender to all the known will of God' is obscured."

Our brother goes on to show that this *obscuration* is occasioned by such preaching of the doctrine of "justification by faith *only*," as "denies the need of the spirit of obedience, even in germ, as necessary to *justification, that is to forgiveness, that is to acceptance with God.*"

This earnest advocacy by him, of the inseparable connection of "the spirit of obedience" with saving faith, would seem to be in exact accordance with all the teaching of the Word of God.

"Lord, *what wilt thou have me to do?*" was the first cry of faith from the lips of even the great champion of justification by faith (Acts ix. 6).

Loss of the joy of pardon.

The following is from a dear sister in the Lord, previously unknown to me:—

"Dear Sir,—I shall be very grateful if you will send me a copy of your 'Scriptural Proofs.'

"Nearly eleven years ago, while telling the way of salvation to some young people, I was myself convinced of sin; and for some days I felt an insupportable load on my conscience. But quite suddenly Isaiah xliii. 25 ('*I, even I, am he that blotteth out thy transgressions for mine own sake, and will not remember thy sins,*') came before me; and the relief I experienced I could not describe.

"But mixing with the world, &c., &c., I lost the *peace* and *assurance* which gave me such unspeakable comfort. This I have never regained.

"Praying your 'Scriptural Proofs' may be blessed to my soul, I remain, yours truly, ———."

No safety but in pressing on.

This letter follows only too well upon our brother's letter in the last section. For it is just one of the sad number of painful illustrations to be met with everywhere of the terrible evil of that view of the Gospel which makes the mere sense of pardon almost its sum and substance; and so causes the convert to be satisfied when that is obtained, instead of pressing on (2 Pet. i. 5–11; Hos. vi. 3; Phil. iii. 13) to the cleansing from all our filthiness and all our idols, which we are considering in this book, and to the obtaining of a new heart and a new spirit, and the receiving of God's Spirit to dwell in us, and cause us to walk in his statutes and keep his judgments and do them (Ezek. xxxvi. 25–27).

A dear minister, when he had believed in Christ for entire sanctification, and had begun to preach it with power and success as God's "gift" (John iv. 10) to us in Christ, and his appointed way of keeping converts faithful to Himself, on then looking back upon years of hard work for the bringing of souls under conviction of sin and into the enjoyment of pardon, had to give the following sad account of the result of such work, even when for the time apparently successful, if not used as a means of entrance into this "more excellent way" (1 Cor. xii. 31).

"I was grieved from year to year, by seeing

what might astonish hell, and fill heaven with lamentation—company after company of young converts *walking into partially backslidden unsanctified churches, first to wonder, then for a while to be grieved, but finally to add another layer to the backslidden stratification* ("Perfect Love," by Rev. J. A. Wood, 29th Edition, p. 318).

"Longing for more light."

The following is also from a dear sister in the Lord, previously unknown to me:—

"Dear Sir,—I should much like a copy of your book, 'Scriptural Proofs.' I have taken great delight in your book, 'Life of Cornelius Cayley,' which was given to me some years ago.

"I am seeking for and longing for more light; and to be raised to a higher platform, as it were, in spiritual life. It may be that your little book may be a help to me in these aspirations."

Hindrances.

Our sister wrote in a later letter:—

"I plainly see the heights and depths of blessedness which are to be obtained, and *are* obtained by some—but, alas! 'what various hindrances we meet' in pressing forward. The things of time and sense, the things that are *seen*, pull you back when your spirit would fain soar—not the least, the cares and anxieties consequent on a large family."

Our sister here rightly expresses a great difficulty. Our Lord named "*the cares of this world*" among the things which "entering in, *choke the word*, and it becometh unfruitful" (Mark iv. 19).

Remedy for this evil.

But is not the remedy for this, our entire acceptance of Him as having given Himself " for our sins, *that he might deliver us from this present evil world, according to the will of God and our Father*" (Gal. i. 4); that the earthliness of our human attachments may be gone, that so we may love all related to us, more dearly indeed than ever before, but now only in God and for God, so that they may all become helps to us instead of hindrances in our heavenly life?

"God is my witness," said one who had not the spiritual advantages that we have, a dear Roman Catholic friend of Madame Guion, as she was bidding her good-bye on her death-bed—"God is my witness, that I have loved you only *in Him*, and *for Him*."

And dear Archbishop Leighton, when one, observing his heavenly life, said to him, "Ah! if you had a wife and family, you would not live such a life!" answered, "I cannot tell what *would* be, but I know what *should* be—*Enoch walked with God, and begat sons and daughters*" (Gen. v. 22).

"*An honest and good heart.*"

Oh! it is the full acceptance of Christ for entire "sanctification" (1 Cor. i. 30), which does away with the difficulty of living a sanctified life, in the midst of any possible attachments and surroundings. What is the "honest and good heart" of which He spoke (Luke viii. 15), as the ground in which the seed, *unchoked by thorns*, grew, and brought forth fruit, but a heart out of which He has Himself turned the devil and all his works (Luke xi. 22; 1 John iii. 8)?

" My great Redeemer's throne,
  Where none but Christ is heard to speak,
  Where Jesus reigns alone."

Doctors administering poison.

The following is from a dear sister in the Lord, previously unknown to me, working for Him among the poor patients in a provincial hospital.

" Thank you much for the copy of 'Scriptural Proofs' you kindly sent me. I like it much because *it is* scriptural, and feel sure it will be useful to many.

" Should you have any copies to spare for free distribution, I should be most glad to receive them at any time, as I have many opportunities for distributing amongst our poorer brothers and sisters in Christ.

" Only yesterday a young girl patient trusted for the blessing of entire sanctification; also another young convert who is a member of my Bible class for mill girls and others.

" Sometimes I fear in the case of such that there is cause to fear backsliding, owing to the teaching heard from too many of our pulpits, &c.: and a little manual such as yours is likely to be helpful. At the same time *I believe in the Holy Ghost* with all my heart, and in his power to keep that which is committed to Him.

"Believe me, yours in the kingdom of Jesus Christ, ———."

Teaching young converts to expect to sin.

That which our sister says here about danger to young converts " owing to the teaching heard from too many of our pulpits, &c.," is most terribly true.

Sinning and repenting.

Here is part of the report, given—evidently with hearty approval—in a Christian paper of high character and certainly considered in the churches thoroughly orthodox, of an " Address to young converts," by a dear brother in Christ, a highly respected minister, a speaker at the Mildmay Park Conferences:—

" Now the first thing I should like to say is, *Christian life means going on as you have begun*" (the italics are our brother's own). " How did you become Christians? By repenting of your sins, and putting your trust in the blessed Son of God. These are just the exercises you must continue. Continually as often as you sin, and that is daily and hourly, and as long as you sin, and that is while you are in the body—for in this life you will never be wholly free from sin and temptation" (surely, a strange thing that our brother should thus class temptation and sin together, as if being subject to temptation like our dear Lord Himself, who, having " suffered being tempted," " is able to succour them that are tempted" Heb. ii. 18, necessarily means falling into sin)—" continually, therefore, you have to keep on repenting of sins and confessing your sins."

And yet our brother goes on, in very sweet and earnest and truly scriptural exhortation, to enforce upon the young converts watchful and continual obedience to our dear Lord's words, "Abide in me;" calling the chapters in which He most enjoins this upon us, namely, the thirteenth to the seventeenth of St. John's Gospel, "*the vade mecum of Christian life.*"

A difficult question.

How he can reconcile his teaching them that they must sin "daily and hourly" "as long as" they "are in the body," with this entreaty to them to *abide in Christ,* taken along with those words of St. John, "WHOSOEVER ABIDETH IN HIM SINNETH NOT" (1 John iii. 6); I must leave to himself to say.

And so, also, I must leave to him the reconciling his instruction to them, that as their course up to their conversion was one of sinning, and their conversion itself a repenting of and confessing their sin, and being pardoned for it, all their Christian life afterwards must be a course of sinning and repenting, and being pardoned, with that word of our Lord, "Go and *sin no more*" (John viii. 11; v. 14), and with that of St. John, "These things write I unto you, *that ye sin not*" (1 John ii. 1); and with that in the epistle to the Hebrews, "Therefore *leaving the principles of the doctrine of Christ, let us go on unto perfection; not laying again the foundation of repentance from dead works*" (Heb. vi. 1).

Meetings for deepening the Christian life.

In "a series of meetings"—to quote from the report in "The Christian,"—"with the expressed object of promoting 'the deepening of Christian life,'" an "object" which that paper further says, "was amply attained as far at least as human calculation can go," one of the most frequent and prominent speakers, who also, like our brother referred to above, is a much respected minister and a speaker at Mildmay, and besides this, a prolific and acceptable writer of books having the same object as that series of meetings, in "an address of solemn and searching power," to continue the quotations from "The Christian" "on CEASING FROM SIN," set himself elaborately to prove that this could not possibly mean *ceasing to have sin in us.*

"It cannot mean," he said, "ceasing from the law of sin which is in our members. It cannot mean ceasing from the nature that has got sin in it as flint has fire." And then he goes on to show that if it did mean this, "it would not be a gospel according to Peter," or "a gospel according to John," or "a gospel according to James," or "according to Paul," as they all repudiate, as he thinks, in passages which he quotes from them, any *such* "ceasing from sin."

Blessedness of even a half Gospel.

But he shows that, notwithstanding this, the Gospel is an exceedingly blessed one. He says:—

"It would be a great thing for society if the miser could cease to love his gold, and the spendthrift cease to be such a fool; that the hot-tempered man should become calm, and the cold-hearted man should become tender, and gentle, and full of sympathy. It would be a glad day to the home, a glad day to the heart of the man himself, when such a change as that should come.

"Such a change may come. We may not only cease from the 'sin that doth so easily beset us,' but we may also 'lay aside every weight,' not only that one fatal sin, but the other sins, the buzzing swarm of sins that torture, and torment, and sting, and poison our life. These, too, may be dealt with and got rid of by the grace of God. The Lord Jesus Christ is near enough, and condescending enough, to come down to the least as well as to the greatest. Over them, too, God giveth us the victory through our Lord Jesus Christ. The nature left, but the brood slain as soon as they are hatched: the sin left, but the sins met and captured, and conquered, the moment they arise, by the grace that is all-sufficient."

"*Make the tree good.*"

"*The nature left, but the brood slain as soon as they are hatched: the sin left, but the sins met and captured, and conquered, the moment they arise, by the grace that is all-sufficient.*" This is, certainly, a far more blessed gospel than that preached by our other dear brother above to those poor young converts, that they must sin daily and hourly as long as they are in the flesh; that the whole of their Christian course is to be a constant sinning and repenting. But still, as I had to leave it to him to reconcile his teaching with the multitude of passages to the direct contrary in the Word of God, of which I quoted a few as specimens, so I must leave to this other dear brother to reconcile his milder teaching in the same direction, his "*nature left*" and only "the brood slain," "*the sin left*" and only "the sins met and captured and conquered," with the great number of passages which we have been considering in this book, showing salvation to be offered to us from "the nature" itself, and not merely from "the brood;" from "the sin" itself, and not merely from "the sins;" and most especially with that Word of our dear Lord, so often quoted above:—

"*Either make the tree good and his fruit good, or else make the tree corrupt and his fruit corrupt*" (Matt. xii. 33).

"*If they drink any deadly thing.*"

Surely, all such teaching—whether that of the first dear brother, that we are doomed as long as we are in the body to be continually sinning, or that of the other, that we must have sin continually brooding in us—is deadly poison to dear young converts just beginning to exercise perhaps a weak trembling faith in our dear Lord, as being indeed their Redeemer "from all iniquity" (Titus ii. 14), their Preserver "from all evil" (Ps. cxxi. 7), their "keeper" "every moment" "night and day" (Isa. xxvii. 3).

But the hope of prevention of mischief to them by it lies, as our dear sister truly says in her letter above, in the power of the Holy Ghost, by whom we may trust, that as regards *this* "deadly thing," they being now believers in our Lord in the full sense—not merely for pardon for the guilt, but also for deliverance from the existence of sin in them— that word of his may be fulfilled in their case, "*If they drink any deadly thing, it shall not hurt them*" (Mark xvi. 18).

May our loving God grant that the effect upon them of all such teaching may be to stir up their hearts to increased thankfulness to Him for the better thing" (Heb. xi. 40) which He has showed them, and to sorrow for the preacher and for the probable mischievous effects of his preaching upon less established ones than themselves, and to prayer for him that he may, like Apollos of old, "an eloquent man, and mighty in the scriptures," and "fervent in the spirit," be brought within reach of some Aquila and Priscilla, by whom to have "the way of God" "more perfectly" "expounded unto him" (Acts xviii. 24–26).

Definite testimony again.

The following little word from a dear brother in the Lord, previously unknown to me, I introduce as another little bit of definite testimony—the value of which was noticed above—to the fact of entire cleansing:—

"Dear brother in Christ,—Having long enjoyed the priceless blessing of purity, and ever feeling deep interest in all literature bearing *directly* on the subject of holiness, I should be glad to receive 'First Sheets of Scriptural Proofs' for my own profit and edification, and more effectually to help dissatisfied believers upwards to a higher plane of Christian experience. Yours fully trusting, ——."

A little bit more.

And the following from a sister in the Lord, previously unknown to me, is also in the same tone of definite testimony:—

"Dear Sir,—Would you receive my best thanks for the copy of your little book which I received some little time since. I should be much obliged if you would kindly send me two more copies. The copy you sent has been sent to India, and I am wishing to send another to China.

"'Where the word of a king is, there is power' (Eccl. viii. 4), and the Lord must abundantly bless your little work. May very many through it step out into the glorious liberty of the children of God, and 'stand fast in the liberty wherewith Christ *hath* made us free.'

"Let us take our stand where God puts us. If God says 'Ye are dead' (Col. iii. 3), let us reply, 'Yes, Lord, we are dead.'

"And 'He that is dead is freed from sin' (Rom. vi. 7).

"Yours faithfully in Christ our *Life*, ——.

"'*Hath* delivered us from the power of darkness, and hath *translated* us into the kingdom of his dear Son' (Col. i. 13)."

And another little bit.

The following sweet little bit of testimony from another sister in the Lord, previously unknown to me, to the perfect keeping power of our dear Lord experienced during five years, has come in just while I am writing this part of the book:—

"Will you please send me 'Scriptural Proofs.' Can you recommend any tracts for distributing?

"I am trusting to the Lord to save me from *all* sin. For five years I have enjoyed perfect peace, and I am longing for others to enjoy this sweet rest and peace in Jesus, ——."

Very definite.

And the following from a dear brother in the Lord is very particularly definite; a good deal too much so, I fear, for some readers. If this should be the case, I must beg them to bear with it for the sake of others, among whom I must include myself, who can receive it, and feel blessed and strengthened in reading it; "comforted together with" our brother "by the mutual faith both of" him and us (Rom. i. 12).

"1 John iii. 2–3, 'Beloved, now are we the sons of God, and it doth not yet appear what we shall be: but we know that, when he shall appear, we shall be like him; for we shall see him as he is. And every man that hath this hope in him purifieth himself, even as he is pure.' My dear brother, — I beg to state that I am one of the Lord's saints, and kept by the power of God from *all* sin. The Lord will not have his blood-washed saints polluted with sin and iniquity; but will have them pure as He is pure. If the saint is not *pure* and *holy* he would not be ready to meet the Lord, should He come suddenly to take the waiting saints home to glory.

"Oh it is most blessed to live in sweet communion with the Lord, to enjoy his fellowship, to abide in Him, and He abiding in us. It is utterly impossible for Christ to dwell in us, and sin at the same time. We cannot have Christ in one hand and the devil in the other. 'Blessed are the pure in heart: for they shall see God' (Matt. v. 8).

"I am living by faith, dear brother, and look to God for all. I am yours in Jesus, ———."

"A little child" (Matt. xviii. 2).

I insert the following letter from a dear sister in the Lord, previously unknown to me, because of the sweet child-like spirit which it breathes, the spirit in which our dear Lord has told us that we need to be for entrance into the kingdom of heaven (Matt. xviii. 3):—

"Dear Friend,—Thank you so much for your little book. I am not in a position to criticise it: but I can say it is a large amount of clear and useful instruction in a concise form. It has helped me to realise more fully the glorious Gospel of Christ, looking at it as you do in all its *glorious simplicity*. Believe me, yours in earnest Christian sympathy, ———."

Limiting God's power to save.

The following is from a dear brother in the Lord, previously unknown to me. After mentioning that he had had some papers on entire sanctification before, and had "lent those said papers to friends who have long known Jesus," he continues:—

"But they repudiate the idea of being freed from sin, while they remain here, quoting the words of St. Paul, 'The good that I would I do not.' But, sir, your explanation of that has so fully convinced me, that I shall lend it to these friends and entreat them to strictly examine it, and shall also bear their indignation if they still pursue me, for I did not always see things thus, yet have read the Scriptures from my youth up.

"Much of the teaching and preaching has fallen short of pointing to a higher life. Blessed be the Lord, his will is better known now. So, dear sir, continue your work. Sow beside all waters. Do not mind obstacles. Life is hard sometimes, but brief.

"Blessed be the Lord Jesus for such a bond of such fellowship, ———."

"*They repudiate the idea of being saved from sin while they remain here.*"—Is not this just a repetition of, "*They believed not in God, and trusted not in his salvation*" (Ps. lxxviii. 22)?

I have heard a dear minister express his great astonishment that dear children of God, who *would not hesitate to die for their faith in the Lord Jesus Christ as the* "MIGHTY GOD"(Isa. ix. 6 ; John i. 1), yet cannot believe that He has power to "*save his people from their sins*" in the sense of destroying all "the works of the devil" (1 John iii. 8) *in* them.

And I have read another bit by another dear minister—in "The King's Highway," I think, but am not quite sure—I wish I could remember, that I might refer to it exactly and give his name, but I cannot—but it was exactly to this effect:—

"The Father expects Christians to be holy. The Lord Jesus Christ expects Christians to be holy. The blessed Spirit expects Christians to be holy. The holy angels expect Christians to be holy. The world expects Christians to be holy. The devils expect Christians to be holy. *The only intelligent being in the universe who does not expect Christians to be holy is the unbelieving believer.*"

Seeing full salvation.

I do not know that I have much excuse for inserting the following letter from a dear sister in the Lord previously unknown to me, except the pleasure it has been to me to receive it. But I hope there will be one good effect of the insertion of letters which, like this, speak of dear brothers and sisters in Jesus longing for more and more of the heavenly life, that some of the children of God who read them here will *remember all such dear ones in prayer.*

"Dear Sir.—Will you kindly send another copy of 'Scriptural Proofs.' We have read it with much profit, and as there are a few friends in —— who, like ourselves (my sister and myself), are just beginning to understand what is the meaning of a full salvation, we are desirous to circulate your little book, feeling sure it is the very thing. We believe much blessing and much light will be the result of a careful perusal. May the Lord bless you. Yours in a risen Saviour, ——."

Even Methodists objecting.

The following is from a dear brother in the Lord previously unknown to me:—

"Dear Sir,—I am quite convinced that the Scriptures do teach full deliverance from all sin. But I find the doctrine opposed by professing Christians even of my own Church—Wesleyan Methodist. I suppose it always will be so. The Lord fill us with love to prove the truth of it. Yours in Christ, ——."

And off-shoots from them.

It is a correct statement that our brother here makes, that many even among Wesleyans—and the same is true also of many belonging to other sections of the Christian Church, off-shoots of Wesleyanism, such as " Primitive Methodists," " Bible Christians," &c.—ignore, or even oppose, the doctrine of entire present deliverance from all sin, inward as well as outward.

Yet surely this is enough almost to startle, so to speak, good old John Wesley out of his grave, if he could be made acquainted with it.

For all these bodies profess to hold, and to teach, all the Gospel which he held and taught. And yet there is not anything in its declarations of what God in his goodness has provided for us, to which he attached more value, next after the free full forgiveness of our sins, and the gift of the Holy Spirit to witness with our spirits that we are the children of God, than to this doctrine of entire present sanctification.

He believed, and loudly and persistently proclaimed his belief, that it was the peculiar " *depositum* " (his own word), put in trust by God with the Methodists for the spread of it in the world, and that they would as a body flourish or fade according to their faithfulness or the want of it to this trust.

" *All the days of Joshua.*"

But it is a true saying that " All the days of Joshua, and all the days of the elders that overlived Joshua " (Josh. xxiv. 31), seems about the limit of full vitality in any human movement in the things of God. Moses had to say to "all Israel," including "all the elders" and "officers," "I know that *after my death* ye will utterly corrupt yourselves, and *turn aside from the way which I have commanded you*": (Deut. xxxi. 1, 28, 29); and St. Paul had to say in his last solemn charge to "the elders" of one of the brightest of the churches founded by him, and one to which he seems to have given more personal supervision than to any other (Acts xx. 31), "I know this, that *after my departing*" "*of your own selves* shall men arise, speaking perverse things, to draw away disciples after them" (Acts xx. 17, 29, 30).

And of John Wesley.

And so, as regards the Wesleyan church—speaking generally, though with blessed exceptions, such, for instance, as William Bramwell, John Smith, David Stoner and others here and there of similar type, for every one of whom God be praised—within but a little while after John Wesley and the last of his fellow-labourers had departed "to be with Christ" (Phil. i. 23), the influential ones in the body seem to have so fallen away from his teaching, that entire present sanctification appears almost to have died out from among them as a *practical reality*! though it may have left its ghost behind it to reappear from time to time in the shape of a lifeless orthodox sermon upon the mere doctrine; and though the reality may happily have continued to exist among individual private members of the body not influential enough to make their voices heard in protest against this falling away of their rulers from the faith of their fathers.

I.   X

Sanctification and Aggressive Power.

And with the departure of entire sanctification, as a reality in heart and life, from among the rulers of the body, there appears to have departed also, to a sad extent, in fulfilment of John Wesley's prophecy, that energy of spiritual life which made the Wesleyans in their early days such a power in God's hand for awakening and evangelising the world.

They gave up in general their aggressive open-air work, and settled down in comfortable chapels, with intellectually trained, human-appointed, instead of Holy Ghost trained, Christ-appointed ministers, and encouraged themselves by reckoning by thousands or tens of thousands, as more recently by hundreds of thousands, the members of their classes, or of their congregations, with little, in a great proportion of them, beyond a mere hope that they were pardoned and going to heaven, and, in the case of many among them, not even so much as that, and, naturally enough, under such circumstances, with little thought as to where the rest of the world were going.

"*Primitives*" and others raised up.

But if through supineness (Prov. xiii. 4) and unbelief (Heb. iii. 19) we will not let God bring us into and keep us in a state of spiritual blessedness, in which He can use us in his work (2 Tim. ii. 21), yet He will not, for want of us, let the work go undone (Luke iii. 8; xix. 40); and so He raised up the "Primitive Methodists," "Bible Christians," and others to continue the attack upon the kingdom of darkness from which those to whom He had first entrusted the conduct of it had—like "the children

EVEN METHODISTS OBJECTING. 307

of Ephraim," who " being armed, and carrying bows, turned back in the day of battle" (Ps. lxxviii. 9) —thus unhappily withdrawn.

And now these more recently raised up ones have had their time of successful aggressive openair work, and have in their turn also—still speaking generally, and with the thankful admission always of blessed individual exceptions—retired from it, ceasing to "go out quickly into the streets and lanes of the city, and bring in" "the poor and the maimed, and the halt, and the blind," and " into the highways and hedges, and compel them to come in" (Luke xiv. 21, 23), and have settled themselves down, like those before them, in comfortable chapels, with well-trained ministers to preach to them " good sermons;" but with what result in sinners converted or believers enabled to enter into entire sanctification, had, in general, better, perhaps, not be asked.

And now " The Salvation Army."

And He has accordingly raised up now in our own day " The Salvation Army," to take up the aggressive work on the devil's kingdom on a greater scale than any who have in modern times gone before them, and to preach everywhere, as in the early days of the Gospel, and as in the case of John Wesley and his like-minded fellow-labourers, along with " the *principles* of the doctrine of Christ" (Heb. vi. 1), entire deliverance also by Him from all sin outward or inward, as our blessed present privilege. (Acts iii. 26; xxvi. 18; Titus ii. 14).

" Scavengers."

Our good Bishop (of Rochester) has called them " The Scavengers," saying that they do the work, which no others of us can touch, of *sweeping the streets*. May God keep them at it, and bless them more and more abundantly in it, and keep the devil from in any way getting in among them to divert them from it. Anything that he does against them—and as long as he sees them making any serious inroads upon his kingdom he is sure to do plenty (Acts xiii. 50; xiv. 2; xvii. 5, 6, &c.)—outside of their own selves, will only help them on in it.

But if they don't keep to their work.

But if the Lord should still delay his coming, and they in their turn should after a while retire from this very hard—and, by many, much despised and condemned, but surely in the sight of God and his holy angels most blessed (Luke xv. 7, 10)—work, and settle themselves down in their "barracks," as the others of us before them in our churches and chapels, may He in his still unfailing (Lam. iii. 22) "compassion on" "the multitudes" "scattered abroad, as sheep having no shepherd" (Matt. ix. 36), then raise up some fresh agency, again to proclaim to "the outcasts of Israel" (Isa. lvi. 8) "the gospel of" his "grace" (Acts xx. 24), "with the Holy Ghost sent down from heaven" (1 Pet. i. 12).

All guilty alike.

"Let us search and try our ways, and turn again to the Lord. Let us lift up our heart with our hands unto God in the heavens. We have transgressed and have rebelled" (Lam. iii. 40–42).

"Yea *all Israel* have transgressed thy law, even by departing, that they might not obey thy voice" (Dan. ix. 11).

In venturing to speak in the last section, as it might appear to some, very depreciatingly—in connection with the remark in the letter of our brother there given, that he found the doctrine of entire deliverance from sin opposed in his, the Wesleyan, Church—of the present generation of Wesleyans, and of " Primitive Methodists," and " Bible Christians," and other off-shoots of Wesleyanism, I was not, thereby, as not belonging to any one of these sections of the universal Church, *bearing false witness against my neighbour*; but was only expressing that which many of the most spiritually minded among them of a past generation lamented to see in prospect, and which many of those so minded of the present generation lament to see as a fact; though, as above said, with blessed exceptions, for every one of which God be praised!

An average congregation.

A dear minister, one of the exceptions, whose whole heart is bent on the spread of holiness among his people, said in deep sorrow, a little time back:—

" *The fact is, the bulk of my people have very little religion: and worse than that, they do not want any more. And they do not like to be told of it. But I must tell them.*"

This was no condemnation of his own ministry; for he had only recently come among them: nor any reflection upon their previous ministers as less efficient than the average; for I do not believe that he at all intended to say that *his people* were in a lower state spiritually than the general run of congregations belonging to his section of the Church.

Dare not throw stones at each other.

And I do not at all mean that the particular denominations I have named are worse than the rest of us, Establishment, Baptists, Congregationalists, Presbyterians, Friends, Close or Open Brethren, or whatever else. If any of us of one denomination were inclined to sit in judgment (Matt. vii. 1) upon those of another in the matters here being spoken of, we should be stopped by " He that is without sin among you, let him first cast a stone " (John viii. 7) : and, " Are there not with you, *even with you*, sins against the Lord your God " (2 Chron. xxviii. 10) ?

A word respecting all of us.

The minister's sad word was spoken with reference to a nonconformist congregation : but here is a yet more sad word by a bishop of our Established Church respecting conformists and nonconformists alike :—

" Let us all awake to a sense of the perilous state of professing Christians : 'without holiness no man shall see the Lord': without sanctification there is no salvation (Heb. xii. 14). Then what an enormous amount of so-called religion there is which is perfectly useless ! What an immense proportion of church-goers and chapel-goers are in the broad road that leadeth to destruction ! The thought is awful, crushing, overwhelming."

"*Guilty concerning our brother.*"

And in this failure of all of us—every section alike of the whole Church—we have not only incurred deep guilt toward God (Ps. li. 4) and our own souls (Num. xvi. 38), but are also "*verily guilty concerning our brother*" (Gen. xlii. 21).

God on the day of Pentecost fulfilled his promise given through the prophet Joel, "*I will pour out my Spirit upon all flesh*" (Joel ii. 28). We know He did so, by those words of St. Peter: "*This is that which was spoken by the prophet Joel*" (Acts ii. 16). And the Church was the channel through which the Spirit was poured out upon all flesh, just as the disciples were the channel through which our Lord fed " the multitude " (Matt. xiv. 19) with the five barley loaves and the two small fishes.

The channel choked.

But the channel has long since become too foul for the sweet blessed stream (Ps. xlvi. 4; John vii. 38, 39) to continue to flow freely through it. It is choked with the filth of our sins. And so by far the greater part of " all flesh " is still lying as " a dry and thirsty land, where no water is " (Ps. lxiii. 1); though God thus set the living water running, which, if we had let it reach its destination, would long ago have made " the wilderness and the solitary place " to be " glad," and " the desert " to " rejoice, and blossom as the rose " (Isa. xxxv. 1).

Through unbelief for full sanctification.

And all this, surely, because of our refusal to believe in and accept our Lord Jesus Christ as made " unto us " " of God " " *sanctification* " (1 Cor. i. 30), to the extent of redeeming us "*from all iniquity,*" and purifying " unto himself a peculiar people " (revised version, " a people for his own possession"), " zealous of good works " (Titus ii.

14); so that through us, as an always perfectly open, clean channel, the "pure river of water of life clear as crystal, proceeding out of the throne of God and of the Lamb" (Rev. xxii. 1) could flow on constantly in its full, fresh, life-giving power, and the sweet word be spiritually fulfilled, that "everything shall live whither the river cometh," and "upon the bank thereof, on this side and on that side, shall grow all trees for meat, whose leaf shall not fade, neither shall the fruit thereof be consumed: it shall bring forth new fruit according to his months, because their waters they issued out of the sanctuary: and the fruit thereof shall be for meat, and the leaf thereof for medicine" (Ezek. xlvii. 9, 12).

Sanctification and Missionary Success.

"Then flew one of the seraphims unto me, having a live coal in his hand, which he had taken with the tongs from off the altar: and he laid it upon my mouth, and said, Lo, this hath touched thy lips; and thine iniquity is taken away, and thy sin purged. Also I heard the voice of the Lord, saying, Whom shall I send, and who will go for us? Then said I, Here am I; send me" (Isa. vi. 6-8).

"If a man therefore purge himself from these, he shall be a vessel unto honour, sanctified, and meet for the master's use, and prepared unto every good work" (2 Tim. ii. 21).

Both the above passages have been partly considered in one or more previous sections. But I bring them in again here because of their bearing on the subject of the last section—the need of entire deliverance from sin, inward as well as outward, for the reception of the Holy Ghost for evangelising power.

Missionary Societies some time back.

This necessity is strikingly illustrated in the history of many modern missions as they were conducted some time back by the large English Societies. We may trust that every one chosen as a member of the " Committee of Management " of any of these Societies was an earnest child of God, but may be equally confident that, in the then state of the Church, he repudiated the idea of entire present deliverance from indwelling sin; and that he, therefore, in all probability, was without that baptism of the Holy Ghost for evangelizing power which, according to the two passages at the head of this section, and very many others to the same effect in the Word of God, it is his rule—though subject, it may be, to exceptions (Matt. vii. 22, 23)—to bestow only on those whom He has prepared as pure vessels for the reception of so blessed a gift.

The choice of missionaries.

And so these dear Christian men appointed to the management of the Societies, being thus in practical ignorance (Acts xix. 2) of that baptism of the Spirit—though it is the most indispensable of all qualifications for evangelising work (John vii. 38, 39)—of course could not take it at all fully into account in their choice of the missionaries; but appear in most cases to have appointed men in much the same spiritual state as themselves; that is, deeply earnest children of God, with their whole hearts set upon carrying out all his blessed will, but living practically on the other side of the day of

Pentecost; and continuing there, because of their not believing in the possibility of a present entire emptying of sin to make room for this filling with the Holy Ghost.

Their comparative failure.

And so these dear earnest children of God thus chosen for missionaries were sent out and supported at very heavy cost, to do, in a sad number of cases, but little except show a noble example of devotedness to our Lord, even, it may be, to the laying down of their lives to carry out his command, " Go ye into all the world, and preach the Gospel to every creature" (Mark xvi. 15), though thus all the while inadvertently ignoring his other command, the obedience to which was such an indispensable requisite for any real success, *"But tarry ye" "until ye be endued with power from on high"* (Luke xxiv. 49).

Cost of some of the converts.

Is it not the case that there have been missionary fields worked in this way in which every convert really worth the name has cost thousands of pounds, years of labour, and the life of one, or perhaps more than one, dear devoted missionary?

And is such a state of things ever contemplated for a moment in the New Testament as possible in the case of any preacher of the Gospel " with the Holy Ghost sent down from heaven " (1 Peter i. 12; 1 Thess. i. 5)? And is any preacher, who preaches otherwise than with the Holy Ghost sent down from heaven, ever recognised in the New Testament as a preacher at all?

And has any child of God any warrant in his

SANCTIFICATION AND MISSIONARY SUCCESS. 315

Word to look for this baptism of the Spirit otherwise than by the acceptance of Christ as his "sanctification" (1 Cor. i. 30), to his entire deliverance from all indwelling sin, that his heart may be a fitting reception-room for so blessed a guest?

Exceptions.

But it may be said that there were cases entirely differing in character from those here described, and in some instances such success in the work that many undoubted converts were made in only a short time, and through the instrumentality of only a single worker.

Yes, God be praised, there were such blessed individual instances of success answering to a happy extent to the examples of the New Testament: but was it not that in these cases God, in his goodness, either led the managing ones in the Society as "the blind by a way that they knew not" (Isa. xlii. 16), to choose those to whom He had given this qualification for the work of which they, in choosing them, knew nothing, or else that when they had chosen, as in other cases, those without this qualification, He afterwards in his goodness endowed them with it while actually engaged in the work?

Happy contrast now.

But now, glory be to God, there are not merely just a few such individual exceptions to the general rule of want of enduement with power for the work, and these brought about unknowingly by the ruling authorities in it, but a glorious number—though not in general, apparently, in connection with the old Societies—of fully equipped ones for service; and these chosen, not in ignorance of their being thus thoroughly qualified for the work, but for the very reason of their being so. And bless his holy name! these God-prepared workers in the Gospel seem to be still rapidly increasing in number, both by fresh ones answering to this character continually being sent out, and by many of those already out who were not in the first instance thus qualified now becoming so by accepting Christ for entire sanctification and for this baptism of the Holy Ghost.

"*To Him the porter openeth.*"

And as it is thus now Christ Himself in them by his Spirit (Eph. iii. 17; Gal. ii. 20; John xx. 21, with xiv. 10), going forth to the work, the Word is fulfilled that to Him, as "the Good Shepherd," "the porter openeth," that He may go in and call his own sheep by name and lead them out (John x. 3). For God, simultaneously with his raising up of such a blessed band of workers, has made so many and such glorious openings for work as must cause the hearts of the dear ones who laid down their lives in the missionary cause—it may be three-quarters, or half, or even only a quarter of a century back, dance for joy—if they are permitted to know what is going on in the earth—to see their happiest dreams of what might, perhaps, come to pass in the very far distant future now already being realised as a glorious matter of fact.

A good little book.

Anything that I ventured to say in the last section, on the failure of so much of the work of many modern missions for the want in most of the missionaries of that baptism of the Holy Ghost of which entire deliverance from sin is, according to God's ordinary way of working, the accompaniment or the preparation—is only an echo of the lament of many of the best of the missionaries themselves.

I will name in this connection a beautiful little book, in the reading of which I have received much blessing, by a very devoted missionary, Mr. Griffith John, who has worked for very many years in China, in connection, I believe, with one of the large London Societies.

The book is published by Morgan & Scott, 12 Paternoster Buildings, London, E.C., price sixpence in a paper cover, or one shilling in cloth. Its title is "*Spiritual Power for Missionary Work*;" but if it had the wider title of "Spiritual Power for *Christian Life*," it would, I think, be at least as rightly named.

I wish that every missionary, home or foreign, every minister, every scripture reader, every Sunday-school teacher, and every other Christian, and indeed, also every one not yet a Christian, could have a copy of it, and would read, mark, learn, and inwardly digest its contents.

Practical unbelief in the Holy Ghost.

He asks:—

"My brethren, do we believe in the Holy Ghost? No doubt we do theoretically; but do we *practically*?

"Have you observed how little is written and said about the Holy Ghost, as compared with other themes? God the Father is a constant theme; God the Son is a constant theme; the morality of the Gospel is ever preached; but God the Holy

Ghost is comparatively forgotten; and Christians are seldom urged to seek the *fulness* of his indwelling as a distinct and available blessing.

"And how little is said about this special endowment of power in our colleges and universities! Whilst the student is ever stimulated to seek every other qualification for his work, how seldom is his attention directed to this, the most essential qualification of all!

Questions put to a missionary candidate.

"Then when a young man offers his services to a Missionary Society, how seldom is he made to feel that every other endowment is absolutely nothing as compared with this.

"He will be asked how much Latin, Greek, and Hebrew he knows; how many books on theology he has read; and what reasons he has for supposing that he is a converted man, and called to be a missionary. But how seldom is this question put to him, 'Are you endued with power from on high?' And how seldom is a man told to go and tarry with his God until the promise of the Father shall have descended upon him!

"Whilst our creed is 'I believe in the Holy Ghost' there is, unquestionably, a real amount of atheism in our practice.

"*Are we filled with the Holy Ghost?*

"Are we filled with the Holy Ghost in the sense in which the Apostles were filled on and after the day of Pentecost?

"Have *we* been endued with power from on high? Is *our* joy in God *full*? Is our gladness in

Jesus complete? Would it be the plain unvarnished truth to speak of the divine life as realised in *our* experience as a fountain ever springing up in the soul and as rivers of living water ever flowing forth to bless?

"God never intended that any one should enter on his life-work as a Christian, or attempt to carry on any Christian work, without being endued with power from on high. It is not only our privilege to seek and obtain this power, but our solemn duty. Oh, if there be a Holy Ghost, if there be an Infinite Spirit in us and around us, and if it be the fact that the Omnipotent Spirit is both able and willing to satisfy our deepest longings, and meet and supply our every need: if all this be so, then we ought to reckon it a sin—not a misfortune, but a *sin*—to offer up a single prayer, to preach a single sermon, or to speak a single word to a single soul, unfilled with his inspiring presence!

Preaching powerless without this.

"Think you that India, China, and Japan are going to be converted by the mere might of preaching and teaching? No, no! 'It is not by might, nor by power, but by my Spirit saith the Lord.' No one can have stronger faith in preaching and teaching than I have myself. Preaching has been my life-work, and, God willing, it is the work to which I shall devote the rest of my days. Let us not, however, close our eyes to the fact that mere preaching will never move those great empires.

"I feel in my inmost soul that our pressing need is a baptism of divine power, and I can add from certain knowledge, that most of our missionaries yonder feel as I do. China is dead—terribly dead.

Our plans and organisations can do but little for that great people. They need life. Christ came to give *life*, and the all-absorbing question with me is, How is this life to be imparted to that dead mass? I know that mere preaching and teaching can never do it. It is simply beating against the air to talk to men without *the* power.

Christ in us the power.

"The secret of the success of the Apostles lay not so much in what they did and said, as in the presence of Christ in them and with them. They saw with the eyes of Christ, felt with his heart, and worked with his energies. They were nothing: Christ was everything. Christ was living, breathing, triumphing in their personal lives. Their entire nature being replete with his life, their spirits bathed in his light, and their souls kindled with the fire of his love, they moved in the midst of men as embodiments of supernatural power.

"They spoke with the demonstration of the Spirit. When they came in contact with men a mysterious energy went out of them, and under their vitalizing touch dead souls started into life.

"Brethren, this is what your missionaries must be if India, China, and Japan are ever to be moved through them; and this is what your pastors must be if Christendom is ever to become Christ-like; and this is what we must all be if God's will is ever to be accomplished in us and through us.

We must all be holy.

"We must be more than good men, we must be *holy* men.

"We must be men full of the Holy Ghost; and the divinity within must energize mightily through us. But, to be this, the throne of grace must be our refuge, the secret place of the Most High must be our daily and hourly habitation. We must take time to become intimately acquainted with God: we must take time to be filled with his power: we must *take time to be holy*. May God help us to wait on Him in earnest persevering prayer! Let us put our desires into one heart-felt petition for a baptism of the Holy Ghost, and not cease to present it until we have prevailed.

"So Elijah prayed—he threw himself on the ground resolved not to rise again till his request was granted. So Jacob prayed—he wrestled with the angel. So Daniel prayed—he set his face to the Lord his God. So the disciples prayed—they continued with one accord in prayer and supplication. And so must we pray, if we would have power with God and with man, and prevail. Let us have faith in God, link our feebleness to his omnipotence, and go forth conquering.

> " ' Faith, mighty faith, the promise sees,
>   And looks to that alone;
> Laughs at impossibilities,
>   And cries, It shall be done.' "

Faith and Holiness: then Power.

"Have faith in God . . . What things soever ye desire, when ye pray, believe that ye receive them, and ye shall have them" (Mark xi. 22-24) —or, as it is in the revised version, "All things whatsoever ye *pray and ask for,* believe that ye *have received* them, and ye shall have them."

" If any of you lack wisdom, let him ask of God, that giveth to all men liberally, and upbraideth not; and it shall be given him. But let him ask in faith, nothing wavering. For he that wavereth is like a wave of the sea driven with the wind and tossed. For let not that man think that he shall receive anything of the Lord (James i. 5–7).

" Ye have not, because ye ask not. Ye ask, and receive not, because ye ask amiss, that ye may consume it upon your lusts " (James iv. 2, 3).

Unsuccessful prayer.

I trust that any of us who may feel the force of our brother Griffith John's exhortation above to make " the throne of grace our refuge, the secret place of the Most High our daily and hourly habitation," and thus to "wait on " God in "*earnest persevering prayer*" for " *power*," " and not cease," " until we have prevailed," will make due note also of his words respecting *faith* and *holiness*.

For there may be some of us in a state of soul in which exhortations to prayer for power, without reference to *holiness* and *faith*, would not be likely to lead us into the life of power which we are seeking, but only into deeper despondency as to any prospect of attaining to it.

The suggestion of such a remedy for our spiritual weakness would sound in our ears like the advice of a good London doctor to a sick girl who had come up from her home in Hastings to consult him: " My dear, what you really need is a time at the seaside. *Now if you could only get away to Hastings——*"

"Oh!" the poor girl answered—her heart sinking within her at a prescription of which she too well knew the uselessness in her case—"*I have just come from Hastings. I have long been living there.*"

And so the dear souls I am now referring to might answer any mere exhortations to earnest prayer: "*I have just come from it. I have long been in the habit of it.*"

Possible clue to our failure.

But that word about holiness and faith may, perhaps, afford to any such of us a clue to the cause of our failing to attain to that which we have thus so earnestly sought, by leading us to consider more carefully than hitherto, the two causes of failure stated by St. James in the passages at the head of this section; namely, either that we do not when praying *believe*—according to our Lord's command, also at the head of this section, and so often previously quoted—*that we receive the things we ask for*, or that we admit *some unholiness* into our motive for asking.

"*Private Thoughts*" *by Thomas Adam.*

In a little book of the last century, "Private Thoughts on Religion, by the Rev. Thomas Adam, late Rector of Wintringham,"—in which the heart of a child of God not yet having accepted Christ for entire sanctification, though having accepted Him for pardon, is laid bare with dreadful skill— there are, in the chapter of "Confessions," the two following passages:—

"I am grievously offended with my flock,

because they will not contribute to my reputation in the world by being converted by me."

" I find upon strict scrutiny into myself, that I am not so much influenced by a sense of reputation as to deny a persecuted truth. Nevertheless, I plainly perceive that, if I could be instrumental in spreading it, *the great motive would not be love of the truth, of Christ, or the souls of men. My chief pleasure would arise from* THE CREDIT OF IT."

And I have read long ago a question I am almost sure by the same writer, though, if so, I cannot find the place just now in order to give the exact words, but it was exactly to this effect. " If I could write a book which God should use to the conversion of the whole world, *could I be content that no one in the world should know that it was I who had written it?* "

Asking amiss.

And are there not many dear children of God, not yet having accepted Christ for entire sanctification, who could not answer " Yes " to such a question? Would not even many who have gone out as missionaries feel in their inmost souls—because of their want of entire sanctification, however devoted they may be to their work—that they could not give this answer?

And may not any of us who feel that we could not give it see in those words of St. James, " *Ye ask and receive not, because ye ask amiss, that ye may consume it on your lusts,*" the reason why our prayers for success in our work, however intensely earnest, and however much we may have striven to believe for their fulfilment, have not been answered? For is it not a mere earthly lust (Ezek. xvi. 17)—

though, bless the Lord! one from which, as from all others, we are entirely delivered (2 Pet. i. 4) by accepting Christ for full sanctification—to desire credit among our fellow-creatures for any good work in which God may see fit to use us? (Ps. cxv. 1; John v. 44; Acts iii. 12; 1 Cor. iii. 5–7).

A bit of ministerial experience.

One who well knows by experience the difference between ministerial work with motives still partially impure, and the same work after Christ has been accepted for their entire purification, as for that of all else within us, describes the blessed change—as one of the many resulting benefits of so accepting Him—in the following words:—

" *The death of personal ambition* :—To all desire of self-promotion and self-aggrandisement, to the glory of God's grace let it be said, I feel as dead as the autumn leaves beneath my feet, as I tread the streets of Lynn on this gusty November day. It was different once. There was once a desire for the applause of men, a name resounding in the trumpet of fame. It was not inordinate and noticeable to my friends: but it existed as an uneasy tenant of my bosom; the spring of many of my actions, and a motive mingling with all my aspirations to serve God. But five years ago this blessed day, an unalloyed spring of action, the motive power of unmingled love to Jesus and the race for which He shed his blood, was fixed within by the Holy Spirit. It is no longer the old nature that lives, but Christ Jesus."—*Dr. Daniel Steele, in* "*Mile stone Papers,*" *already quoted from above.*

No longer the old nature.

"*It is no longer the old nature that lives, but Christ Jesus.*" Is not this just that which we have considered so much above, "I am crucified with Christ: nevertheless I live; yet not I, but *Christ liveth in me?*" (Gal. ii. 20).

And is not Christ God's gift (John iii. 16; iv. 10) to us that it may be so with every one of us?

And is not the seeking to have it so with us the only scriptural way of seeking spiritual power?

Case of Holiness before Power.

"Seek ye first the kingdom of God, and his righteousness" (Matt. vi. 33).

"Be ye clean, that bear the vessels of the Lord" (Isa. lii. 11).

Working hard in the Gospel.

A dear brother in the Lord worked hard in the Gospel all his spare time from his daily earthly work in the neighbourhood of London for many years; and worked hard also in it in a place at a distance from London in his holiday time, in each of three successive summers. And then seeing the great necessity of more continuous work in that place, he at length left London to give himself up to work there in the Gospel.

But thirsting for power.

And there he worked in it with all his heart and soul, and with acceptance among the people; but still with a deep sense of the need of much

more "power" (Acts i. 8) in his work. Soon after settling there, he wrote to a friend:—
"I have but one need: I am thirsting, praying, longing for more *living* Holy Ghost power. It's no use my staying here unless to bring souls to Jesus. He has given me two as yet; *an earnest.*"

But needing holiness first.

His friend answered that in saying that he had "but one need," that of "living Holy Ghost power," he mistook his real, or, at any rate, his *first* need; that what he really needed first of all was *a clean heart* (Ezek. xxxvi. 25, 26), and that when once he had come to God for that, and had by faith received it, by accepting Christ for it (2 Cor. i. 20; Eph. i. 3), there would be no fear but that the Holy Ghost would come and fill it, and so fully endow him for any work to which He might see fit to call him.

Case in point.

And he told him that he himself had only just before seen the way of perfect heart purification—though for many years believing that there was such a thing, only not knowing how it was to be obtained—by simple faith in our Lord for it, as before for pardon; and quoted to him, as now his own experience, the chorus of a sweet hymn by Mrs. Palmer, No. 192 in "Hymns of Consecration and Faith":—

> "*The cleansing stream I see, I see!*
> *I plunge, and oh, it cleanseth me!*
> *Oh praise the Lord! it cleanseth me!*
> *It cleanseth me! yes, cleanseth me!*"

This letter was used of God to lead him to see that a clean heart was really his most pressing need, and to such a sense of the necessity of its being supplied (Phil. iv. 19), that it was with him almost as with Rachael in the want pressing upon her, " Give .... or else I die " (Gen. xxx. 1.)

Deep soul trouble.

" I am," he wrote again to his friend, "in deep soul trial, and spend not only my days but my nights in tears. I know in sorrow and pain, and only too well, that my heart is not clean.

" The dear Lord whom I *do* love, enables me to keep myself pure in the *eyes of men*, and indeed to be free from the grosser kinds of sin that would bring dishonour on his dear name; and I am enabled to preach the gospel of his love in some power: but my poor sick, weak, unclean heart, has never known perfect deliverance from sinful inclinations, desires, and imaginations, however much I may have been enabled to keep them under.

" Your letter came to me so distinctly from the Lord, that I cried for nearly an hour after reading it. It tells me *exactly what I want*; and sets my poor weary soul longing more and more, and praying more and more. But I am, I fear, in a more hopeless state than ever. I do not mean that I am in any state of sin of act or thought worse than in times past: but I feel in utter weakness and helplessness to do anything towards getting cleanness of heart."

The want supplied.

But eleven days afterwards, he wrote again:—
" It is with very much joy that I write to tell

you that the dear and loving Saviour has enabled me to believe in Him, as my *indwelling Master*: and so my heart is filled with Himself; and I feel that He *rules* in me and subdues my heart to his own loving, joyful will.

"When I wrote my last letter to you, I little thought how near I was to the obtaining of that which I have always sought for, but *never believed in*, a pure heart. I fear that I never really believed that I could be filled with Christ. And so sin really ruled in me; though I had much controlling power to prevent all that was in me coming out in actions.

"I do so thank you for the letter you sent me some days back. It came to me as from God: so distinctly so that it proved his all-seeing and loving care for my poor but precious soul. After reading it, I passed much time in prayer about it: I am certain that when I *really believed in* a clean heart, and asked for it, our loving God blessed me with a sense of purity of heart that I had never before known.

To the praise of God's grace.

"I thought I was going to keep the fact to myself: but on Sunday morning I was compelled to tell out all my newly found joy; and I am already conscious of the sweet power of the Holy Spirit in the testimony. Oh, how many among brethren long for a new and clean heart, but dare not say so, because they, *theologically*, don't believe in a new heart!

"I have had a sweet time to-night with twenty young people. I am compelled to preach now deliverance from the power of sin as well as its punishment. Do pray still for me. Jesus is almighty *to keep.* This is all my hope for holiness within. The dear Lord bless you! Yours in grateful love."

About a fortnight later he wrote again:—

"I am grateful to our loving Saviour to say that I am always full of joy in Him. The dear Lord gave me happy liberty in speaking of his precious blood and the fulness of the Holy Spirit twice last night, and once to-night."

About this time his wife also entered into the same fulness of "joy and peace in blessing" (Rom. xv. 13).

Still increasing blessedness.

A little later he wrote again:—

"The dear Lord still *keeps* me in the conscious joy of cleanness within. I am always happy; and sometimes cannot contain myself, but walk along the streets *crying* with joy. The dear Lord makes me so happy, that the very brightness of my face first led to questions as to the cause of my extra happiness."

Again, about five weeks later:—

"I find the path I am in very trying: but my dear Saviour is more than all I need. I am cast upon Him *continually*; and the joy, the sweet precious joy of conscious cleanness within is mine abidingly. Satan tries me fearfully: but I am hourly more than conqueror. I feel the power of the words '*And that wicked one toucheth him not,*' ever dwelling in me in divine strength.

Increased power of testimony.

"The dear Lord is constraining me more and more to use the power He has given me, and spread the truth—the peculiar truth—of his own full sanctifying power. I have a meeting somewhere every night.

"Last Thursday afternoon I had a holiness meeting at a lady's house in the country. Some were much opposed to the truth of sanctification as I understand it. One acknowledged her unwillingness to give up all for Jesus; and so did not expect purity within. On Sunday morning the same lady told me by a messenger that she had done what she could not before accomplish. I understood that to mean that she had given up all for Jesus.

"Will you kindly remember me in Christian love to all who know me in your meetings. Tell them I am further in the thick of the fight against sin than ever: but Jesus is a living power within me, and is always more than all that be against me. I am held up and kept always."

Again, a little later:—

"My heart overflows with love and praise to our kind and loving Father who watches over me continually. The dear Lord gives me constant liberty from heart-plagues; and I write now with tears of joy as I delight in the sweetness of the precious peace that reigns in my heart.

"I shall never be able to tell you, or any one, the *greatness* of the change which has been wrought *within* me. Now I can praise his name that *He has cast the unclean spirit out*, and He Himself guides me and works within me."

Fresh opportunities for service.

Again, a little later:—

"I am still pressing forward in the Master's work; and new opportunities are opening for this blessed and sweet service. My heart is occupied with talking and singing of Him; and I feel very near the glory. The dear Lord has led me in a wondrous way the last four months; and my heart is melted within me as I think of his loving, full, bountifully providing hand to me, the very *very* least of all his saints. In fond and grateful love, yours in the joy of Christ."

And again a little later:—

"The dear Lord knows all that was in my poor heart when I came to ———, and, indeed, for years before; and I see the answer to many prayers slowly, mysteriously, and wonderfully opening out. So much so that I should feel sometimes *frightened* could I not fall back upon the everlasting grace, and everlasting mercy of my God."

And again about three weeks later:—

"I am kept hourly; much tried at times, little encouragement around" (he means "little encouragement" in the way of help or sympathy in his work from the professing Christians around, not little encouragement as regards success in the work, for, as regards *that,* the good Lord was always giving him *much* encouragement); "but still 'occupying.' My heart is fixed; and all I am and have is *his*. My dear wife and I are living for Jesus only. The dear Lord ever bless you and all yours. Yours in ever grateful love."

Subsequent testimony and service.

At the time at which I am now writing (May 1886), more than four years have elapsed since the date of the last of the letters from which the above extracts have been made.

During this time our dear brother has been used

of the Lord to bring many souls to Him, and to bring many children of God up into that life "more abundantly" (John x. 10), into which the Lord brought him at that deeply important crisis in his spiritual history of which the account is given above.

For he was very intimate with many in much the same state that he himself was in before "God Almighty" so "appeared unto" him, as to Jacob of old, "in the day of" his "distress," and "answered" him, "and blessed" him (Gen. xxxv. 3; xlviii. 3); the state referred to by him in those words in one of the above extracts, "*How many among brethren long for a new and clean heart, but dare not say so, because they theologically don't believe in a new heart!*"

Especially among "Brethren."

Having been many years an acceptable speaker in their gatherings, in which he was always a strenuous supporter of the—according to their views—orthodox doctrine of the not only utter, but utterly unchangeable, even by the almighty power of God, depravity of the human heart, he knows the heart of a brother (Exod. xxiii. 9). And so, going among them, refusing all controversy, but lovingly and humbly, to the glory of the grace of God (Ps. cxv. 1; Eph. i. 6), declaring what He has done for his soul (Ps. lxvi. 16), he has been used of Him to lead many of them to seek and find the same blessed deliverance in which he himself is rejoicing (Ps. cxxiv. 7).

And if any dear brother expresses doubt about the fact of his deliverance as stated by him, he still **refuses** any dispute about it; saying lovingly,

"Brother, I know you are truthful; and I receive undoubtingly all your statement of your experience: and ought you not so to receive my statement of mine?"

All included in love.

"Knowledge puffeth up, but *love buildeth up*" (1 Cor. viii. 1; margin, revised version).

"The end of the charge is love out of a pure heart and a good conscience and faith unfeigned" (1 Tim. i. 5, revised version).

"Love is the fulfilling of the law" (Rom. xiii. 10).

"Beloved, let us love one another: for love is of God; and every one that loveth is born of God, and knoweth God. He that loveth not knoweth not God; for God is love" (1 John iv. 7, 8).

"God is love; and he that dwelleth in love dwelleth in God, and God in him" (1 John iv. 16).

After purity, only more love.

There is a little bit in our Wesleyan brother's letter given a few sections back, too sweet to be passed over without remark. After naming the opposition in his church to the doctrine of entire present sanctification, he added:—

"*The Lord fill us with love, to prove the truth of it.*"

To which devout wish, let all of us who venture to speak at all in support of the doctrine say a hearty AMEN!

Dear John Wesley, in the sight of wild work

going on among some who professed to be entirely sanctified, said :—

"The very desire of growing in grace may, sometimes, be an inlet of enthusiasm. As it continually leads us to seek new grace, it may lead us unawares to seek something else new besides new degrees of love to God and man. So it has led some to seek, and fancy they had received, gifts of a new kind after a new heart.

" Another ground of these and a thousand mistakes, is the not considering deeply that *love is the highest gift of God*; humble, patient, gentle love; that all visions, revelations, manifestations whatever are little things compared to love.

Seek nothing else.

" There is nothing higher in religion. There is in effect nothing else. If you look for anything but more love, you are looking wide of the mark, you are getting out of the royal way.

" And when you are asking others, ' Have you received this or that blessing?' if you mean anything but more love, you mean wrong. You are leading them out of the way, and putting them upon a false scent.

" Settle it then in your heart, that from the moment God has saved you from all sin, you are to aim at nothing more but more of that love described in the thirteenth of the Corinthians. You can go no higher than this till you are carried into Abraham's bosom."

And again, he said :—

" There is nothing deeper, there is nothing better in heaven or earth, than love. There cannot be, unless there were something higher than the

God of love. So that we see distinctly what we have to aim at. We see the prize, and the way to it. Here is the height, here is the depth, of Christian experience, 'God is love; and he that dwelleth in love, dwelleth in God, and God in him.'"

Another witness.

And dear Thomas Mitchell, one of Wesley's fellow-labourers in the Gospel, looking back in weakness and infirmity caused partly by age, but, probably, more by the hardships he had endured in the Lord's work, in which he had several times been in danger of his life, wrote:—

"I now look back on the labour of three and thirty years, and do not repent of it. I am not grown weary either of my Master, or of the work I am engaged in. Though I am weak in body and in the decline of life, my heart is still engaged in the cause of God. I am never more happy than when I feel the love of Christ in my heart, and am declaring his praise to others. There is nothing like the love of Christ in the heart to make us holy and happy.

"It is love alone that expels all sin out of the heart. Wherever love is wanting there is hell: and where love fills the heart there is heaven. This has been a medicine to me ever since I set out. When sin and Satan beset me on every side, it was this that drove them away.

"'O Love, how cheering is thy ray,
    All pain before thy presence flies
  Care, anguish, sorrow melt away,
    Where'er thy healing beams arise.
  O Jesus, nothing may I see,
    Nothing desire, or seek, but Thee.'"

"Now abideth faith, hope, love, these three; and *the greatest of these is love.* FOLLOW AFTER LOVE" (1 Cor. xiii. 13—xiv. 1, revised version).

"If we let God make us holy ——."

The following is from a sister in the Lord in lowly earthly circumstances; but always working hard in the things of his kingdom, and always rejoicing in Him (Phil. iii. 1; iv. 4; 1 Thess. v. 16), though suffering from weakness of body, and having to beg that her "bad writing" may be excused, "as *I am*," she says, "*nearly blind with one of my eyes.*"

She speaks of some meetings she is privileged to attend on the Saturday nights, after her week's hard work, as "real Holy Ghost meetings." "I do," she says, "so love them. I always feel that the very God of peace reigns there in our midst; and my poor heart leaps for joy.

"I thank you very much for the book you kindly sent me. I mean to lend it out all I can. It is what I wanted to convince some that we can live holily. If we let God make us holy, He will keep us holy."

All blessings in Christ.

Those words of our sister, "*If we let God* make us holy," show that she had learned to good purpose, in the matter of holiness, the lesson which the African boy spoken of some time back had learned to *no* purpose in the matter of forgiveness of sins (Ps. cxxx 4), when he answered William Taylor's question, how it was that God, though He was Almighty and wanted to save him, yet did not save him? "Mr. Taylor, it is *because I won't let Him.*"

I mean the lesson so frequently referred to more or less directly above, that most of us have been so slow to learn, that God does not require us to *do* anything for the obtaining of his blessings, whether pardon, sanctification, or whatever else, but simply to *accept* them *by accepting his Son*, in his one gift of whom they are all included, according to that word of St. Peter, " His divine power hath granted unto us all things that pertain unto life and godliness, *through the knowledge of him that called us by his own glory and virtue* " (2 Peter i. 3, revised version); and that of St. John so often quoted above, " God hath given to us eternal life, and this life *is in his Son*. He that hath the Son hath life: and he that hath not the Son of God hath not life " (1 John v. 11, 12); and those words of St. Paul, "hath blessed us with all spiritual blessings in heavenly places *in Christ*" (Eph. i. 3); " For it pleased the Father that *in him* should all fulness dwell" (Col. i. 19); " And ye are complete *in him* " (Col. ii. 10); and " All the promises of God *in him* are yea, and *in him* Amen, unto the glory of God by us" (2 Cor. i. 20); and *He* " of God is made unto us wisdom, and righteousness, and sanctification, and redemption : that, according as it is written, he that glorieth, let him glory *in the Lord*" (1 Cor. i. 30, 31).

With Him in us right working begins.

And when we have thus accepted Him, and "all spiritual blessings " in Him, then our *doing* of the right sort begins. For He dwelling in our heart by faith (Eph. iii. 17), is now to us "the power of God" (1 Cor. i. 24), working in us "to will and to do of his good pleasure," so that we "work out" our own "salvation with"—not painful, but reverent and earnestly joyful (Ps. ii. 11; lxxxix. 7; Heb. xii. 28)—"fear and trembling" (Phil. ii. 12, 13), lest we should lose anything of such a precious possession (Matt. xiii. 44, 46); "striving according to his working which worketh in" us "mightily" (Col. i. 29); and proving (Rom. xii. 2). as a blessed fact in our own personal experience, that God "is able to do exceeding abundantly above all that we ask or think, *according to the power that worketh in us*" (Eph. iii. 20).

This life of blessedness and power, by no doings of our own, but by Christ dwelling in us, is just that described above by Mr. Griffith John as that of the Apostles after the day of Pentecost, in those words:—

"The secret of the success of the Apostles lay not so much in what they did and said, as in the presence of Christ in them and with them. They saw with the eyes of Christ, felt with his heart, and worked with his energies. They were nothing: Christ was everything. *Christ was living, breathing, triumphing in their personal lives.*"

And it is that described by St. Paul in those words so often in part quoted above:—

"I through the law am dead to the law, that I might live unto God. I am crucified with Christ: nevertheless I live; yet not I, but CHRIST LIVETH IN ME: and the life which I now live in the flesh I live by the faith of the Son of God, who loved me, and gave himself for me" (Gal. ii. 19, 20).

Not yet "established."

"Now to him that is of *power to stablish you* according to my gospel . . . be glory through Jesus Christ for ever. Amen." (Rom. xvi. 25, 27.)

"The Lord make you to increase and abound in love one toward another, and toward all men, even as we do toward you: to the end he may *stablish your hearts* unblameable in holiness before God, even our Father, at the coming of our Lord Jesus Christ with all his saints" (1 Thess. iii. 12, 13).

"The Lord is faithful, who shall *stablish you* and keep you from evil" (2 Thess. iii. 3).

"The God of all grace, who hath called us unto his eternal glory by Christ Jesus, after that ye have suffered a while, make you perfect, *stablish, strengthen, settle you.* To him be glory and dominion for ever and ever. Amen." (1 Pet. v. 10, 11.)

"As ye have therefore received Christ Jesus the Lord, so walk ye in him: rooted and built up in him, *stablished in the faith*, as ye have been taught, abounding therein with thanksgiving" (Col. ii. 6, 7).

Statement of a common experience.

A dear sister in the Lord, previously unknown to me, writes that she had been at a "convention," where she had "received great blessing, clearly seeing that such a thing as a clean heart can be had in this life, and is to be had by faith." But she continues:—

"Ever since my return I have found it more than difficult to get any of my friends to believe it. All say there is no one can truthfully declare at night that they have not sinned if but once through the day, and say, though they may not show temper outwardly, they feel it, and that God looks to the heart. This is just an example.

"I still believe it is not necessary to sin; though I cannot truthfully say I have not sinned since receiving the blessing. I think it is because my eye got away from looking at Christ; not having learned to keep looking without interruption.

"I feel I have yet a great deal to learn; and it seems to me as though I cannot help on those I love to see the truth. Will you remember me in prayer that I may be kept, and daily live, as far as I see the light, the life of a clean heart, and learn what yet I do not see."

I have copied out this much of our sister's letter because it expresses so clearly an experience which I should think almost all of us who have seen the truth that our Lord "gave himself for us *that he might redeem us from all iniquity*, and purify unto himself a peculiar people zealous of good works" (Titus ii. 14), and have sought to have it fulfilled in us, know only too well.

And of the cause of it.

And our sister not only thus clearly sets forth our failure, but also in those words, "I think it is because *my eye got away from Christ*, not having learned to keep looking without interruption," expresses clearly the undoubted cause of it.

I think there is danger that our very anxiety about having and keeping a "clean heart," and being preserved from falling into the least sin, may be the very means of our failing to obtain a clean heart, or of our losing it if we have it, and of our failing to walk free from sin; and this just because of this anxiety so taking up our attention, as to cause our "eye," according to our sister's words, to get "away," in a greater or less degree, "from looking at Christ," so that we do not "keep looking without interruption."

Peter walked firmly on the waves as long as he did not think about them, nor about his own walking upon them, but was attending only to our Lord's word "Come." But directly he became anxious lest they should be too much for him they indeed proved so (Matt. xiv. 29, 30).

This matter of our being liable to fail of perfect and constant salvation from all sin because of our very earnestness leading us to seek it too directly, that is, otherwise than in Christ—so that in fact we really are seeking an "experience" instead of accepting Christ to dwell in our hearts by faith (Eph. iii. 17), and *so* to be to us God's fulfilment of this, as of our "every need," "according to his riches in glory IN CHRIST JESUS" (Phil. iv. 19, revised version)—is so important that I must give another section to it, showing the case of one who was for some time kept out of the full blessing through this mistake; but who at length seeing it, and being delivered from it, entered gloriously into the blessing as one of the "all spiritual blessings" with which God has indeed "blessed us" already "in heavenly places *in Christ*;" but to enter into which we need to see them and accept them IN HIM.

Not an "experience," but Christ.

The case I have here to give is that of a dear brother in the Lord associated with Dr. Cullis in his "Work of Faith" in Boston, America, but over here for the International Conference on Holiness

and Faith Healing. He wrote to me for a copy of the " First Sheets " and afterwards wrote again :—
"I have received your little book, and am delighted with its contents: may our gracious God be pleased to bless it to thousands."

And he enclosed to me a little book giving an account of the way God had led him to see and accept, as his gift to us in Christ, salvation from all sin, and of his state of continued blessedness consequent upon his entering into this salvation.

The little book, of a size suitable for inclosing in a letter, is published in England as well as America. Its title is:—

"BELIEVE AND RECEIVE,"

By Rev. F. D. Sanford. London, Bethshan, 10 Drayton Park, Highbury, N. Price one penny each, or 9d. per doz.

I am going here to copy it out because of the practical illustration contained in it of the mistake spoken of in the last section of seeking a happy " experience," instead of first accepting all God's spiritual blessings given to us in Christ (Eph. i. 3), and leaving it to Him to give us how, and when, and in what shape He sees good, a happy " experience," as a consequence of our having accepted Him.

I shall be very glad if my giving its contents should lead those who may read them here to write to " Bethshan " for copies of the little book itself to give away.

Many longing for rest from sin.

" From the Church of Christ in every direction comes the inquiry, ' What are the scriptural possibilities of faith to be enjoyed in this present life?'

"Many of such inquirers are in spiritual bondage, groaning to be delivered from besetting sins, and find a blessed rest promised in the words, 'We which have believed do enter into rest' (Heb. iv. 3).

"But no sooner is the soul aroused by spiritual hunger to seek the fulness there is in Christ for every believer, than the arch-enemy endeavours to persuade them that such rest pertains only to their eternal state, or, that it is attainable only by those who are advanced in the Christian life. There is a failure to observe the present tense used in the passage, 'do enter' *now*, conditioned on simply believing God's Word.

"I was once a seeker of this rest; and, finding it, now delight to relate my experience of entering therein.

Clear conversion, but wanting something more.

"When brought by the Blessed Spirit to see myself a lost sinner, helpless and undone, I was pointed to the Lord Jesus, 'who loved me, and gave himself for me.' Under deep conviction I took the precious promise, 'Him that cometh to me I will in no wise cast out' (John vi. 37), and penitently pleading it in Jesus' name, and believing in Him as my only Saviour, I was made a new creature in Him. My conversion was remarkably clear. Not a doubt had I of forgiveness of sins and of eternal life.

Wrongly directed by one brother.

"The blessed Word of God afforded me great joy and comfort. Still, I was unsatisfied, and said to an older Christian, 'My soul is reaching out after something more to satisfy these intense desires;' but was put off with the answer, 'We can never be satisfied here,' and was given to understand I must go on in my hungry condition till death.

"How absolutely contrary to the teachings of Scripture, which declare, 'He *satisfieth* the longing soul, and filleth the hungry soul with goodness' (Ps. cvii. 9); 'He satisfieth the desire of every living thing' (Ps. cxlv. 16).

But then rightly by another.

"Shortly after this, another brother—in answer to the question, 'What does the Lord Jesus mean when He says, "Blessed are they which do hunger and thirst after righteousness?"'—pointed out to me the glorious possibility of being so filled with the Holy Ghost as to find a continual satisfaction in Christ's fulness. He replied, 'Why, just what He says. Blessed are they already; and He promises that they shall be filled.'

"Wonderful promise! little did I realise its richness and fulness, neither did I thank the Blessed Spirit for such desires begotten by Himself only to satisfy.

Early fervour gradually subsiding.

"Four months passed away, in which God poured upon me rich blessing. But—for all I had no doubt regarding the pardon of actual transgressions—yet was I daily brought into bondage by the uprisings of inbred sin, in the forms of anger, impatience, pride, unbelief, and love of the world: and being engaged in active business, I found the love and fervour which so graciously marked my early experience subsiding. Gradually, but surely, was a deadness and coldness creeping into my soul regarding spiritual things; and, although I never for a day ceased reading the Scriptures and praying for more and more holiness, yet had I been asked regarding Christ's yoke, I could not have said I found it ' easy ' nor his ' burden light ' (Matt. xi. 30).

Earnest struggles for deliverance.

"In this condition the Blessed Lord brought to me a little tract, in which I plainly saw *deliverance from the power of sin* ' through sanctification of the Spirit and belief of the truth ' (2 Thess. ii. 13); but not understanding how to act faith, I thought such an experience could not be mine. Here I fell into legality, day after day trying in some way to arrive at this state. So much did I ' wrestle ' in prayer, and so great were my efforts to improve my spiritual condition, that I became physically worn.

"The doctrine of 'Holiness,' 'Entire Sanctification through faith,' or 'The Higher Christian Life,' was studied almost continuously; and I was thoroughly convinced by God's Word of the possibility of a life of unclouded communion with a living Christ, as a result of uniform victory over sin, through Him. Just here came in Satan with the insinuation that, although such a life was possible, yet it would be presumptuous for so young a Christian as I to expect to reach a state which only those who had been Christians for years could enjoy. For a short time I believed this to be true, while I looked forward to coming days, and, perhaps, years, with sorrow: for such bondage as I endured would have rendered me most miserable.

Clearer sight of Christ as the Way.

"While in this state of mind, the Precious Jesus one day brought me great comfort through one of his true followers, by showing me from his Word that I could be delivered from the power and inbeing of sin, and have soul-rest that very moment, would I but give over all my own efforts and let Christ *have all* and *do all* for me; that I was limiting the power of the Holy One of Israel when I entertained the thought that He could not fully deliver me then and there, as well as at some future day.

"One evening about this time, in the quiet of my room, I was reading with deep interest the experience of a dear soul who was delivered from the bondage of inbred sin, in answer to the prayer, 'O Lord, give me purity of heart at any cost: make the cleansing complete.' This was what my soul panted for—*purity*. But such a prayer—would I dare offer it? 'At any cost!' I might be reduced to the lowest poverty, or become a helpless cripple, or even pass the remainder of my life in insanity.

Help coming in a strange disguise.

"While under these base temptations the words so sweetly came to me, 'As thy days, so shall thy strength be' (Deut. xxxiii. 25); 'My grace is sufficient for thee' (2 Cor. xii. 9). Oh! the confidence these words produced towards my precious Saviour! drawing me unto Him with the cry, 'Give me purity of heart *at any cost*: make the cleansing complete. I can and do trust Thee, dear Jesus.'

"The God who inspired this prayer heard it, and, blessed be his name! answered it; but in a way I little anticipated. Late in the afternoon of the day following, while engaged in my occupation—a situation in a large mercantile house, which I highly prized—I was told that on account of depression in business, my services would not be required longer than that week. What could it mean? Discharged on less than a week's notice! All was so strange: but unto Jesus did I fly, and underneath my soul He placed the promise, 'All things work together for good to them that love God' (Rom. viii. 28), which kept me from murmuring at his dealings with me.

Able to attend a Holiness Convention.

"While going to my home in a neighbouring city the week following, the prayer which I had offered for entire cleansing 'at any cost' came back to my mind for the first time since it went up from my burdened heart: and with it came also the fact that the way was now all open for me to attend a Convention for Scriptural Holiness which was soon to be held at F——. Had I retained my position this would have been impossible. Thanksgiving and praise went up to our loving God for so blessedly working for me. A few days later found me at this Convention an earnest and sincere seeker of holiness of heart.

But still seeking wrongly.

"I fully expected to receive this great blessing; but, as was soon shown me, I was seeking it in a

NOT AN "EXPERIENCE," BUT CHRIST. 349

way of my own devising. Having consecrated myself to God, I looked immediately for an overwhelming manifestation, which *some* experience at the time of a full surrender; thus unconsciously seeking joy and peace as an evidence that the sacrifice was accepted, and overlooking the precious truth, 'The just shall live by faith' (Rom. i. 17).

"At every opportunity I went to the altar with other seekers of entire sanctification: but instead of seeking *Christ* as my sanctification, I was simply seeking *an experience*, and was therefore only plunged into doubt and discouragement.

"'It's no use,' I said to one; 'there's no rest of soul for me.'

"'Have you given up all?' he asked.

"'All,' I replied.

"'Then, according to God's Word, "The altar sanctifieth the gift" (Ex. xxix. 37; Matt. xxiii. 19; 2 Cor. vi. 17), 'and you are received.'

"'But I do not *feel* any different.'

"Straight came back the truth to me, 'You will never have soul-rest till you *believe God*.'

"How blind I was! like Israel entering not in 'because of unbelief' (Heb. iii. 19): but working and struggling, when I should have read, 'He that is entered into his' (God's) 'rest, hath also ceased from his own works, as God did from his' (Heb. iv. 10).

Putting away the "evil heart of unbelief."

"At one of the evening services, a dear brother spoke briefly from 2 Cor. vi. 17. He was aware, he said, of the error some were in as to the witness of the Spirit to the grace of sanctification. They were expecting this before they fully believed God accepted the sacrifice they brought Him. Such were touching '*the unclean thing*;' and should the Holy Ghost give the witness to them, He would be witnessing to a lie.

"The Lord through these words revealed to me 'the unclean thing' I was touching—the blackest, foulest sin man ever committed, viz., unbelief, doubting God's Holy Word. Instantly I exclaimed, 'I am received! The blood cleanseth; and now by God's grace I will continue to believe Him, irrespective of any emotion.'

Not to seek gifts, but the Giver.

"After reaching my home some days after, I was shown an unconscious reaching-out after peace and joy, seeking the *gifts* instead of the *Giver*, when the words, 'How shall he not with him, also freely give us all things?' (Rom. viii. 32) were powerfully applied to my soul, together with other passages teaching the same truth—'All things are yours' (1 Cor. iii. 21), '*Christ* is ALL' (Col. iii. 11). From this moment I sought all in Christ.

"The desire for a deeper consecration here arising in my heart, I at once wrote out a complete dedication which included body, soul, spirit, time, talents, possessions, friends, reputation—all I had or ever should have. My 'feelings' had been the cause of so much stumbling, that it seemed a relief to place them at the divine disposal, which was done. This offering I knew was accepted by the witness of the Word 'acceptable unto God' (Rom. xii. 1). And obedience to the blessed command to 'present the body a living sacrifice' was immediately rewarded by *rest in Jesus*.

Trusting only in Christ.

"Thus was all yielded to the Blessed Lord. My soul was in his dear hands for a perfect cleansing. Nothing less would be an answer to my prayers. Faith well knew that in God's own time would be given the direct witness of the Holy Ghost that this work was accomplished through the precious blood of Christ.

"This act of consecration and faith was followed at once by severe and furious temptations. On every side I was assailed by the angry hosts of hell. The chief point of attack was faith: doubts regarding my abiding in Christ, and the efficacy of his cleansing blood, were literally poured upon my soul: but oh! such a heavenly calm as reigned within as faith rose triumphantly above all, through 'the greatness of his power to us-ward who believe' (Eph. i. 19). And the 'Lo, I am with you alway' (Matt. xxviii. 20) was spoken in tones of such sweetness as only Jesus can speak.

"Waiting for the fire."

"Five days passed since my consecration, and still no direct witness of purity. Words of God again brought comfort. 'Fear not: for I have redeemed thee, I have called thee by thy name; thou art mine' (Isa. xliii. 1).

"Nine days of acting faith. The blessing was still held in the promise—no emotion, no overflowing joy. The temptation to discouragement was banished by the whisperings of the Spirit, 'Ye have need of patience, that, after ye have done the will of God, ye might receive the promise' (Heb. x. 36). 'The trial of your faith worketh patience' (James i 3).

"Two weeks elapsed; my all was on the altar, I was 'waiting, waiting for the fire.' Still I had no sensible manifestations. I had come to think none would be given, and was willing there should be none—delighted with whatever my Lord gave. His precious Word was enough. Oh, the rest it afforded me as He told me to 'fear not,' but 'believe only.'

"*Joy unspeakable, and full of glory.*"

"Thus was I led in simple faith, after an entire consecration, *nineteen days*. The trial of faith was now to be rewarded by great blessing. On the morning of this nineteenth day, while alone in my room writing to a child of God, I was suddenly stopped by a shock of divine power and glory coming upon me, as the words flashed through my mind and reached the depths of my soul, '*Said I not unto thee, that, if thou wouldst believe, thou shouldst see the glory of God?*' (John xi. 40).

"Oh, wonderful! Instantly I seemed to be floating in an ocean of glory: wave after wave rolled over and through my spiritual being, the veins of which were almost bursting with 'joy unspeakable.' Never had I conceived it possible for a human being to be so flooded and dazzled with glory. Human words are inadequate to describe the experience of that hour; 'Eye hath not seen, nor ear heard, neither have entered into the heart of man, the things which God hath prepared for them that love him. But God *hath* revealed them unto us by his Spirit' (1 Cor. ii. 9, 10).

In fulfilment of the promises.

"On my table lay my open Bible: raising it without turning a leaf, my eye fell on the words, 'the Father of glory may give unto you the spirit of wisdom and revelation in the knowledge of him: the eyes of your understanding being enlightened; that ye may know what is the hope of his calling, and what the riches of the glory of his inheritance in the saints, and what the exceeding greatness of his power to us-ward who believe' (Eph. i. 17–19).

"Every letter and word of all this blessed truth, seemed to stand out in letters of shining gold. The eyes of my understanding being opened, this truth was easily received, and its reception caused an inflowing of the life and nature of the Holy One who was in it. And with this came such a love for the Blessed Word, as I have never been able to describe. I read also, 'In whom also after that ye believed, ye were sealed with that holy Spirit of promise, which is the earnest of our inheritance until the redemption of the purchased possession' (Eph. i. 13, 14).

To the perfect satisfying of his soul.

"Streams of praise flowed out spontaneously to the Adorable Trinity for such unutterably precious manifestations of glory and truth. For the first time in all my life, I was fully satisfied, not with my experience, but with *Him* whom the precious Spirit now revealed within me as *my Saviour from all sin.* Hungering and thirsting was turned into full consciousness of inwrought holiness and purity, of which I was as well assured as of my own existence. From my heart I could sing:—

"'Precious Saviour, precious Saviour,
    Thou hast sweetly saved my soul;
 Cleansed me from inbred corruption,
    Sanctified and made me whole.

Glory, glory, Jesus saves me,
Glory, glory, to the Lamb!
Oh, the cleansing blood has reached me,
Glory, glory, to the Lamb.'

Subsequent experience.

" Since this memorable era in my Christian life four years have passed away, and still 'the blood cleanseth from all sin' (1 John i. 7). It has been a period of blissful communion with the precious Jesus. 'Peace passing all understanding' (Phil. iv. 7), with 'joy unspeakable' (1 Pet. i. 8), have by the continued influx of the 'life more abundantly' (John x. 10) kept and filled the soul. Progress in the divine life has been blessedly realised, purity having laid the basis for a rapid, unobstructed and unhindered growth in grace.

Temptations and trials in abundance.

" Do not for a moment, dear reader, entertain the thought that there has been a cessation of solicitations to sin. On the contrary, powerful temptations have been permitted; but coming from a foe no longer within the heart, but from one without and from one already conquered (Luke iv.; John xvi. 33) by the Captain of our Salvation, the victories have been glorious through faith in Him 'who *always* causeth us to triumpth' (2 Cor. ii. 14).

" Have there been no trials? Ah! yes, almost without number; bringing to a severe test the work wrought within by the blessed Sanctifier: but in them has that wondrous promise been fulfilled to faith, 'God is able to make *all* grace abound toward you, that ye, *always* having *all* sufficiency in *all* things, may abound to every good work' (2 Cor. ix. 8); thereby working for me the 'far more exceeding and eternal weight of glory' (2 Cor. iv. 17). Infirmities, mistakes, and failings are all eternally covered by the infinitely precious blood of Christ, which makes 'whiter than snow.'

"The future is with 'Him who is able to keep us from falling' (Jude 24), and through whose mighty power we may be 'more than conquerors' (Rom. viii. 37).

Caution to the reader.

"Beloved child of God, do not make the mistake of expecting an experience similar to mine. No two have the same manifestation; but *the end* is the same—CHRIST JESUS *in his fulness.*

"Hast thou *rest in Jesus* from all unholiness? Does the blessed Comforter *abide* in a soul wholly sanctified? Is *victory through Christ* thy daily experience? Is the sweet Lord of glory the satisfying portion of thy soul? And thy communion with Him, is it uninterrupted?

"All this, and much, *much* more shall be thine, wilt thou but give Him thy whole heart and believe his every promise; as within thee shall dwell 'Him who is able to do exceeding abundantly above all we ask or think, according to the power that worketh in us' (Eph. iii. 20).

"Boston, Mass., U. S. A., October 1879."

Out of Galatians into Ephesians.

In the last section we had the account of how our brother Sanford, some time after his clear and bright conversion, passed, without any conscious wilful unfaithfulness to God, and in spite of all his efforts to keep up the fervour of his spiritual life, into comparative darkness and bondage, in which he long remained helpless and almost hopeless; and then of the way in which he was led out of this unhappy state (Isa. xli. 17; xlii. 16), into bright light and liberty in Christ.

There is an article by him in the number for May, 1886, of that excellent little periodical, "*Times of Refreshing*"—" a monthly record of Christian life and Christian testimony, edited by Dr. Charles Cullis, of Beacon Hill Church, Boston, America"— bearing on his happy deliverance: out of which I shall therefore here make some extracts; though to do so will involve the repetition of a little of the above account, and also of a little of what was said further back in the section headed "Prayers and Armour in Ephesians." The article is headed "*Out of and Into*," and is published also in tract form, price two cents, or twenty cents per dozen.

First out of Egypt: then into Canaan.

"The epistles to the Ephesians, Philippians, and Colossians may be looked upon as the New Testament counterpart of the description of the land of Canaan, which flowed 'with milk and honey.'

"There are two distinct epochs in the life of the children of Israel: the departure from Egypt, and the entrance into the promised land.

"So it is with many Christians at the present day. We first come to Jesus for pardon; but before long we become aware of the presence of inherited evil. Satan says, 'There is nothing better than an up and down life'" (the counterpart of the wandering of the children of Israel hither and thither those forty years in the wilderness), "'it is what all the best saints have experienced.' Perhaps the earnest inquirer, with intense spiritual hunger and thirst, goes to some one for counsel, and is told as I was, 'Nobody will ever be satisfied here; if they were they would not want to go to heaven.'

"The man told me the best he knew; but I afterwards went to another, who knew what it was to be *satisfied with Jesus Christ*, and I asked him, 'What did our Lord mean when He said, "Blessed are they which do hunger and thirst after righteousness, for they shall be filled"?' 'Mean!' he replied, 'why, He meant just what He said. Why don't you get filled? *He* is all you want.'

Risk of missing our way.

"The temptation again is, 'This is to be a gradual work.' The enemy desires to keep us running on the gradual line, looking for improvement all the way along: which would never be anything else than self-improvement. Sanctification does not run on that line. We cannot remove sin from our hearts by gradualism: God wants a *re-creation*, a new creation in answer to a prayer like David's, '*Create* in me a clean heart.'

"Again the enemy will point to some one's experience and say, 'That is what you want,' and endeavour to persuade the soul to seek an experience, a state or condition, instead of Jesus Christ Himself to come into the heart and remove the element that is causing the trouble, and in the place of it to bestow his own glorious life.

Need of being definite.

"This is a definite work. Wesley says, that out of six hundred persons he examined" (whom he believed to have accepted Christ for entire deliverance from sin), "not one professed to have received sanctification by a gradual process. They all testified to having received it by simple faith, by taking Jesus at his word. And the same testimony is world-wide—'I came to Jesus and took Him as my Saviour. I afterwards felt the need of something more. And I then sought as definitely for a clean heart as I had before sought pardon. And as I yielded all to Christ and leaned upon his promise, He came in and cleansed me by his precious blood. And then the Spirit of God filled me, and worked out in me all "the good pleasure of his will."'

"We lose many blessings because we are not definite. A lack here will hinder people all the way along. Whether healing or anything else be our need, God wants us to be definite. And when a man *seeks definitely* and *believes definitely* he gets something—even Jesus Himself, who is revealed to meet the present need.

Canaan a type of Ephesians.

"The place of receiving is Canaan, even living in the epistle to the Ephesians. I used only to be able to take this epistle judicially. I could see the blessings described were all mine in Christ, but how I longed for the experience! to have what was revealed as God's purpose for me brought into my life, and made a reality there.

"But when by his grace He brought me to the

place of yielding and of believing, and thus letting Him work in me, I then entered into the life of this epistle, and knew what it was to have Him come into his temple and cast out all that offended—come like the priests and Levites in Hezekiah's days into the *inner place*, and bring out the uncleanness, carry it out and have it destroyed, that the glory of God might fill the house.

Ephesians as real as Galatians.

"No one will ever know the blessedness of Canaan until they really get into it. One reason why so many fail to enter into 'the fulness of the blessing' is because they continue to live in Galatians. Galatians is to them practical, while Ephesians is judicial. Is Ephesians as literally true to you as Galatians? Galatians is *intensely real* to very many: 'for the flesh lusteth against the Spirit, and the Spirit against the flesh.' But Ephesians may be just as real. We may cross over Jordan and come into Canaan and possess the land.

"It was said to Joshua, 'Every place that the sole of your foot shall tread upon, that have I given unto you.' The children of Israel had this promise before they had practical possession of the land. Judicially it was theirs: but they had to march forward and take it before it was practically theirs. And so have we to take by faith entire deliverance, and then God makes it real to us.

Difference of the two conflicts.

"And here comes the conflict of faith. Notice the difference. In Galatians it is a conflict *with the flesh*: but in Ephesians, 'we wrestle not against flesh and blood, but against principalities, against powers, against the rulers of the darkness of this world, against spiritual wickedness in high places.' The blessed aim of the Epistle to the Galatians is to bring us to the end of the conflict with the flesh. And then we come to Ephesians, to soul-rest in Jesus when God will *fill the whole man.*

"The Apostle's prayer in Ephesians iii. is wonderfully clear. *Not a word about sin.* He does not tell us to keep sin down—to repress it. Why? Because those to whom he wrote had come where their whole beings were emptied, that they might be 'filled with all the fulness of God.' Then in chapter vi. we have the true Christian conflict with foes without. This blessed armour (Eph. vi. 11, 13) would be no security if the enemy were still within. A foe within under the panoply of God would overthrow the soul continually.

All victory when Jesus has come in.

"But Galatians once passed and Ephesians really and practically entered, Jesus our glorious Deliverer will fill the whole hemisphere of our being, and thus save us from interior antagonisms; and, also, by 'the whole armour of God' keep us in all the attacks of Satan. Our only safety then is to get out of Galatians into Ephesians, and to have it become just as real to us as Galatians has ever been.

"As long as we have a foe within—a civil war in our hearts—there is too often sad defeat. But after Jesus comes into us and reveals Himself as our sanctification, instead of turmoil and defeat, all is quiet, because He reigns, rules, and delivers.

And He desires to come in and bring forth in us the blessed antitype of the land that flowed 'with milk and honey.'

Enemies all the way along.

"The enemies will come and try their best to defeat us and hinder our progress. We shall meet with them all the way along. For, although we have passed the wilderness enemies, yet there are those in the land. But what we have to do is simply to 'stand' behind 'the shield of faith' and use 'the sword of the Spirit,' and the victory is sure. We can never thus stand if we have foes within. But once let the inward foes be cast out by the power of Christ, and He will take their place, live the life, and do the overcoming.

"Are you longing for this perfect salvation, this continual victory over sin? If so, *seek Jesus*, and seek Him to do something *definite* for you; to cleanse your heart and occupy it with his glorious presence, thus making you more than conqueror, and saving you to the uttermost."

"All the way 'long it is Jesus."

"For, as by one man's disobedience many were made sinners, so by the obedience of one shall many be made righteous" (Rom. v. 19).

[Dean Alford says on this text, in his Greek Testament: "'*Be made righteous*,' not by imputation merely, any more than in the other case, but shall be made *really and actually* righteous; as completely so as the others were made really and actually sinners. When we say that man has no righteousness of his own, we speak of him as *out of Christ*. But *in Christ*, and united to Him, he is *made righteous*: not by a fiction or *imputation only* of Christ's righteousness; but by a real and living spiritual union with a righteous Head, as a righteous member; righteous *by means of*, as an effect of, the righteousness of that Head, but not merely righteous by transference of the righteousness of that Head: just as in his natural state he is united to a sinful head, as a sinful member; sinful by means of, as an effect of, the sinfulness of that head, but not merely by *transference* of the sinfulness of that head."]

" Then shall the lame man leap as a hart, and the tongue of the dumb sing: for in the wilderness shall waters break out, and streams in the desert. And the parched ground shall become a pool, and the thirsty land springs of water: in the habitation of dragons, where each lay, shall be grass with reeds and rushes. *And a highway shall be there, and a way, and it shall be called The way of holiness; the unclean shall not pass over it*" (Isa. xxxv. 6–8).

" The path of the just is as the shining light, that shineth more and more unto the perfect day" (Prov. iv. 18).

" I'm on my journey up Zion's hill,
All the way 'long it is Jesus.
The way grows brighter and brighter still,
All the way 'long it is Jesus.
Jesus! Jesus!
All the way 'long it is Jesus."

(Hymn No. 269 in *Sacred Songs and Solos*, and No. 446 in *Hymns of Consecration and Faith*.)

"Yes, in me abroad He sheddeth
  Joys unearthly, love, and light;
And to cover me He spreadeth
  His paternal wing of might.

Yes, in me, *in me He dwelleth,*
  I in Him and He in me;
And my empty soul He filleth
  Here and through eternity."
    (Dr. Horatius Bonar; Hymn No. 136 in *Hymns of Consecration and Faith.*)

"*The gift of God.*"

The above passages from the Epistle to the Romans, the prophecy of Isaiah, and the Proverbs, and the accompanying extracts from hymns, express "the gift of God" the "living water" "given" by our Lord to our brother Sanford, on his so earnestly and perseveringly seeking and asking for it (John iv. 10; Luke xi. 8–10); the "life" "more abundantly" (John x. 10) into which He brought him after he had been so long and so vainly trying to find the way into it himself (Eccl. x. 15).

We have seen that when he wrote the account in October, 1879, he had then already been in the enjoyment of the power and happiness of that life four years. He has now (May, 1886), had six and a half years' further experience of its blessedness; and he is able, in the meetings which he is holding in different parts of England for the purpose of bringing all that he can of his fellow-believers in our Lord into the same happy experience, to declare—and no one who hears him can doubt that it is a reality that he is declaring—that "the way" does indeed "grow brighter and brighter still;" and this just because indeed "All the way 'long it is Jesus."

Christ Himself the gift.

I shall presently give extracts from other hymns, setting forth the truth which our brother is so anxious to impress upon us, which he himself was so slow to learn, and in the apprehension (Phil. iii. 12) of which many others of us have doubtless been at least equally dull scholars (Luke xxiv. 25); namely, that the true object of pursuit (Phil. iii. 7–10), the real "pearl of great price" for which to sell all that we may buy it (Matt. xiii. 46), is *Christ Himself*, and not any happiness, power, holiness, or anything else in ourselves, otherwise than by *our being so truly and fully in Him and He in us* (John xv. 4; Eph. iii. 17; &c.), that we are altogether *one with Him*: one, that is, not in any mere shadowy oneness—the mere idea in our mind because of our holding it as a doctrine in our creed that God makes us righteous by, as Dean Alford says in the passage quoted above, "a *fiction*, an *imputation only*, of Christ's righteousness"—but one with Him in very "nature" (2 Pet. i. 4; Gal. iv. 6, ii. 20; Rom. viii. 9; 2 Cor. xiii. 5; &c.), He and we "one spirit" (1 Cor. vi. 17; John xvii. 21), and even also "one flesh" (Eph. v. 31, 32; Matt. xix. 6; John i. 14; Heb. ii. 14).

Mere doctrinal oneness with Christ.

I allude to that mere shadowy doctrinal oneness, because there is such danger of our taking up with it to quiet our consciences, while living consciously unholy lives. I have heard it said of God's salvation of us in Christ that it is like this; that if you look at an object through coloured glass, you see it of the colour of the glass, though all the while it has no such colour in itself; and so, God looking at us through Christ, sees us righteous in his righteousness, though *we remain as unrighteous as before*, no change whatever in our own selves by that faith in Christ which causes God thus to see us only through Him; our Lord having, as Alford says on Gal. ii. 17, ("Is therefore Christ the minister of sin? God forbid!") according to this view, "*done all his work only to minister to a state of sin*"—as if He had received his "name" of "Jesus," not because He should "*save his people from their sins*" (Matt. i. 21), but because God wanted to be able to *tolerate sin in them*—instead of to destroy it all out of them (1 John iii. 8), saving us "according to his mercy," "BY THE WASHING OF REGENERATION, AND RENEWING OF THE HOLY GHOST; which he shed on us abundantly through Jesus Christ our Saviour; that being justified by his grace, we should be made heirs according to the hope of eternal life" (Titus iii. 5–7).

I shall give in the next section a practical illustration of the passing out of the merely doctrinal into the real living oneness with our Lord Jesus Christ.

Living union with Christ.

Two hundred years ago, one who had entered the ministry with nothing but the shadowy doctrinal oneness with Christ alluded to above was preparing a sermon to be preached in the course of a few weeks in St. John's Church in Luneburg.

"My mind was," he says, "in such a state that I had not the mere exercise of preaching in view, but the edification of my hearers. Whilst reflecting upon this subject I hit upon the words 'These are written that ye might believe that Jesus is the Christ, the Son of God, and that believing, ye might have life through his name" (John xx. 31). My intention in selecting this text was to treat of true and living faith, and how it is distinguished from a mere human and imaginary belief. Whilst revolving the subject in my mind with all seriousness, I felt that I myself was still devoid of that faith which would be required in my sermon. I therefore relinquished meditating upon the sermon, and found enough to do with myself."

"He sought," his biographer says, "to compose himself by a variety of means, and to convince himself of the reality of his faith on rational grounds, but the more he endeavoured to help himself, the higher rose his distress and his scruples. He had recourse to dogmatical and practical writings, and even to the holy Scriptures, but could derive no benefit either from the Word of God or the word of man, and found just as little efficacy in the one as in the other. 'The whole of my life,' says he, 'presented itself to my view like the prospect of a large city from a lofty tower. First of all I was able to number, as it were, my sins; but soon the principal source from which they sprang unfolded itself—I mean unbelief, or *mere imaginary faith, with which I had hitherto deceived myself.*'"

God shining into his heart.

Of the way in which God in his goodness led him, as he was kneeling, after many days of, as he says, "anguish of soul," in intensely earnest but almost despairing prayer, into true and living faith, and thereby into real and vital union with our Lord Jesus, he says:—

"His paternal love was so great that He would not divest me by degrees of my heartfelt distress and doubts, with which I might well have been satisfied; but that I might be the more thoroughly convinced, and that my reason might have nothing to object to his power and faithfulness, He answered me all at once. Every doubt disappeared. I was assured in my heart of the favour of God in Christ Jesus. I could not only call Him God, but could also call Him Father. All sorrow and distress of mind was removed. I was animated with a flood of joy, so that I blessed and praised God with an overflowing heart and tongue, who had manifested such mercy to me. I knelt down in great distress and doubt, and rose up again with unspeakable joy and certainty. It seemed to me as if I had spent all my life in a deep sleep—as if I had done everything only as in a dream—and had now for the first time awoke from it. I was perfectly convinced that the world, with all its pleasures and delights, could not excite such sweet felicity in the human heart as that which I then enjoyed."

And his mouth showing forth God's praise.

It was on the Sunday next before the day on which he was to preach that he thus blessedly entered "into rest" (Heb. iv. 3). He had been on that day reflecting "upon the propriety of declining the invitation to preach if no change manifested itself; because I could not," he says, "preach against my conscience nor deceive the people with respect to my state." But "the following Wednesday he delivered," his biographer says, "his discourse upon

John xx. 31 with heartfelt satisfaction; for he could now say with Paul, 'we having the same spirit of faith, according as it is written, I believed, and therefore have I spoken; we also believe, and therefore speak'" (2 Cor. iv. 13).

"Living Water."

"It was from this decisive hour that Franké dated his real conversion. Forty years after, he said in his last prayer, in the garden of the Orphan House at Hallé, that God, at that time, had dug in his heart the well of the VITAL KNOWLEDGE OF JESUS CHRIST, from which never-failing source streams of consolation and joy had abundantly flowed forth during the whole of his life."

He was during those forty years gloriously used of God for the extension of his kingdom in Germany, and by his converts as missionaries in other parts of the world. Schwartz, one of the greatest missionaries of modern times, who used to preach to the heathen the love of Christ till the tears ran down his cheeks, and then they soon began to run down the cheeks of his hearers, was converted through a book of Franké's.—[*Narrative of the Conversion of Augustus Herman Franké, Founder of the Orphan House at Hallé, in " Gladness of Heart,"* the contents of which are taken from his Life by H. E. F. Guerike, translated by Samuel Jackson. London: Seeley & Burnside, 1837.]

"Jesus only."

In a hymn headed "None but Christ can satisfy," by B—— E——, No. 328 in " Sacred Songs and

Solos," there is a statement of the happy consequence of deliverance out of the mistake of seeking "spiritual blessings" otherwise than "in Christ" (Eph. i. 3):—

"O Christ, in Thee my soul hath found,
　And found in Thee alone,
The peace, the joy, I sought so long,
　The bliss till now unknown.

I sighed for rest and happiness,
　I yearned for them, not Thee;
But while I passed my Saviour by,
　His love laid hold on me.

Now, none but Christ can satisfy;
　No other name for me;
There's love, and life, and lasting joy,
　Lord Jesus, found in Thee."

"Jesus comes, He fills my soul."

The hymn by W. Macdonald, headed "I am coming to the cross," No. 54 in " Songs and Solos," sweetly expresses the long-continued consciousness of evil within, and the coming to the cross and meeting with Jesus there to come in and bring in with Him perfect salvation (Rev. iii. 20):—

"Long my heart has sighed for Thee,
　Long has evil reigned within;
Jesus sweetly speaks to me,
　I will cleanse you from all sin.

In the promises I trust,
　Now I know the blood applied,
I am prostrate in the dust,
　I with Christ am crucified.

> *Jesus comes, He fills my soul,*
> *Perfected in Him I am;*
> *I am every whit made whole;*
> *Glory, glory to the Lamb!"*

"*Simply trusting.*"

A sweet hymn by Louise M. Rouse, No. 198 in "Hymns of Consecration and Faith," expresses the blessedness of the change from struggling to trusting:—

> " Long my yearning heart was striving
> To obtain this precious rest;
> But when all my *struggles* ended,
> Simply *trusting* I was blessed.
>
> Trusting, trusting, every moment,
> Feeling now the blood applied,
> Lying in the cleansing fountain,
> Dwelling in my Saviour's side.
>
> Consecrated to thy service,
> I will live and die for Thee,
> I will witness, to thy glory,
> Of salvation full and free.
>
> Glory to the Lord who bought me,
> Glory for his saving power;
> Glory to the Lord who keeps me,
> Glory, glory evermore.
>
> > Glory, glory, Hallelujah!
> > Glory, glory to the Lamb!
> > Oh, the cleansing blood hath reached me!
> > Glory, glory to the Lamb!"

"*I struggled and wrestled.*"

And another sweet hymn by W. F. Crafts, No. 234 in the same book, also expresses the blessedness of the change:—

"I struggled and wrestled to win it,
The blessing that setteth me free;
But when I had ceased from my struggles,
His peace Jesus gave unto me.

He laid his hand on me and healed me,
And bade me be *every whit whole;*
I touched the hem of his garment,
And *glory came thrilling my soul.*

  The cross now covers my sins,
   The past is under the blood;
  I'm trusting in Jesus for all,
   My will is the will of my God."

"*Jesus saves me now.*"

But of all the hymns expressing trust in God's salvation of us in Jesus, without waiting for any feelings or any other "sign" (Matt. xii. 38, 39; John iv. 48) of any sort whatever, I do not know one that is clearer and brighter than the following by Parker, No. 200 in the same book. I must copy out the whole of it to wind up this section on hymns of trust, because from the first line to the last it expresses such fulness of absolute trust in spite of everything outward or inward that would discourage us from trusting. May our loving God strengthen every one of us, feeling in need of salvation from anything whatever, or in any respect whatever, just, in reading it, to accept our dear Lord as God's gift to us for the supply of every possible need (Phil. iv. 19), and by saying in the strength of the Lord "Jesus saves me now," to have as a blessed fact in Him not only all the salvation we are seeking, but "exceeding abundantly above all that we ask or think" (Eph. iii. 20; Heb. vii. 25).

"I'm more than conqueror through his blood,
    Jesus saves me now!
I rest beneath the shield of God,
    Jesus saves me now!
I go a kingdom to obtain,
I shall through Him the victory gain,
    Jesus saves me now!

Before the battle lines are spread,
    Jesus saves me now!
Before the boasting foe is dead,
    Jesus saves me now!
I win the fight though not begun,
I'll trust and shout still marching on,
    Jesus saves me now!

I'll ask no more that I may see,
    Jesus saves me now!
His promise is enough for me,
    Jesus saves me now!
Though foes be strong and walls be high,
I'll shout, He gives the victory,
    Jesus saves me now!

Why should I ask a sign from God,
    Jesus saves me now!
Can I not trust the precious blood?
    Jesus saves me now!
Strong in his word, I meet the foe,
And shouting, win without a blow,
    Jesus saves me now!

Should Satan come like 'whelming waves,
    Jesus saves me now!
Ere trials crush, my Father saves,
    Jesus saves me now!

He hides me till the storm is past,
For me He tempers every blast,
   Jesus saves me now!"

Bless his holy name, He "saves me now."

Jehoshaphat's Victory.

"Have faith in God" (Mark xi. 22).

The hymn, in the end of the last section, of sweet rejoicing in God by faith in his bare Word without any "token for good" (Ps. lxxxvi. 17) in ourselves or our surroundings (John iv. 48), is taken in part from the triumph of Jehoshaphat, by just such faith, over the "huge host" (2 Chron. xvi. 8) of enemies who had come up with "their wrath" "kindled against" him, and in a human point of view, abundantly able to swallow him up quick (Ps. cxxiv. 3) and all Judah with him.

His sin against God.

His faith shone out all the more brightly because of the circumstances tending to discourage him from exercising it, especially the fact that it was doubtless on account of the "wrath" that was "upon" him "from before the Lord" for his own wrong-doing (2 Chron. xix. 2), that the great multitude had been permitted to come up against him.

In his faithfulness to God in the beginning of his reign, he was safe from any such attacks. For it is written of him then, not only that "he had riches and honour in abundance, and his heart was lifted up in the ways of the Lord;" but also, that "the fear of the Lord fell upon all the kingdoms of the lands that were round about Judah, so that they made no war against Jehoshaphat" (xvii. 5, 6, 10).

Caught in a snare.

But he "joined affinity with Ahab. And after certain years he went down to Ahab to Samaria. And Ahab killed sheep and oxen for him in abundance, and for the people that he had with him, and persuaded him to go up with him to Ramoth-Gilead. And Ahab king of Israel said unto Jehoshaphat king of Judah, Wilt thou go with me to Ramoth-Gilead? And he answered him, I am as thou art, and my people as thy people; and we will be with thee in the war.

" And Jehoshaphat said unto the king of Israel, Enquire, I pray thee, at the word of the Lord to-day. Therefore the king of Israel gathered together of prophets four hundred men, and said unto them, Shall we go to Ramoth-Gilead to battle, or shall I forbear? And they said, Go up; for God will deliver it into the king's hand.

Inquiring of a prophet of the Lord.

"But Jehoshaphat said, Is there not here a prophet of the Lord besides, that we might enquire of him? And the king of Israel said unto Jehoshaphat, There is yet one man, by whom we may enquire of the Lord: but I hate him; for he never prophesied good unto me, but always evil: the same is Micaiah the son of Imla. And Jehoshaphat said, Let not the king say so. And the king of Israel called for one of his officers, and said, Fetch quickly Micaiah the son of Imla" (xviii. 1-8).

"And when he was come to the king, the king said unto him, Micaiah, shall we go to Ramoth-Gilead to battle, or shall I forbear? And he said, Go ye up, and prosper, and they shall be delivered into your hand. And the king said to him, How many times shall I adjure thee that thou say nothing but the truth to me in the name of the Lord? Then he said, I did see all Israel scattered upon the mountains, as sheep that have no shepherd: and the Lord said, These have no master; let them return therefore every man to his house in peace" (xviii. 14–16).

Going on in spite of warning.

But in spite of this warning from the Lord, Jehoshaphat still went on in his "fellowship" (2 Cor. vi. 14) with Ahab, and "so the king of Israel and Jehoshaphat the king of Judah went up to Ramoth-gilead.

"And the king of Israel said unto Jehoshaphat, I will disguise myself, and will go to the battle; but put thou on thy robes. So the king of Israel disguised himself; and they went to the battle.

"Now the king of Syria had commanded the captains of the chariots that were with him, saying, Fight ye not with small or great, save only with the king of Israel.

"And it came to pass, when the captains of the chariots saw Jehoshaphat, that they said, It is the king of Israel. Therefore they compassed about him to fight: but Jehoshaphat cried out, and the Lord helped him; and God moved them to depart from him. For it came to pass, that, when the captains of the chariots perceived that it was not the king of Israel, they turned back again from pursuing him.

Death of Ahab.

"And a certain man drew a bow at a venture, and smote the king of Israel between the joints of the harness: therefore he said to his chariot man, Turn thine hand, that thou mayest carry me out of the host; for I am wounded.

"And the battle increased that day: howbeit the king of Israel stayed himself up in his chariot against the Syrians until the even: and about the time of the sun going down he died (xviii. 28–34).

God's reproof of Jehoshaphat.

"And Jehoshaphat the king of Judah returned to his house in peace to Jerusalem. And Jehu the son of Hanani the seer went out to meet him, and said to king Jehoshaphat, Shouldst thou help the ungodly, and love them that hate the Lord? therefore is wrath upon thee from before the Lord. Nevertheless there are good things found in thee, in that thou hast taken away the groves out of the land, and hast prepared thine heart to seek God.

"And Jehoshaphat dwelt at Jerusalem, and he went out again through the people from Beer-sheba to mount Ephraim, and brought them back unto the Lord God of their fathers" (xix. 1–5).

"A great multitude" come up against him.

"It came to pass after this also, that the children of Ammon, and with them other besides the Ammonites, came against Jehoshaphat to battle. Then there came some that told Jehoshaphat, saying, There cometh a great multitude against thee from beyond the sea on this side Syria; and, behold, they be in Hazazon-tamar, which is Engedi.

"And Jehoshaphat feared, and set himself to seek the Lord, and proclaimed a fast throughout all Judah. And Judah gathered themselves together, to ask help of the Lord: even out of all the cities of Judah they came to seek the Lord.

"And Jehoshaphat stood in the congregation of Judah and Jerusalem, in the house of the Lord, before the new court, and said, O Lord God of our fathers, art not thou God in heaven? and rulest not thou over all the kingdoms of the heathen? and in thine hand is there not power and might, so that none is able to withstand thee? Art not thou our God, who didst drive out the inhabitants of this land before thy people Israel, and gavest it to the seed of Abraham thy friend for ever? . . . . . And now, behold, the children of Ammon and Moab and mount Seir, whom thou wouldest not let Israel invade, when they came out of the land of Egypt, but they turned from them, and destroyed them not; behold, I say, how they reward us, to come to cast us out of thy possession, which thou hast given us to inherit. O our God, wilt thou not judge them? for *we have no might against this great company that cometh against us ; neither know we what to do : but our eyes are upon thee.*

"And all Judah stood before the Lord, with their little ones, their wives, and their children.

God's promise of deliverance.

"Then upon Jahaziel, the son of Zechariah, the son of Benaiah, the son of Jeiel, the son of Mattaniah, a Levite of the sons of Asaph, came the

Spirit of the Lord in the midst of the congregation; and he said:—

"Hearken ye, all Judah, and ye inhabitants of Jerusalem, and thou king Jehoshaphat, Thus saith the Lord unto you, *Be not afraid nor dismayed by reason of this great multitude; for the battle is not yours, but God's.* To-morrow go ye down against them: behold they come up by the cliff of Ziz; and ye shall find them by the end of the brook, before the wilderness of Jeruel. *Ye shall not need to fight in this battle: set yourselves, stand ye still, and see the salvation of the Lord with you, O Judah and Jerusalem: fear not, nor be dismayed; to-morrow go out against them: for the Lord will be with you.*

They believe and praise the Lord.

"And Jehoshaphat bowed his head with his face to the ground: and all Judah and the inhabitants of Jerusalem fell before the Lord, worshipping the Lord. And the Levites, of the children of the Kohathites, and of the children of the Korhites, stood up to praise the Lord God of Israel with a loud voice on high.

"And they rose early in the morning, and went forth into the wilderness of Tekoa: and as they went forth, Jehoshaphat stood and said, Hear me, O Judah, and ye inhabitants of Jerusalem; Believe in the Lord your God, so shall ye be established; believe his prophets, so shall ye prosper.

"And when he had consulted with the people, he appointed singers unto the Lord, and that should praise the beauty of holiness, as they went out before the army, and to say, Praise the Lord; for his mercy endureth for ever.

And God fulfils his promise.

"And when they began to sing and to praise, the Lord set ambushments against the children of Ammon, Moab, and mount Seir, which were come against Judah; and they were smitten. For the children of Ammon and Moab stood up against the inhabitants of mount Seir, utterly to slay and destroy them: and when they had made an end to the inhabitants of Seir, every one helped to destroy another. And when Judah came toward the watch tower in the wilderness, they looked unto the multitude, and, behold, they were dead bodies fallen to the earth, and none escaped.

And " exceeding abundantly " more.

"And when Jehoshaphat and his people came to take away the spoil of them, they found among them in abundance both riches with the dead bodies, and precious jewels, which they stripped off for themselves, more than they could carry away: and they were three days in gathering of the spoil, it was so much.

"And on the fourth day they assembled themselves in the valley of Berachah" (margin "*Blessing*"); "for there they blessed the Lord: therefore the name of the same place was called, The valley of Berachah, unto this day.

"Then they returned, every man of Judah and Jerusalem, and Jehoshaphat in the forefront of them, to go again to Jerusalem with joy; for the Lord had made them to rejoice over their enemies. And they came to Jerusalem with psalteries and harps and trumpets unto the house of the Lord.

"And the fear of the Lord was on all the

kingdoms of those countries, when they had heard that the Lord fought against the enemies of Israel. So the realm of Jehoshaphat was quiet: for his God gave him rest round about" (xx. 1–7, 10–30).

Faith in God's bare Word.

This seems one of the sweetest instances in all the Bible of faith in the bare Word of God, in spite of all appearances against the possibility of its being fulfilled.

There were the enemies still in front abundantly able in any human point of view utterly to destroy poor, weak Judah—not a single earthly circumstance changed from the state of things which had only just now made Jehoshaphat cry out, " *We have no might against this great company that cometh against us, neither know we what to do* "—and yet because of the Word from the Lord, that the battle was not theirs but his, so that they should not need to fight in it, but were to stand still and see the salvation of the Lord, they at once without waiting for any sign of its fulfilment, or asking any question as to how this was to be brought about, " *stood up to praise the Lord God of Israel with a loud voice on high.*"

His answer to it.

And in the morning " when he had consulted with the people " and " appointed singers unto the Lord, and that should praise the beauty of holiness as they went out before the army and to say, *Praise the Lord; for his mercy endureth for ever* ": the Lord fulfilled the Word gloriously, giving them not only entire deliverance from the threatened destruction, but also very great enrichment through their enemies having come up to destroy them; for when they "came to take away the spoil of them, they found among them in *abundance both riches with the dead bodies, and precious jewels,* which they stripped off for themselves, *more than they could carry away: and they were three days in gathering the spoil, it was so much.*"

Jehoshaphat "staggered not at the promise of God through unbelief; but was strong in faith, giving glory to God; and being fully persuaded that, what he had promised, he was able also to perform" (Rom. iv. 20, 21); and he proved the truth of the Word, "*HE spake, it was done; HE commanded, and it stood fast*" (Ps. xxxiii. 9).

Bearing upon our own case.

And do not all objections to the certainty of the fulfilment to us, on our simply believing them, of God's, humanly speaking, impossible promises, so many of which we have been considering in this book, of our present entire deliverance from sin, receive their perfect answer in the fulfilment, on Jehoshaphat's simply believing it, of the humanly speaking, impossible promise made to him?

For are not all objections to their fulfilment to us and in us founded either upon something in our own state—our powerlessness, for instance, and our utterly ruined, bankrupt condition spiritually (Isa. i. 5-9; lxiv. 6, 7)—or else upon some such supposed power in our spiritual enemies—such exceeding strength in the devil and his works, sin around us, and upon us, and in us—as makes our present entire victory over them impossible? And is not **every objection of either of these two sorts absolutely met in that case of Jehoshaphat?**

No matter what his weakness.

For is it not plain that any powerlessness in him and his people, had nothing to do with the question of whether they were to be victorious over their enemies or not—that if they had been a thousand times weaker than they actually were, it would not in the smallest degree have affected the certainty of their complete victory?

Or the power of his enemies.

And is it not also equally plain that if "the children of Moab and children of Ammon, and with them other besides the Ammonites," "the great multitude" "from beyond the sea," had been a thousand times more in number, and each individual of them if it were possible a thousand times stronger, still this would have had absolutely no bearing of any sort whatever upon the question of on which side the victory was to be?

If only he believed.

But this of course always on the assumption that any such increased disparity of power between Jehoshaphat and Judah and their enemies, did not affect the one only thing in them (Acts iii. 12, 16) bearing upon the question of whether they were to be victorious or vanquished, namely, their *faith in that Word of God by which, if trusted to, the victory was secured to them.* For if it had had the effect of causing them to look away from the almighty power of God to fulfil his Word, doubtless then it would not have been fulfilled to them (Numb. xiv. 30), for while "with God all things are possible" (Matt. xix. 26), yet in the application of this his, in itself, unlimited power to our deliverance the limitation comes in of, "All things are possible TO HIM THAT BELIEVETH" (Mark ix. 23).

And so with us.

And so with us, if only it did not affect our "faith in God" (Mark xi. 22), and in his Word to us of assured present victory in our Lord Jesus Christ, by the power of the blessed Spirit revealing Him in us for it, over all our spiritual enemies (Luke i. 71, 74; 1 Cor. i. 30, 31), it would be wholly immaterial, as regards our realisation of present entire deliverance from all sin, outward and inward, if our indwelling sin were a thousand times deeper, our actual sins a thousand times greater, our bad habits a thousand times stronger, and our surroundings a thousand times more against us, than as a matter of fact they are. The blessed words would still hold good to us, "*Be not afraid, only believe*" (Mark v. 36). "*All things are possible to him that believeth*" (Mark ix. 23). "*Said I not unto thee, that,* IF THOU WOULDEST BELIEVE, *thou shouldest see the glory of God?*" (John xi. 40).

And the *want of such faith* would render our *failure* to obtain the deliverance absolutely certain, however much less desperate our case might be than that above supposed. And, indeed—always, of course, pre-supposing that we have made the entire consecration of ourselves to God, without which, the exercise of any such faith is impossible—this want is the ONLY reason why any of us fail of always realising in all its blessedness the perfect present deliverance.

Conclusion of this Volume.

In sending out the first part of this book—pages 1 to 128—as "*First Sheets of Scriptural Proofs,*" and the second part—pages 129 to 256—as "*Further Sheets of Scriptural Proofs,*" I begged for "brotherly and sisterly criticisms, to enable me to add any necessary qualifications or explanations in the remaining sheets, or in the introduction."

I have received many most kind letters respecting the contents of those two parts, but only few of them containing criticisms. Some of the most interesting are of a private character; but others are such as there can be no objection to print, though of course without the name or address of the writer. I have put some of this latter sort into the latter part of this volume; but to avoid increasing it to an inconvenient size, I keep back many more in hope of being able to send them out hereafter in another volume, with remarks upon them, and further "Scriptural Proofs," in answer to difficulties expressed or explanations asked in them.

In the prospect of issuing, should our heavenly Father permit it, such a further volume, I now earnestly renew my request for free communications from readers of this one, to guide me to anything that I ought to add to its contents, whether, as above said, in the way only of qualification or explanation, or in that of the admission and correction of positive error, if, *on the authority of the Word of God alone,* apart from all human toning down of its statements, any can be pointed out to me.

Spottiswoode & Co., Printers, New-street Square, London.

www.ingramcontent.com/pod-product-compliance
Lightning Source LLC
Chambersburg PA
CBHW022118290426
44112CB00008B/726